W9-DIW-939

ISTANBUL
INTRIGUES

ALSO BY BARRY RUBIN

THE ARAB STATES AND THE PALESTINE CONFLICT

THE GREAT POWERS IN THE MIDDLE EAST, 1941–1947:
The Road to the Cold War

PAVED WITH GOOD INTENTIONS:
The American Experience and Iran

SECRETS OF STATE:
The State Department and the Struggle over
U.S. Foreign Policy

MODERN DICTATORS:
Third World Coup Makers, Strongmen,
and Populist Tyrants

ISTANBUL INTRIGUES

Barry Rubin

PHAROS BOOKS
A SCRIPPS HOWARD COMPANY
NEW YORK

This Pharos paperback edition of *Istanbul Intrigues* is an unabridged republication of the edition published by McGraw-Hill in 1989, here supplemented with corrections and a new foreword by the author. It is reprinted by arrangement with Barry Rubin.

First Pharos Books Edition: March 1992

Library of Congress Cataloging-in-Publication Data
Rubin, Barry M.
  Istanbul intrigues / Barry Rubin.
     p.   cm.
  Originally published: New York : McGraw-Hill, © 1989.
  Includes bibliographical references (pp. 282–91) and index.
  ISBN 0-88687-656-7
  1. World War,—1939–1945—Anecdotes. 2. Istanbul (Turkey)—History—Anecdotes. 3. Turkey—Nonalignment—Anecdotes.
I. Title.
[DR731.R82   1992]
940.54′85′09563—dc20   91-33346   CIP

Printed in the United States of America

Pharos Books
A Scripps Howard Company
200 Park Avenue
New York, NY 10166

10 9 8 7 6 5 4 3 2 1

CONTENTS

FOREWORD TO THE PAPERBACK EDITION

The story of the World War Two intrigues in Istanbul has only just ended. Until their recent liberation, the East European countries had enjoyed no true springtime since 1940. For exactly a half-century, they were engulfed in war and then the Cold War, a foreign occupation first by Germany, then by the USSR. The Soviet troops who finally left after Communism's collapse had first arrived chasing the Germans in 1944 and 1945.

As *Istanbul Intrigues* shows, the struggle over Bulgaria, Czechoslovakia, Hungary, Poland, and Romania was a major battle in the intelligence war fought from Istanbul. The Allies had tried unsuccessfully to keep the Germans from conquering the Balkans, and then, more effectively, to force them out. The end of World War Two melted into a Cold War between the USSR and the democracies to determine whether these same lands would be independent or Soviet satellites.

It is not yet clear whether the Balkan states have learned the lessons of that earlier era. They fell to the Germans and the Russians in the 1940s largely because of their own internal disorders. The end of Communist rule has again revived the same problems that had wrought destruction before. The old ethnic and border conflicts included hatreds ripping up Yugoslavia, between Hungary and Romania, among Czechs and Slovaks in Czechoslovakia, and anti-Semitism. By provoking instability and opening the way for foreign influence, this strife proved as suicidal to practitioners as it was fatal to the victims. Understanding the high cost of these conflicts in the 1940s would show the folly of repeating the same mistakes.

During World War Two's last years, patriots from East European countries and anti-Nazi Germans contacted U.S. and British intelligence in Istanbul, desperately trying to push the Nazis out of their countries without letting the Soviets replace them. Rival Communist and anti-Communist Yugoslav and Greek guerrilla groups also came to press competing claims for aid to fight the Germans.

On orders from their governments in Washington and London, American and British intelligence operatives encouraged these resistance efforts against the Germans as contributions to the war effort. But they did not wish—and did not dare—to take any step that might endanger the alliance with Moscow. While the United States and Britain were sensitive to Soviet concerns, Stalin never let the alliance of convenience against Berlin make him forget his own ambition to conquer Europe.

One of Stalin's first objectives was to take over Turkey. Obsessed with the threat from Moscow, the Turks stayed neutral to avoid falling victim to either Berlin or Moscow. In retaliation, the Soviets tried to kill German Ambassador Franz Von Papen and pin the murder on Turks in order to foment war between Germany and Turkey. Turkey secretly helped the British and Americans, hoping they would protect it from both dictators.

In the end, American diplomatic and intelligence officials learned lessons in Turkey and the Balkans that would long mark U.S. foreign policy. Watching the German advance, Americans saw their country's duty to take a leading international role. Observing Soviet behavior forced them to recognize that only America could bear the burden of the long Cold War struggle to block Soviet expansionism.

The most heartening response to the publication of *Istanbul Intrigues* came from those who had lived as soldiers, spies, and statemen in the Balkans and Istanbul during World War Two. Many of them contacted me to say that the book accurately conveyed the flavor of their adventures in days that thrust ordinary people onto the world's center stage.

These events stayed secret for fifty years, yet few mysteries can long elude the insatiable thirst to decipher the story of espionage. It is a remarkable narrative of daring and foolish schemes, brave and cowardly deeds, won and lost opportunities, noble and despicable people. These all-true tales are far more colorful than the well-known narrative of highly disciplined armies and diplomacy.

Spying is a strange blend of the last remnant of chivalry and an officially sanctioned type of thuggery. It is the era's last untold story, freeing the imagination from our reality's seeming inevitability, being as different from history as a novel is from a textbook.

—*Barry Rubin*
Washington, 1991

PREFACE

This is a book about Istanbul and about those who conducted political and espionage missions there during the Second World War. It is a work of nonfiction based on extensive archival research and interviews. Each event and every conversation is reconstructed as accurately as possible.

Whenever I interviewed those involved, four decades after the events herein described, there always came a moment when these Americans, Austrians, Czechs, Germans, Hungarians, Israelis, Russians, and Turks would almost visibly reach back in time. Their eyes would light up in recalling those remarkable days that had forever marked their lives. To some, these were moments of great achievement and romance; to others, searing tragedy. For all of them, it was an era of great perils and passionate idealism when they hoped their actions would shape a new world.

One of Istanbul's most intriguing wartime characters was Wilhelm Hamburger. A highly successful German intelligence officer who later defected to the British, Hamburger then disappeared from history until I found—on my last day of research in the OSS archives—one of his letters that the OSS had intercepted in 1945. In a postscript, Hamburger mentioned the new name he was taking. After checking a Vienna telephone book, I had his address within an hour.

It was particularly meaningful for me to visit Vienna a century to the day after my great-grandfather left there for America. I walked to Hamburger's apartment down streets named for the city's great composers. Wiry and charming, as described in Allied intelligence reports forty years earlier, he spoke with me for six hours.

Hamburger's wealthy, sophisticated upbringing made him self-confident and poised. He spoke candidly about his experiences. After defecting, he worked on psychological warfare in Cairo until the mistrustful British exiled him to Sudan. By 1945, Hamburger was exhausted and angry. His beloved Vienna was wrecked, and he feared his scattered family was dead or in the hands of the Soviets. Over the years, he rebuilt his fortunes, as the luxuriously furnished flat showed.

For Hamburger, his secret contact with George Earle in wartime Istanbul had been a central event in his life. An American politician and friend of President Roosevelt, Earle also thought himself a great spy. One American diplomat described Earle this way: "The most bizarre and despicable character I had ever known." Hamburger and other Austrian patriots had spent a great deal of time cultivating Earle as what they hoped would be a reliable channel to the White House.

Like so many who had performed espionage and counterintelligence work during the war, Hamburger had spent decades pondering a painful question. Finally, he turned to me and asked if "anything we did made any difference?"

Events in Istanbul did greatly affect the war and the world that emerged from it. Defeating German efforts to seduce Turkey and conquer the Middle East was essential for Allied victory. Failure to subvert Berlin's Balkan allies quickly enough doomed millions of people and made inevitable Soviet domination of eastern Europe. Intelligence sent from Istanbul helped Allied bombers devastate German industry and shorten the war. Frictions there were catalysts in the Cold War; experience gained there formed a foundation for building the postwar U.S. intelligence agencies.

It became possible to discover the truth about these events only after a treasure trove of information became available when the CIA released the vast archives of its predecessor, the Office of Strategic Services (OSS).

But Freedom of Information requests were necessary to obtain more material, and there were additional tens of thousands of pages of embassy cables, army and navy intelligence reports, prisoner interrogations, and captured German records to examine. The most difficult task was to uncover the people behind the code names. Like a counterintelligence officer, one had to seek some slip in a cable or detail in an interview that made possible a breakthrough. There were also journalists' accounts, Turkish newspapers, British military and diplomatic records, and the correspondence of the Zionist delegation in Istanbul. I interviewed dozens of people now living on three continents and in twenty American states.

Among those I most wanted to meet was Lanning Macfarland, wartime head of the OSS in Turkey. I knew he was from Chicago but had no luck locating him. One day I discovered Macfarland's 1942 application to join the OSS, which mentioned he was a trustee of a small Iowa college. I wrote a letter to the school and received Macfarland's obituary and his son's address. By coincidence, the son was visiting Washington the day before I left on a long research trip abroad. Inspired by my letter, Lanning Macfarland Jr. had opened a locked suitcase left by his father and found a 180-page memoir detailing his father's operations in Istanbul. He graciously gave me a copy.

And so it went, interviewing people in an attempt to reconstruct life in wartime Istanbul: an appointment to meet with an ex-OSS man in a cafeteria; a visit to one former U.S. diplomat at his New Hampshire retirement home, to another at his New York club; a drive up to Nyack, New York (whose beautiful Hudson River vista bears a striking similarity to Istanbul) to see a Turkish official's widow; an accidental meeting at a California reception with a German-born refugee who had been a professor in Istanbul. In southern Virginia, Robert St. John—one of the great foreign correspondents—told me about his experiences in the Balkans. In England, I took a train to a retired British diplomat's country estate to resolve the mysterious, world-famous case of the British ambassador's valet who spied for the Germans. We spoke in his dining room amid 200-year-old pictures of his ancestors. A Soviet defector, forty-five years after fleeing Stalin, insisted we meet in a way that allowed him to reconnoiter the place to ensure I was not a KGB agent. I drove two hours through Israel's Negev desert to meet one leader of Istanbul's

Zionist rescue mission and went to Jerusalem's city hall for an interview with another, Mayor Teddy Kollek.

In Washington, I met a former Hungarian diplomat, Aladar Szegedy, who lived only a few blocks from where I grew up. Well into his eighties, Szegedy served coffee with a sure hand and then pulled out reams of Hungarian articles and documents and recounted with remarkable accuracy his experiences as a Foreign Ministry official active in secret peace contacts with the Allies in Istanbul. He described, as if it had happened only yesterday, being thrown into the Gestapo's Budapest prison.

A few lines from Tom Stoppard's remarkable play *Travesties*, about Zurich during World War I, were an inspiration: "Great days . . . Zurich during the war. Refugees, spies, exiles, painters, poets, writers, radicals of all kinds. I knew them all. Used to argue far into the night . . . at the Odeon, the Terrasse. . . ." The lines fascinated me. Stoppard masterfully brought to life the relations between famous and obscure people, the ways that memory recalls or distorts life, and those particular moments when history is at a crossroads and all the onlookers know it.

The dramatic story of a neutral city as a center of intrigue during World War II provided the plot for one of the best American films ever made. Yet many of the scenes fictionalized for *Casablanca* actually did take place in an Istanbul swarming with diplomats, spies, refugees, and intelligence merchants.

I recalled those ideas while boarding the Zurich-Lucerne train with Professor Yehuda Bauer. We had talked in Jerusalem and Washington about our parallel research on the period, debating over the meaning of events and speaking—as one would of old friends—about long-dead spies and agents we had never met. We were on our way to see Alfred Schwarz who, under the code name "Dogwood," had run the largest U.S. intelligence operation in Nazi-occupied Europe.

Schwarz had never before granted an interview. His very existence was a secret. Anthony Cave Brown had written in his book on the OSS that Dogwood's "real name . . . has never been revealed anywhere, and he may have died suddenly and mysteriously." He went on to hint that the man had either defected to the Russians at war's end or been murdered by the OSS.

Actually, Schwarz remained in Istanbul for many years and then became a banker in Austria and Switzerland; some of his former associates helped me locate him. It was merely a short taxi trip from the Lucerne station to his home. On the left was the city's famous medieval bridge with its paintings of the dance of death memorializing the black plague; on the right were the lake's clear waters and, beyond, the massive snow-covered Alps.

A few minutes later, I had the rare thrill—after a two-year search—of meeting one of my main "characters." The 83-year-old Schwarz was articulate and hospitable. He spent the whole day talking freely of relevant events—at least up to a point. The Dogwood spy ring had ended in debacle in the autumn of 1944, but Schwarz insisted he had voluntarily quit in "December 1943 or January 1944." A proud man and himself a student of psychology, Schwarz had either rewritten or successfully blotted out large portions of his past.

Schwarz had some bitter reminiscences. His entire family was wiped out in the Holocaust. He sincerely believed in 1943—as he did that day—that if the Americans had responded to secret German peace offers at the time, the war could have ended years sooner with millions of lives saved. At a moment in time, Schwarz felt the world's future rested on his shoulders. He was forced to conclude in retrospect that either he failed this test or that the Americans were criminally foolish in refusing to listen to him.

Schwarz also felt strongly about another failure. Like other central Europeans opposing Nazi tyranny, he was equally averse to Soviet control of his country. Schwarz's fellow Czechs and the Hungarians, Poles, Bulgarians, and Romanians in Istanbul dealing secretly with the Allies all faced this paradox. Schwarz angrily recalled how OSS officials told him that either the Soviets would tire of occupying eastern Europe or the local people would expel them. Another example, he felt, of American naïveté.

He was much less willing to talk about Dogwood's problems. In one U.S. military intelligence report on German agents in Istanbul, I had come across the name of Luther Kovess. I guessed that Kovess was also a key American agent. Finally, I discovered a single sentence in an OSS cable nestled among a thousand others instructing the Washington office to deposit $100 in Kovess's bank account. Further research showed that Kovess was the mysterious "Jacaranda," the liaison man between the

OSS and Hungarian anti-Nazi officials and officers. But Kovess had been the Istanbul representative for a company that was a front for German intelligence. In addition to Kovess, there were a half-dozen other suspicious agents employed by both OSS-Istanbul and its German enemy.

Schwarz admitted knowing Kovess but was convinced that he was absolutely reliable. Another double agent, Frantisek Laufer, was described in the files as a "close friend" of Schwarz. Schwarz claimed to have met Laufer only two or three times, although, over forty years later, Schwarz could still accurately describe him. Obviously, Schwarz, with all his sophistication and experience, had been fooled by German double agents.

Yet it was hardly surprising that so many people had betrayed so many causes in those years. Istanbul was a neutral city where enemies fighting to the death sat table by table in elegant restaurants listening to Gypsy orchestras. It was a city where a German and an American intelligence agent fell in love with the same beautiful Hungarian singer. Those who had barely escaped from lands of bombed-out buildings, shortages, and fear came to a place of bounteous peace. For people daily risking their lives elsewhere, as one of them put it, the most urgent question in Istanbul might be the waiter's query, "Do you prefer red wine or champagne with your dinner?"

Great days . . . Istanbul during the war. Refugees, spies, exiles, painters, poets, writers, radicals of all kinds . . .

ACKNOWLEDGMENTS

I owe a great debt to a large number of people for their time and unselfish assistance.

I would particularly like to thank Professor Yehuda Bauer for his scholarly generosity in our exchanges of information on the Dogwood and Hungary stories contained in Chapters 11 and 12.

The staff of the National Archives' Modern Military and Diplomatic branches and of the Washington National Records Center, particularly John Taylor, Larry MacDonald, Bill Lewis, and George Chalou, were most helpful in dealing with dozens of my inquiries. Many historians have benefited from their commitment to public service and their dedication to the creation of an accurate history of these events.

A number of people made useful suggestions. Among those who were so kind as to assist this project were Christopher Andrew, Fritz Arndt, Bilge Criss, Ann and Bill Edmonds, Steven Emerson, Charles Fenyvesi, Talat Halman, Eve Jacobson, David Kahn, Bruce Kuniholm, Heath Lowry, Lanning Macfarland Jr., Robert Minor, Daniel Newberry, Dalia Ofer, Dan Rustow, Philip Stoddard, and Aladar Szegedy.

Proficiency in many languages was necessary in researching this book. Among those who assisted were Rozella Dillon on Czech sources, Lizou Fenyvesi on Hungarian, Jennifer Noyon on Turkish, Anita Mallinckrodt on German, Maya Latynski on Polish, and Anat Lapidot on Hebrew. Additional archival research was done by Sibel Irzik in the Burton Berry papers and Petra Marquardt in German-language records. I would also like to thank Mrs. Rose Vali for permission to quote from her husband's unpublished memoirs.

Patrick Clawson and Jennifer Noyon were particularly generous with their time in reading the entire manuscript at an early stage and in giving very useful comments, corrections, and criticisms. Dr. Noyon's knowledge of Turkey and its people was invaluable.

Suzanne Singer devoted a great deal of time to helping edit the final manuscript. Her literary insight made an important improvement in the quality of this work. My editor, Dan Weaver, supported this project from the time it was a brief proposal. His backing throughout several years of research and writing is, once again, very much appreciated.

I decided that the use of footnotes would take up too much space and be of limited interest. I want to stress, however, that the book is based on primary source material and depends heavily on a careful reading of State Department, OSS, U.S. military intelligence, and British Foreign Office records, as well as on interviews, memoirs, and contemporary accounts.

The guardian shore is under threat,
its waters lit by fire,
reflecting off each minaret,
then leaping up far higher.
On drifting, unwelcome shipwrecks flee,
refugees to doors half shut,
and those upon the ramparts fear,
that all escape is cut.
Counselors heatedly debate,
while envoys speak with charm,
so none can help but hesitate,
between such hope and harm.
Spies do gather, purchase, bribe,
inside the city walls.
Can one hope faithfully to describe,
that which then befalls?

"BOO, BOO, BABY, I'M A SPY"

I'm involved in a dangerous game,
Every other day I change my name,
The face is different but the body's the same,
Boo, boo, baby, I'm a spy!
You have heard of Mata Hari,
We did business cash and carry,
Poppa caught us and we had to marry,
Boo, boo, baby, I'm a spy!
Now, as a lad, I'm not so bad,
In fact, I'm a darn good lover,
But look my sweet, let's be discreet,
And do this under cover.
I'm so cocky I could swagger,
The things I know would make you stagger,
I'm ten percent cloak and ninety percent dagger,
Boo, boo, baby, I'm a spy!
—*popular song in Istanbul during World War II*

1 | Diplomacy by Murder

Neither vineyards, nor gardens
Do I ask.
Nor horses, nor sheep.
Don't take my soul away,
O God!
I am curious.
I must see how this game ends!
　　　　　　　—Ilhami Bekir

In a hurry, the neatly dressed little man was panting as he carried a bulky package down Atatürk Boulevard in Ankara, Turkey's capital city. It was 10 o'clock on the pleasant morning of February 24, 1942, a good day for a walk after the oppressive, positively Siberian winter. There was little diversion in that city plopped in the midst of the desolate Anatolian plateau. For entertainment, people might have a drink at the railroad station and watch a train leave. Ankara was jokingly called a diplomatic concentration camp. Turkey was neutral, but this fact and the country's physical isolation from the war raging in Europe did not prevent that titanic struggle from being the city's main preoccupation.

Distances were long in Ankara and there were many gaps between buildings. It had been a mere village fifteen years earlier when it was chosen as the new capital, and it still looked like an unfinished real estate development. Britain's ambassador, Hughe Knatchbull-Hugessen, thought Ankara "like the realization of one of H. G. Wells's dreams of the future," but it was still an incomplete one. The broad boulevards, local wits said, began nowhere and ran past nothing to end nowhere. Each summer, government officials and foreign diplomats fled Ankara's baking heat, sandstorms, and sirocco wind on the overnight train for the cool breezes of cosmopolitan Istanbul.

No such escape was possible in the winter when the city was imprisoned by deep snows and wolves prowled in the outer suburbs. The lights burned late into the night in the missions of Allied, Axis, and neutral countries—whose buildings often adjoined each other along Atatürk Boulevard—as those within worked to win the ferocious war that raged all around Turkey's borders.

That January the terrible weather had distracted everyone. It snowed every day for a week. Bus and train service collapsed; food rations were reduced. Newspapers gave lessons on how to follow the European custom of standing in line at stores. People shivered in their homes because there was not enough wood or coal. Life was very hard.

Cabdrivers found few fares, since Turks took buses and foreign diplomats had their own cars. For the taxi driver on Atatürk Boulevard, the man struggling with an oversize package appeared as a miraculous opportunity. The Turk blocked the sidewalk. "Wouldn't you like a cab, sir?" he asked politely.

"Get out of my way," the man replied, pushing past him.

"But your burden is heavy and the fare is cheap," the driver insisted, opening his car's door. The man ignored him, pressing on, and the driver could only shrug his shoulders and lean back against his automobile. He had a peasant's patience. Something else would turn up.

A fashionably dressed couple strolled on the other side of the boulevard about 10 yards away. The taxi driver watched the rude man hurriedly walk to a point directly across from the couple and lift his package. A single car passed down the empty street. Constantino Liberali, the Italian embassy's concierge, stood outside that building's gate waiting for a bus.

Suddenly, there was a tremendous explosion. The package had blown up, disintegrating its bearer. Window glass shattered for several blocks in all directions. The couple was thrown to the ground. The shaken Liberali ran up and recognized the two people immediately as German Ambassador Franz von Papen and his wife. The wiry, gray-haired ambassador was impeccably dressed in a well-cut suit, bow tie and monogrammed handkerchief. "Are you hurt?" Liberali asked in Italian. "No," von Papen replied. Somewhat reassured, Liberali looked up and saw nearby the would-be assassin's amputated foot lying on the sidewalk.

Von Papen's personal secretary, who had also been walking to work, helped the ambassador stand up. "Damn it!" von Papen complained. "My best suit!" A trickle of crimson ran down his neck from a broken eardrum. Bits of the assassin's flesh and spots of his blood covered the von Papens. Officials rushed out of the nearby German embassy. They saw a large pool of blood on the opposite pavement and a battered revolver. Von Papen's survival seemed incredible.

After the attack, all the byzantine complexity of Turkey during World War II came into play. Ankara was full of rumors as to the assassin's identity, motives, and employers. There was no shortage of suspects, as spies and saboteurs rubbed shoulders in every hotel, restaurant, and nightclub. There were many refugees whose great sufferings at German hands might induce them to choose von Papen as a target.

Von Papen's unpopularity sprang from his personal record as well as his post as Hitler's representative in Turkey. In Germany, von Papen had been a leader of the Catholic Center party. But in 1932 he betrayed his party to become Germany's chancellor and one of those conservatives who had helped Hitler into power. Von Papen was part pillar, part prisoner of the Nazi regime. Some friends became early critics of Hitler; his own assistant was executed in a 1934 purge. But von Papen collaborated, first as vice-chancellor and then as ambassador to Austria, which he helped Germany annex in 1938. Von Papen then became ambassador to Turkey. His mission was to bring the country into the German orbit or at least keep it from joining Berlin's enemies.

A few months before the assassination attempt, von Papen visited Berlin—where rumors of his secret contacts with the Allies were common—to shore up relations with Hitler. Ulrich von Hassell, a German diplomat who despised the Nazis, wrote about von Papen in his diary: "He again impressed me as weak. On the other hand, he apparently still has a lot of ambition. At the proper time he would like to take German foreign policy in hand and make peace for Hitler." If, von Hassell added, von Papen thought Hitler would compromise, he was living in a fantasy world. And if von Papen believed that new German victories in Russia would persuade the Allies to make concessions, he did not know the truth about the faltering German war effort. Time, von Hassell concluded, was on the Allies' side.

The smooth, well-mannered von Papen was an effective representative of Hitler's regime. Many anti-Nazis thought him to be both a brilliant tactician and a powerful, evil genius. One author called him "Satan in a top hat." Yet despite the popular belief that von Papen was a strong influence behind Hitler's throne, Berlin's cliques held him in low regard. Von Papen exaggerated his own power and thought himself Hitler's most likely successor. This strange combination of subservience and ambition made him both a successful servant of the Nazi regime and a man willing to toy with betraying it, though he never committed himself to supporting the resistance.

Given all this ambiguity, it was difficult to determine which side had sought to assassinate him on that February morning. The Germans blamed the Allies and particularly the Russians for the assassination attempt. Some of von Papen's subordinates suspected elements in Berlin; the ambassador himself thought the British were responsible. Moscow hinted that the Gestapo was behind the attack and wasted no time cranking up a propaganda barrage. The Tass news agency falsely reported, "Papers found in the clothing of the person killed in the explosion . . . showed stamps of the German Embassy." Equally inaccurate was the Soviet ambassador's claim that the Americans had "irrefutable evidence" of the Gestapo's responsibility.

More bizarre was the fact that while millions of people were being killed in battle or murdered in concentration camps, the would-be assassin's breach of diplomatic norms was deemed shocking. At a Berlin dinner party—between discussions about kidnapping French children and raising them as Germans and about the "good news" that the massive deaths of Russians would allow German repopulation of the Soviet Union—Hitler commented that the attempt on von Papen's life showed the Soviets' depravity. Not only was the deed itself dastardly, he complained, but Moscow arranged it so that the killer's bomb would destroy himself as well as his victims, leaving no evidence for tracing the crime.

In the midst of total war, belligerent countries continued to observe diplomatic niceties. This situation had a comic, even farcical, side. On Turkey's national day, guests at the president's reception were divided between two rooms: Germany and its partners were in one; the Allies were in another. The neutrals shuttled between them. In 1943, Italy quit the Axis and joined the Allies, posing a complication. When the Italian ambassador was shown into the Axis room, von Papen led a walkout, complaining of the "traitor's" presence. But the Greek and Yugoslav envoys, whose countries had been occupied by Italy, also objected to the hapless Italian's presence among the Allies. He was forced to wander the corridor.

Both sides recognized Turkey's strategic importance. The Germans needed a foothold in order to defeat the Soviets and penetrate the Middle East. The British and Americans sought bases in Turkey to liberate the Balkans from German control. The Russians, Turkey's main enemy for over a century, wanted Istanbul and its straits in order to control the Black Sea and ensure their access to the Mediterranean. From Istanbul, the British and Americans ran spy and paramilitary operations into Nazi-occupied eastern Europe. The Germans bribed officials to gain influence and to gather information; the Russians recruited agents. Each of them established secret bases and fought a tug-of-war with the others to win Turkey for its side.

Istanbul also became a haven for a steady stream of dazed refugees from war and persecution in Yugoslavia, Hungary, Bulgaria, Romania, and Greece. Members of the German underground came to inform the Allies of their plans to overthrow Hitler. The valet of the British ambassador worked as a German agent photographing the Allies' most secret documents. Balkan and neutral businessmen were courted with requests for data on German-ruled Europe. One of them obtained the Reich's secret industrial address book, invaluable for locating bombing targets. Another produced a map of the Romanian oil fields, Germany's main source of petroleum. An Austrian engineer provided data on Nazi synthetic-rubber production. German agents were infiltrated into the Arab Middle East to organize uprisings. Delegates from Zionist groups in Palestine worked day and night to smuggle Jews out of danger. Romanian, Bulgarian, and Hungarian officials arrived with mandates from their Axis satellite regimes to negotiate secret surrenders to the Allies. A whole industry arose on the basis of forged and phony information sold to multiple clients. No less than seventeen foreign intelligence services operated in Turkey during the war. The stakes were high, and the measures taken were desperate.

Investigating who had tried to kill von Papen posed dangerous political issues as well as apparently unsolvable investigative problems for the Turkish authorities. To accuse any state of responsibility was to risk not just diplomatic but perhaps military retaliation. As long as agents observed the ground rules, they had been allowed to function freely, but those attacking von Papen had gone too far. The omnipotent Turkish secret police, the Emniyet (National Security Service), had a well-deserved reputation for effectively countering subversion. With their famous tenacity, the Turks were determined to solve the case and punish the perpetrators, no matter who they might be.

But the scanty evidence did not look promising. The serial number of the revolver recovered at the scene had been filed off. Few fragments remained of the assailant, although it was said that the discovery of a circumcised penis in a nearby tree allowed police to identify him as a Moslem. Investigators discovered that his shoes had been purchased in Ankara about two weeks earlier and that he had been smoking a cigar in a holder, had brownish hair, and had been wearing a hat. The police also had the taxi driver's description, but with all the ambiguous evidence they could not even be sure that von Papen was the intended victim. After all, several high-ranking Turkish officials had driven by the spot within a few moments of the explosion, and the British military attaché might have been killed if he had not left his apartment, under whose balcony the assassin stood, ten minutes before the bomb wrecked it. Sherlock Holmes would have been stymied.

Within two days, however, an incredible breakthrough occurred, bringing some amazing surprises. The Turkish police identified the killer and arrested several alleged accomplices. The assailant was a 25-year-old Yugoslav Moslem named Omer Tokat. A teacher's son, Tokat had joined the underground Yugoslav Communist party as a student. He moved to Turkey in October 1940, enrolled in Istanbul University's law school, and became a Turkish citizen.

The identification of Tokat was only the beginning. The police then surrounded the Soviet consulate in Istanbul. They demanded that George Pavlov, an employee listed as archivist, be surrendered for questioning. After a two-week siege, Pavlov was given up to the authorities. A second Russian, Leonid Kornilov, a transportation expert for the Soviet trade delegation, was arrested on a train near the Soviet-Turkish border while trying to sneak out of the country. Two other men—Suleiman Sagol, a barber, and Abdurrahman Sayman, a medical student—were also taken into custody; both, like Tokat, were Yugoslav Moslems and Communists who had taken Turkish nationality.

The Russian press launched an all-out campaign attacking Turkey for, according to *Pravda,* "yielding to the demands and indulging the interests of the German Fascist circles, which are attempting to cover the traces of those really guilty of the provocation." Soviet diplomats told their colleagues that the charges were slanderous German propaganda, part of the Nazi effort against the Allies. Why were the Turks furthering this farce? Why didn't the British and Americans protest?

Soviet Ambassador Sergei Vinogradov asked the Turks to release the two Russians in order to improve relations, and he gave his personal assurance of the men's innocence. The Turkish foreign minister replied that this satisfied him but, unfortunately, was not sufficient for the judges. Characteristically, the U.S. government believed in the innocence of its Soviet ally, while the British felt that political expediency, not guilt or innocence, should deter prosecution. The case was turning into an international incident that might threaten the Allies' strategic position. London and Washington agreed that the Turks were being too rigid and should drop the whole matter.

Although angry about Soviet pressure, Turkish leaders nonetheless told newspaper editors to tone down criticisms of the U.S.S.R. since the situation was so delicate and fraught with danger. But the Turks were proud and stubborn. As a contemporary U.S. Army intelligence report put it, "The Turks cannot be driven to anything. . . . They are conspicuous among the human creation for their obstinacy." Amidst his own warnings for calm, the head of the Turkish government press bureau could not restrain himself from adding, "If necessary we will fight the Russians!"

The trial began April 2, 1942, with a startling revelation: the two Turkish defendants confessed that the Soviet government had ordered the assassination "to disturb the good relations between Turkey and Germany and to assure the entrance of Turkey into the war to the advantage of the Russians." Tokat was recruited because his nationality and religion would direct Berlin's suspicions toward Turkey. He agreed to be the triggerman after being told that his fiancée in German-occupied Yugoslavia had been mistreated.

In addition to a revolver, the Russians gave Tokat a package they said contained a smoke bomb which he was supposed to set off after the shooting to cover his escape. The overcautious Tokat had pressed the device's button just as he took a pistol shot at von Papen. But the "bomb," filled with dynamite rather than smoke, exploded with such a devastating blast that only after police recovered a bullet from the scene did anyone realize a gun had been fired.

The political situation became increasingly tense. On April 18, Turkey's foreign minister told the British ambassador, "Even if it comes to war we shall not change our attitude!" When a Soviet embassy car accidentally knocked down a Turkish soldier outside the courtroom, an officer incited the crowd and a riot was narrowly averted. Meanwhile, the invading German army continued to drive deeper into the U.S.S.R., breaking through into the Caucasus Mountains on Turkey's northern border. The Turks moved three army divisions to that frontier to oppose any incursion from German or Soviet troops.

As the trial continued, prosecution witnesses—some of doubtful credibility—tied together the four defendants, the dead gunman, and the assassination attempt. A clerk from Tokat's hotel in Ankara identified clothing recovered from the scene of the crime. Experts found a wart between the deceased's eyebrows matching that in photographs of Tokat. A tobacco shop owner said he saw Pavlov talking to Sayman near Istanbul's Azak cinema; another man recounted having observed Kornilov and Sagol meeting at the Marcel hairdresser's shop in Istanbul one morning. The taxi driver who had witnessed the explosion testified that he saw Kornilov, shortly before the event, sitting in the driver's seat of a red car, license plate number 320, belonging to the Soviet embassy.

The plot, said the prosecutor in his closing statement, was "prepared lengthily, slyly and treacherously." The two Russians were actually agents of the Soviet secret police (NKVD,) who organized the conspiracy. They were helped by a third Yugoslav Communist who came from the U.S.S.R. in October 1941, feigned illness, and obtained a temporary residence permit for Istanbul. This man was an assassination expert who trained Tokat. Two months later, he ostensibly left for Cairo to join the Yugoslav army-in-exile there. But he was never seen again.

Moscow's motive, continued the prosecutor, was to have von Papen's murder set off a German-Turkish conflict that would relieve pressure on a Soviet Union hard-pressed by the German invaders. If Turkey went to war, the Russians could use Turkish territory as a base to defend their southern flank, their oil fields, and the Black Sea. The plot failed, concluded the prosecution, "only thanks to a stroke of great luck."

In rebuttal, Pavlov proclaimed, "The despicable slanderers sitting here in the dock are being used by the enemies of my country for provocative purposes against the Soviet Union and for undermining Soviet-Turkish relations." Both Russians denied knowing Tokat or their fellow defendants. Sagol identified him, Pavlov claimed, because the police had showed him a photo earlier. The case, Pavlov said mockingly, "was something like the stories found in fashionable detective novels."

Despite Pavlov's speech, on June 17 the court found all four defendants guilty. Kornilov and Pavlov were sentenced to twenty years, and the two Turks were given ten years despite their cooperation with the prosecution.

The Soviets were not alone in questioning the verdict. U.S. Ambassador Laurence Steinhardt commented, "The state has not only failed to establish the guilt of the Soviet defendants beyond a reasonable doubt but has not even made out a prima facie case against them." A number of British observers agreed. British and American skepticism could only have been heightened during the next few months as the prosecution's case appeared to fall apart.

The two Russians appealed their sentences and again appeared in court on November 4. Looking healthier than they had at the original trial despite months in prison, Pavlov and Kornilov cheerfully gave the Communist clenched-fist salute to Soviet diplomats and journalists. Again, they claimed to be victims of a frame-up, complaining that there was no direct proof of guilt and that some of the defense lawyers were incompetent or corrupt. They asked for twenty-five new witnesses and demanded new judges. All their motions were denied. The appeal dragged on with much repetition, little new evidence, and a great deal of vituperation. At one point, Pavlov claimed Sagol's testimony was unreliable because Sagol suffered from venereal disease.

In December, however, came a dramatic confrontation amidst another dull exchange of charges and countercharges. Sagol rose to his feet and addressed the judges: "The man disintegrated by the explosion is not Tokat. I can cite witnesses who have seen Omer in Ankara since the explosion." The courtroom buzzed with excitement as journalists scribbled notes. Sagol remained calm; the prosecutors conferred. Kornilov whispered a translation in Pavlov's ear.

"My previous depositions were all false. Sayman succeeded in convincing me that it was necessary to make these depositions. I am ready to name the organization that prepared the attack. . . . I will prove to you that I never introduced Sayman to the Russians. I never set foot in the Russian embassy. . . . During my first deposition, I had spoken of a Russian whose nose was shaped like an eggplant. I ask you Mr. President, look at Kornilov's nose, does it look like an eggplant?" The tension dissolved into laughter which quickly quieted when Sagol claimed he had confessed only after being tortured.

The chief judge tried to maintain order. "Here in this tribunal, you are not the object of such torture. You have for months been sworn to speak the truth. And you always kept silence. You could speak freely and you did not do it. Why didn't you speak from the first day?"

"I didn't know Turkish well enough," Sagol replied. His real contact had been neither Pavlov nor Kornilov but a man with "blond hair and with an eggplant nose" to whom Sayman introduced him in Istanbul's Taksim Square Park. The rattled judge asked, "What is the opinion of the prosecutor?"

"Mr. President, members of the court, Suleiman Sagol pretends to having lied and not spoken the truth until now. Now he is lying, lying openly. I have on several occasions questioned him directly. He was sincere in his depositions."

"No! No!" exclaimed Sagol.

"Be quiet!" demanded the judge. The spectators moved their heads back and forth as if watching a tennis match.

"Mr. President," interjected Sayman, "Sagol changed his story because he understood that everything had been discovered." After the last session, Sayman added, Pavlov told him, "All is not lost." They could still save themselves by denouncing their earlier testimony.

Amidst this pandemonium, the court adjourned for lunch. At 2 o'clock, when it reconvened, the Palace of Justice was packed. The Court of Appeals' judges refused to accept Sagol's new statement; they confirmed the guilty verdict but reduced the two Russians' sentences to sixteen years and eight months. The case was closed. Although the Russian prisoners were released as a goodwill gesture in August 1944, the von Papen assassination affair became part of a legacy of Soviet-Turkish antagonism that would contribute to the onset of the Cold War between them.

Yet the mystery and confusion around the case persisted. Why had the Turks taken such a tremendous risk in arresting and prosecuting Kornilov and Pavlov on such limited evidence? Who was really responsible for the attempted assassination?

Only many decades later could the real story be pieced together. In fact, the Turkish authorities had secret information from two witnesses who could not be called to testify but who rightfully convinced them of Soviet responsibility.

One of them was Milos Hanak, the Czech ambassador to Turkey. After the German empire swallowed his country in 1939, Hanak lost his diplomatic standing. In a miniature blitzkrieg that antagonized many other diplomats, von Papen evicted Hanak from the Czech ambassadorial residence and seized it for his own use.

Refused diplomatic license plates, the Hanaks gave up their car. Nearly impoverished, they moved to a little apartment from which they struggled on behalf of their government-in-exile to maintain links with the underground resistance movement at home. Cooperating with their British and American allies, the Hanaks and a small band of refugee Czech intelligence officers made a disproportionately large contribution to the anti-Nazi war effort.

The policy of the Czech government-in-exile in London was to cooperate closely with Moscow. Of all the Allied governments and intelligence agencies, the Czechs had the best relations with the Soviets. The Czech leaders were convinced that the Russians would dominate central Europe after the war and that Czech independence would depend on Moscow's tolerance.

One day, early in 1942, this connection gave Hanak an unexpected opportunity to strike another blow against Germany. Soviet Ambassador Sergei Vinogradov met Hanak at a diplomatic reception and asked him to invite the Soviet press attaché in Ankara to lunch. Hanak complied. At the appropriate time, Leonid Naumov, a stout man with baggy clothes, knocked on Hanak's door. Naumov had come to Turkey a few months earlier as the NKVD chief. He bragged that his orders came directly from Stalin. His mission was to arrange von Papen's assassination.

Naumov was confident that Hanak would help him. As they finished lunch and sat over coffee, Naumov invited Hanak to "collaborate" in the plot to kill von Papen. Czech resistance militants could be brought to Ankara as "students" to act as triggermen. Hanak, shocked and angry, shouted, "I am not a murderer! Get out!" Unaccustomed to being so addressed, Naumov vowed revenge and stormed out the door. Deprived of Czech help, Naumov decided to use Yugoslav Communists instead. He traveled between Istanbul and Ankara seven times to make the arrangements.

The Soviets would remember Hanak's behavior. A few weeks later, he was swimming near Istanbul and saw a man paddling powerfully toward him and carrying a knife. Hanak raced toward shore. Suddenly, a passing boat came between them. The Czech widened his lead and safely reached the beach. He told the Turkish authorities about the conversation with Naumov.

After the war, Moscow demanded that Hanak be fired from his position as ambassador to Turkey. The Czech government complied but then named him ambassador to Belgium. Again, the Soviets objected and Prague fired him once more. Hanak returned home. When the Communists took over Czechoslovakia in 1948, he was on the arrest list. Laurence Steinhardt, the U.S. ambassador in Prague at that time, had befriended Hanak during the war when he was the U.S. ambassador to Turkey. Steinhardt had the Hanaks smuggled across the border in his own car. Mrs. Hanak lay on the back seat under a blanket while her husband hid in the trunk. They settled in Washington.

The other informant on the von Papen case took even greater risks. He was Ismail Akhmedov, the short, powerfully built Soviet press attaché in Istanbul. The 38-year-old Akhmedov, a Soviet Turk from a small town, had grown up in an atmosphere of traditional Islam, one in which a sentimental love for Istanbul was combined with his people's tough independent character. His family suffered greatly in the Bolshevik revolution and ensuing civil war. The world of his youth disappeared. Akhmedov eventually joined the Soviet army and became a military intelligence operative. One of his assignments in the 1930s was to run agents across the wild Soviet-Turkish border.

He was sent to Berlin in May 1941, nominally as a Tass reporter, to study the German army. When the Nazis invaded the U.S.S.R. a few weeks later, Akhmedov was interned with other Soviet personnel. Since he was circumcised, the Germans thought he was Jewish and harassed him. Akhmedov learned three things in Germany: the Nazi regime's bestiality, Stalin's stupid refusal to heed warnings of the impending invasion, and Moscow's view that the United States and Britain were only temporary allies who would be treated as enemies once the war ended.

Germany and the U.S.S.R. finally exchanged their interned citizens through Turkey. And so Akhmedov for the first time reached Istanbul, the fabulous city he had heard about so often as a boy. He was not disappointed. Entering the city, he gazed in wonder at its minarets, mosques, old palaces, and beautiful natural setting. But Moscow's repressive hand quickly descended. Akhmedov and his colleagues were confined to the Soviet embassy's summer residence. Never again might he see Istanbul, Akhmedov thought, as he boarded a train back to Russia. When it stopped in Ankara, however, he was taken to a meeting with Vinogradov. The ambassador told him he was being transferred to Istanbul.

It was a dream come true. Akhmedov now pursued three simultaneous callings. As press attaché, he dealt with foreign journalists, trying to influence them according to Moscow's directives. As a lieutenant colonel in Soviet military intelligence, he recruited agents and ran spy networks into German-held areas. For himself, Akhmedov basked in the city and culture that was his own heritage.

Akhmedov spent much time with new Turkish friends at restaurants, nightclubs, museums, mosques, and the university. Vinogradov warned him that "Turkey is our enemy and one day she is going to pay for it. Remember that." But Akhmedov began to identify with the country, particularly after hearing about his wife's death in the U.S.S.R. The Soviet authorities gave him no explanation. He wondered if the NKVD might have murdered her.

Akhmedov knew Naumov's true mission and Pavlov's expertise at staging murders and kidnappings. "I guess they are cooking up something extraordinary," a colleague said when Naumov and Pavlov arrived in Istanbul. One of Akhmedov's men was the Soviet agent who introduced Pavlov to Sagol and Sayman.

"Naumov" was the cover name for none other than Leonid Eitingon, whose still-mysterious career was one of the most remarkable in the history of twentieth-century espionage. He had been a Soviet operative in China during the 1920s and then Istanbul resident for the secret police in 1929. Next, he was assigned to the NKVD's "Special Tasks" section, which carried out Stalin's bloodiest deeds. He went to Spain in 1936 to kill anti-Stalin leftists during the civil war; the next year found him as a Soviet military attaché in Paris, where he kidnapped the leader of the most important anti-Communist Russian émigré group.

His greatest achievement, however, won him promotion to the rank of deputy director for Soviet military intelligence. In 1940 he went to Mexico to organize the murder of Leon Trotsky. A first assassination attempt in May, involving the world-famous Mexican muralist David Siqueiros as triggerman, failed, though one of Trotsky's bodyguards was killed. Eitingon planned more carefully the second time, recruiting the son of his Spanish Communist mistress to commit the crime. In August, the plot was successful and Eitingon escaped back to the U.S.S.R. The killing of von Papen was his next assignment.

Akhmedov participated in the debate at the U.S.S.R.'s Istanbul consulate when Naumov wanted to resist the Turkish police by force, but cooler heads in Moscow ordered the consulate to surrender Pavlov. The delay, however, gave Naumov enough time to invent a cover story and coach Pavlov on his testimony. During the trial, when Moscow sent the NKVD general in charge of violent operations to investigate what had gone wrong in Turkey, Vinogradov told him that Akhmedov was to blame for revealing the plan to the Turks. It was agreed that Akhmedov was to be the scapegoat for the mess.

Vinogradov ordered Akhmedov to come from Istanbul to Ankara for a meeting in the embassy. The ambassador told the press attaché that he must return to Moscow escorted "for his own safety" by two armed Soviet couriers. Akhmedov took the train back to Istanbul to wind up his affairs. The express clattered over the featureless Anatolian plateau. Next to him sat one of his closest friends and coworkers. He was not afraid to go home, Akhmedov said, and was quite willing to be sent to the front.

"Look, my dear friend," his colleague interrupted, "you are in big, big trouble. If I were you, I would not go back. . . . You are finished. You will never see Moscow as a free man." Everyone else in the embassy already knew that Naumov, needing a scapegoat, was claiming that Akhmedov had tipped off the Turks, British, and Yugoslavs about the plot. Vinogradov was reporting that Akhmedov was pro-Turkish. "People bigger than you, generals and marshals of the Red Army, prominent party members, and untold thousands of others" had died in the secret police's cellars, his colleague continued. His only way out was to defect.

Akhmedov smiled. Perhaps this was merely an attempt to discover his true feelings. Years of intelligence work and of life in Stalin's Russia had made him suspicious. He had no intention of running away, Akhmedov retorted. But whether or not the warning was sincere—Akhmedov later concluded that it was—its accuracy was apparent.

Soon after returning to Istanbul, Akhmedov left the consulate, made sure he was not being followed, and hailed the first passing taxi. He got out near Istanbul's labyrinthine bazaar, bought a pack of cigarettes, walked a bit further, and then took another cab over the Galata Bridge. At the first public telephone, he called the Yugoslav military attaché and a British intelligence man.

He met them clandestinely—the former in a busy cafe, the latter on a local train going to the city's beach—and told them of his plan to defect. Then Akhmedov returned to his apartment and tried to sleep, but he tossed and turned most of the night. The next day he went to the consulate offices, where he typed a farewell note denouncing the Soviet system and balanced his accounts to forestall charges of embezzlement. Then he told everyone that he was going to lunch and walked outside, across the courtyard to the consulate gate. Just before Akhmedov reached the exit, a colleague stopped him. Akhmedov thought he was about to be arrested, but the man merely wanted to ask if they could dine together. Some other time, Akhmedov replied.

Once out the gate, he made his way to police headquarters to request asylum. He was given six bodyguards under orders to shoot if Soviet agents tried a kidnapping. A small boat took him across the Bosporus to a safe house, where he was debriefed by the Turkish army and Emniyet. No Turkish leader could now doubt that Moscow had ordered von Papen's assassination or ignore the Soviet effort to subvert Turkey.

These hidden events revealed a complex pattern of deceit. The Soviet authorities, of course, assumed that Akhmedov and Hanak had told the Turks about the plot. Thus, the Kremlin understood that its guilt was fully known to Ankara. All the bluster and threats, then, were not expressions of innocent outrage or even just propaganda; rather, they were a campaign to intimidate the Turks so that they would back down and bury the facts.

The Turks did not want a confrontation with the Russians, but they pursued the case to make crystal-clear their rejection of Soviet subversion. Turkey's refusal to knuckle under was a prelude to standing firm against the Soviet attacks on its sovereignty that would occur after the war.

The attempt on von Papen's life was only one of many events that made the covert battles in Turkey so vital to the war's outcome. The entanglement of motives, spies, and plots meant that Istanbul, whose name was already redolent of espionage and romance, fulfilled its reputation.

2 | Sailing to Istanbul

He who has burnt his tongue on hot soup, blows on his cold yoghurt.
—Turkish proverb

The small, dirty old Romanian ship chugged southward from the Black Sea. The sun reflected in bright gashes from the blue Bosporus's little waves and made Istanbul's minarets and mosque domes glisten brightly. "On the hills of Asia to the left, on those of Europe to the right, the ancient stone buildings gave off the warm glow of permanence. It was peace, bright and quiet peace. It was strange, disturbing and shameful. . . . It made me nervous. It felt unnatural that from those shores came no vibrations of fear and grimness, no odor of death." Thus wrote CBS radio correspondent Cecil Brown, in his diary, of his arrival in Istanbul during World War II.

To the north, an hour's sailing up the Bosporus waterway, was Russia. Only two hours' drive to the west was the Bulgarian border. Istanbul remained a city still at peace, but it was on the inferno's edge. During the war years, the grand art deco dining room of Istanbul's best hotel, the Park, was a truce zone where Britons and Germans, Americans and Japanese, Hungarians and Greeks, businesspeople, soldiers, journalists, diplomats, and spies of every nation and description eyed each other from adjacent tables. The food was good, there were no wartime shortages, and drink flowed freely in the adjoining wood-paneled bar.

| 17

Across the broad Ayas Pasha Boulevard from the stucco Park Hotel stood the German consulate. From his study, Ambassador Franz von Papen had a fine view of the hotel and the Bosporus strait beyond. Fishing boats, brusque freighters, and boxy ferries moved north, south, and between the European and Asian shores. The ships performed an unending dance. In the distance, Asian Anatolia's green hills rose behind the Shemshi Pasha and Mehmed Pasha mosques. On the eve of World War II, about 740,000 people lived in the city and nearby villages.

Istanbul was a worthy successor to its earlier incarnations as the great imperial capital of Constantinople and Byzantium. No city in the world had a more beautiful—or more strategically powerful—setting than those hills along the Bosporus. The waterway threaded like a strong, broad river south from the wine-dark Black Sea to the Sea of Marmara and thence to the Mediterranean. The word "bosporus" originally meant "the inside of the throat," an unpoetic but accurate description of the waterway's value. The city was fought over so often because it controlled the main land route between Europe, Asia, and the Middle East, as well as the door to and from southern Russia.

On each shore villages famous for their fine fish and mussels punctuated the Asian east coast, where ancient Greece's great cities and many-towered Troy once flourished. Up the Bosporus sailed the Argonauts in search of the Golden Fleece. The powerful currents ran past the pure springs of the Sweet Waters of Asia, the ruins of abandoned palaces and fortresses, the village of Bebek, the plush yacht club and the foreign ambassadors' summer retreats, the narrow roads, the antique wooden mansions of princelings and merchants, and the old sultans' palaces and mighty cathedral mosques.

The city's waterways resembled the letter "Y." Forming the long northeast arm, the Bosporus flowed past Istanbul's modern Beyoglu district, where most foreigners lived, and then by old Galata's steep streets and cramped houses. There it met the shorter, upper-left arm: the narrow Golden Horn, a natural canal that stretched 4½ miles to the northwest. It provided, a French visitor wrote in 1635, "the goodliest, the deepest, and the most commodious [port] in Europe." The Y's stem was the Sea of Marmara, through which the passage continued southward toward the Mediterranean.

Thus, Istanbul had every conceivable natural advantage. It was located on the trade and strategic crossroads of Europe, Asia, and the Middle East while it also linked the Black Sea to the Mediterranean. There were fresh springs, abundant fish, and a generally mild climate. Snow was rare and the summer heat was cut by cool breezes. No city, or emperor, could ask for more.

Constantine, the Roman emperor, founded the city in 413 A.D. as capital of his realm's eastern provinces. After the empire split, Emperor Theodosus III expanded and rebuilt Constantinople as Byzantium, capital of the surviving, Greek-speaking Byzantine empire. For a thousand years thereafter, the strengthened walls withstood numerous assaults— by Goths in 478, Persians in 616 and 626, Arabs in 668 and 716 to 718, Russians four times between the ninth and eleventh centuries, and Turks in 1422. It was captured and plundered only in 1204 by rapacious Christian crusaders who had supposedly come to save it from Moslem conquest.

Byzantium's power decayed due to internal divisions and the westward advance of the Ottoman Turks. Its complex, conspiracy-ridden politics gave the world a new word, "byzantine," to describe such a situation. In 1453, the city was again besieged by the Turks this time led by the dynamic Sultan Mehmed II. Farmlands that furnished the city's food were captured or put to the torch. When the Byzantines stretched a chain across the Golden Horn to keep out the Ottoman fleet, the sultan ordered that seventy ships be built and then dragged over the hills above the city one night in May. At dawn, seemingly by magic, this Turkish fleet appeared in the Golden Horn. Cut off and attacked from all directions, Byzantium fell as church bells tolled its death. Mehmed entered triumphantly and was afterward known in the West as "the Conquerer."

The city itself, however, did not suffer by this defeat. As Istanbul, it became the capital of the Ottomans' empire. Mehmed and his successors proved apt builders as well as generals. The Aya Sophia Cathedral, built in 538, was transformed into a place of Islamic worship. Gigantic new Moslem mosques—the famed Blue and Fatih, Süleymaniye, Kariya, and Koca Mustafa Pasha—were built on the adjoining hills.

The Galata district, given by a Byzantine emperor to Genoese merchants in the thirteenth century, continued to be a commercial center.

Jews expelled from Spain in 1492 by Christian persecution were welcomed and well-treated. The Great Bazaar prospered; palaces were built with harems and treasure houses. The empire's tribute flowed into the capital; artists and artisans adorned it. Through Istanbul's gates marched armies to conquer all the lands from Egypt in the south to the border of Persia in the east and onto the very doorstep of Vienna in the west.

The city flourished for over 450 years until the empire finally collapsed after World War I. Having sided with Germany, the Ottomans suffered a terrible defeat. Millions of Turks were dead from war, disease, and famine. Most of the large Armenian Christian minority had been slaughtered by the Moslems or had fled. The British and French took over the Arab lands, occupied Istanbul in 1919, and enthroned a puppet sultan there. The Turks had lost the half-millennium-old empire which had given them their identity and institutions. A Greek army occupied much of the remaining territory.

At this moment of national catastrophe, General Mustafha Kemal led a revolt from the interior, drove out the Greek army, and established Turkey as a republic in the early 1920s. He was not only the savior of a totally prostrate country but also a reformer determined to make it a modern nation. One of his innovations was to select Ankara over Istanbul as capital in order to develop hitherto neglected Anatolia, Turkey's eastern hinterland. "Henceforth," he declared in 1919, "Istanbul does not control Anatolia, but Anatolia Istanbul." Yet although Istanbul's 1500-year reign as a capital ended, its economic and cultural power survived.

The handsome leader radiated power and authority. A man of immense energy, he would drink and gamble all night and then arise after a short nap to conduct the nation's affairs. In 1921, a U.S. Navy officer described him as strikingly youthful, with "high cheek bones, somewhat hollow cheeks, small reddish and very trim mustache, steel blue eyes." His face was "not intellectual but subtle and mercuric. . . . You got a sense of concentration . . . with immense possibilities of inexorability, cruelty even, yet [with empathy] and a broad outlook."

An absolute faith in his own mission rallied a dispirited, disoriented people. With the help of his friend İsmet İnönü, he began rebuilding the country and forging its new self-image. Previously, "Turk" had been a word of opprobrium applied to backward provincials. The elite saw itself as Ottoman; the majority thought of themselves as Moslem. Now a new slogan was proclaimed: "It is great to be a Turk!"

"We now belong to the West," the leader said, and must adopt new customs. The Turkish language was simplified and written with Roman rather than Arabic letters, the Moslem clergy's power was broken, the legal code was revised, and the wearing of the veil by women was banned. The fez, the brimless headdress which the new leader called "a sign of ignorance, of fanaticism, of hatred against progress and civilization," was replaced with European-style hats. He also decreed for the first time that everyone must choose a last name. Lists of suggested ones were posted everywhere. Parliament voted him the name "Atatürk," that is, "Father of the Turks." A parliamentary regime was established, but there was only one party and Atatürk was the state's unquestioned master.

Yet even with all these changes, Istanbul remained a symbol of exoticism and romance for Westerners. The romantic route for those wishing to visit Istanbul was via the world's most famous train, the *Orient Express*. Running from Paris to Istanbul twice a week, the Express took fifty-six hours to complete the 2000-mile trip across seven countries. Its passengers included emperors and crooks, diplomats and maharajas, spies and diplomatic couriers. King Boris of Bulgaria and Romania's King Carol, alongside his famous mistress Magda Lupescu, sometimes took the controls when the train passed through their countries. The millionaire arms' merchant, Basil Zaharoff, and Calouste Gulbenkian, son of the world's wealthiest man, were frequent passengers who met their wives on the train.

Agatha Christie, Graham Greene, Eric Ambler, and John Dos Passos were among the writers it inspired. Dos Passos once described the trip east in his distinctive newsreel-poetry style: "Day by day the hills get scrawnier and dryer and the train goes more and more slowly and the stationmasters have longer and longer moustaches and seedier and seedier uniforms until at last we are winding between a bright-green sea and yellow sunburned capes. Suddenly the train is trapped between mustard-colored crumbling walls, the line runs among rubbish heaps and cypresses. The train is hardly moving at all, it stops imperceptibly as if on a siding. Is it? No, yes, it must be . . . Constantinople."

The first view of the city from the train's windows was the Fort of the Seven Towers. The Sea of Marmara and then the great mosques appeared. As the train rounded Seraglio Point, it steamed past the sultan's old harem and the fifteenth-century Topkapi Palace. There was magic in the clean lines of the wooden houses, mosques, and palaces. The hills gave way to startling vistas of blue waters, old Ottoman cemeteries with stone turbans atop the pillar tombstones, and the crowded bazaar full of enough gold, jewelry, and carpets to furnish the whole world.

One of the city's true admirers was a rotund little Italian peasant named Angelo Giuseppe Roncalli, whose modest house was only a few blocks away from the Park Hotel and von Papen's consulate. Roncalli rode regularly on the *Orient Express*. "In the train," he wrote, "you can relax, read, pray, observe the beauties of nature and the variety of people." He was the Vatican's legate and apostolic vicar to Istanbul's few Catholics. Fifty-eight years old in 1939, Roncalli came from an Italian village where his family had lived for four and a half centuries. His desk was adorned only with photos of relatives and a Phillips radio for listening to shortwave broadcasts. Forbidden by Turkey's secularist regime to wear clerical garb, he donned a sober coat, unfashionable suit, and bowler hat. But spartan habits did not bar his enjoyment of a garden ablaze with roses and magnolias.

Roncalli's simple, sincere piety was inherited from his humble background as a peasant child, scholarship student, and then a hospital orderly and chaplain in World War I. He emerged from this experience a modernist and supporter of the incipient Christian Democratic movement in Italy.

Many years later, as Pope John XXIII, he would put his beliefs into practice, but now Roncalli was in disfavor. After making a speech in 1925 critical of Italian dictator Benito Mussolini, with whom the church was on excellent terms, Roncalli was exiled first to Bulgaria for ten years and then to Istanbul. His years in Greek Orthodox and Moslem lands would make him ecumenical; from exile in the provinces he gained the perspective of a parish priest rather than that of a Vatican prince.

Yet the prospects for Roncalli's career during his time in Istanbul could not have been poorer. It was not merely humility that prompted him to write on first coming to Istanbul, "I have achieved very little. . . . I feel humbled and ashamed before the Lord . . . but I look to the future with imperturbable and confident serenity." With a self-deprecating sense of humor, Roncalli called himself the "Vatican's postman in the Middle East."

"I am fond of the Turks," he noted in his journal, and he added, "It is my special intention, as an exercise in mortification, to learn the Turkish language." He drew inspiration from watching the hundreds of fishing boats strung with lights on the Bosporus each night. The cheerfulness of the fishermen, who labored even in the pouring rain, made him remark, "Oh how ashamed we should feel, we priests, 'fishers of men,' before such an example! . . . We must do as the fishermen of the Bosporus do, work night and day with our torches lit, each in his own little boat."

But Roncalli also learned from the tragedy of an era so full of war and dictatorship. A state's greatness, he concluded, could not be measured by "military enterprises, diplomatic agreements or economic successes," but only by "justice embodied in law." Amid ruins of the vanished Greeks, Romans, and Ottomans who once governed from Istanbul, Roncalli concluded that Catholicism could survive only by adapting to changing times rather than by imitating the unbending but mortal empires of the past.

While Roncalli sought spiritual lessons from Istanbul, more worldly visitors saw the city as romance incarnate. A Hungarian writer recorded an enchanting twilight in the old quarter: "A mélange of tightly built, dilapidated Turkish houses with closed balconies, primitive caravanseries, modern buildings, churches and ruins of all ages, densely and capriciously grown together along large squares and narrow, meandering, badly paved streets, that silhouette of many thousand years of glory and squalor [under] the immaculate minarets and the compact domes of Aya Sophia and the Blue Mosque."

An American navy officer rhapsodized: "I have seen Istanbul from many points of vantage: from Haydarpasha, in the morning haze, when it is a city out of an Eastern fairy tale; from the minaret of the Blue Mosque at midday, when it is hard and clear like a Canaletto; and from the Seraglio point at sunset, when the towers and minarets cast strange shadows. It remains for me the most beautiful city in the world; blessed in its God-given setting . . . majestic in its man-made mosques and palaces; fascinating in its variety; mysterious in its contrasts of quiet gardens and milling crowds."

The more skeptical *New York Times* correspondent C. L. Sulzberger thought of Istanbul as "sixteen centuries of empire piled on empire in ramshackled hodgepodge, rimmed by rushing waters and jerry-built filth, pierced by the thrust of minarets." President Atatürk had introduced some new features: gardens, Taksim Square, and straight modern avenues to accommodate trolleys and motor cars. Most important of the latter was Istiklal Caddesi (Independence Boulevard). The Aya Sophia was now transformed from mosque to museum as a secularist symbol. The sultan's palaces—the Mideast-style Topkapi and European-style Dolmabahce—became museums as symbols of republicanism. Istanbul University, opened in 1453 as a school of religious studies, was refurbished to promote modern learning and science.

The orderly, disciplined character of the people made it easier for Atatürk to rule. Turks, a British intelligence report accurately noted, "have inherited a natural dignity, restraint, and courtesy, but keenly resent injustice or insult. There is great personal courage, frugality, hardihood, and loyalty to a trusted leader." They were proud, stubborn, respectful of hierarchy, and secretive. Impervious to threats, Turks were quick to take offense but steadfast in friendship.

These same military virtues, however, also constrained progress. As in the sultan's court, personal success depended on winning favor from the powerful. Subordinates feared taking the smallest initiative. An American visitor saw this system in action when the director of a large hospital took him on a tour. Seeing many flies entering the wards through open windows, the guest expressed surprise that no one closed them. His host explained this was not how things worked. Unless the director ordered something, even the closing of a window, no nurse or orderly would dream of being so disrespectful as to do it.

Officials would delegate no power but were loathe to accept responsibility. Asked why Turkey's cabinet ministers stayed a month or two in Europe for medical treatment every summer, an American diplomat explained, "Lectured by the prime minister and plagued with questions by their own subordinates it is no wonder that they show signs of wear and tear."

Foreigners were hospitably but suspiciously received. The Turks were secretive, highly sensitive to dissent, and quick to suspect subversion. The smallest details of army operations and government deliberations were jealously concealed. The ubiquitous secret police (Emniyet) watched everyone and everything with a quiet effectiveness that made other intelligence agencies seem amateurish. It kept detailed files on foreign residents and tourists in Istanbul, gathering information from numerous hotel, restaurant, embassy, and transport workers, as well as others, on its payroll.

Istanbul's people themselves mixed the ethnic groups and cultures of East and West. The Turks passionately embraced European clothes, manners, and secularism. Communities of Greeks, Jews, and Armenians also maintained their own customs, languages, and dress. The champion relay-race team of Protestant-run Robert College, reflecting this mélange, included a Turk, a Greek, an Armenian, and a Bulgarian.

In this cosmopolitan atmosphere, foreign institutions were permitted as long as they did not interfere with Turkish politics. In addition to Robert College, run by American Protestant missionaries, there were German, French, and Italian schools. Italian Fascist and German Nazi party cells operated freely among their nationals; foreign governments subsidized Istanbul newspapers in their own languages. Several long-settled "Levantine" British families played an important role in Istanbul's commerce and later with British diplomacy and intelligence. The American community in Istanbul included the often wild, heavy-drinking adventure seekers working for Socony-Vacuum Oil or Liggett & Myers Tobacco and the earnest midwestern teetotalers from the missionary institutions. Both groups later provided cadre for U.S. intelligence operations.

During the summer months, ambassadors escaped from Ankara's heat to Istanbul's breezes. Each of them had his own yacht. The American vessel the *Hiawatha* hosted such visiting dignitaries as Douglas MacArthur and Eleanor Roosevelt. During the war, these boats would take ambassadors on Bosporus "fishing trips" that concealed secret meetings.

The diplomats and their families passed the summer days of the late 1930s in rounds of parties, receptions, tennis games, and picnics, as well as swimming, fishing, or hunting expeditions. There was always time to go to the yacht club, headquarters of local high society. Rejans, the White Russian restaurant favored by Atatürk, featured waitresses who reputedly were former czarist duchesses. And Istanbul was where

Hungarian-born Zsa-Zsa Gabor, then married to a Turkish diplomat, learned to be glamorous.

Diplomatic work was rarely urgent. As late as 1941, much of the U.S. embassy's correspondence with Washington concerned efforts to sell a piano belonging to an embassy couple who had been transferred home. The ambassador also lashed out at the frustrations of life in Ankara: "I suppose that I am getting the jitters having had to live a better part of my three years in the intellectually and spiritually sterile climate of this cardboard capital in the wilds . . . having had to send away first my children and more recently my wife, and to make out with the companionship of a couple of lovable but ungovernable native dogs— having pleaded in vain with the Department for more than a year to equip us with the personnel to meet a situation of predictably increasing difficulty, having received from the Department scarcely a word of guidance or of help." He concluded that the only time State was interested in his post was when it suspected "some scullduggery about furniture." The secretary of state's "main preoccupation" seemed to be Mrs. Gillespie's piano, he complained, concluding, "To hell with Mrs. Gillespie's piano!"

The Turkish government's main objective in the late 1930s was to ensure that the country remained this quiet. It wanted to prevent war or avoid being dragged into one. World War I was remembered as an unmitigated disaster in which, in Atatürk's words, "millions of men were sacrificed for no purpose." Moreover, while Turks made fine soldiers, their military equipment was obsolete. Istanbul's wooden houses were kindling for a conflagration if bombed from the air. The country had no stockpiles of supplies. Consequently, Turkey tried to stay on good terms with all the powers, including Germany, its World War I ally, which had trained much of its army. The Nazis sought to tie Turkey to Germany by economic means, buying 62 percent of its exports in 1937.

Fear and hatred of Moscow was Turkey's underlying incentive for cultivating London and Berlin. Turkish mothers made their children behave by threatening that the Russians would get them if they were bad. But Russia's historic ambitions, rather than its Communist ideology, were the source of this attitude. Turks remembered the czars' steady advance southward. Throughout the eighteenth and nineteenth centuries, a dozen Russo-Turkish wars had cost the Turks much of their territory and hundreds of thousands of Turkish refugees who fled Russian-occupied lands. Moscow had wanted to conquer Istanbul and control the Bosporus strait which held the key to Russia's southern flank. The Turks knew that the Russian Revolution had not changed those goals.

During the late 1930s, Turkey's leaders knew that their country was in danger as a powerful Germany and U.S.S.R. sought to extend their influence. The Balkans, as southeast Europe was often called, were again—as they had been in 1914—a tinderbox. On September 29, 1938, the British and French surrendered western Czechoslovakia to Hitler at Munich. This concession, British Prime Minister Neville Chamberlain proclaimed, preserved "peace in our time." In contrast, small countries like Turkey saw the betrayal of Czechoslovakia by the bigger powers as an intimation of their own impending mortality.

Winston Churchill advocated a British alliance with all the "smaller states that are menaced, who are going to be devoured one by one by the Nazi tyranny." But he was out of power and out of step with Britain's policy of appeasing Hitler. Even if London had behaved differently, the southeast European states were individually too weak and divided among themselves to resist. Only Atatürk's continued presence at the helm calmed his nation amid these dangers. When rumors began circulating in Istanbul that Atatürk was ill, the government censored any publication of them. A newspaper that dared mention his absence from an October 1938 event was closed for three months.

Censoring reports of Atatürk's illness, however, could not preserve his health. At 10 a.m. on the morning of November 10, 1938, the 58-year-old Atatürk died in his room at the Dolmabahce Palace. The entire nation was traumatized. Work ceased and everything closed. In Istanbul, crowds of frightened, weeping people poured into the streets and milled around for hours. Some reverently listened to a recital of Atatürk's life; others grabbed newspapers as they appeared on the stands. "We have lost our leader at a very inopportune time," a Turkish diplomat dryly wrote in his diary.

A new leader was needed quickly. The next morning, 200 miles to the east, in Ankara, parliament elected İsmet İnönü as the new president. He was the logical choice.

During World War I, İnönü had fought the Russians and served in the War Ministry. But he refused to stay a single day in Istanbul when foreign troops occupied it in 1919, so he defected to Atatürk's nationalist forces. İnönü rose steadily in that army and directed its great victory over the Greeks at İnönü, from which he later took his name.

During the republic's first fifteen years, İnönü was Atatürk's prime minister. A few months before Atatürk's death, the two proud men quarreled over a minor issue. İnönü resigned. But Atatürk spoke well of him even during their estrangement. When İnönü became president, a leading politician noted in his diary, "Only from this point on will his true political character become clear because up until now you could not understand what he did on his own initiative or on Atatürk's." Compared with the handsome, energetic Atatürk, İnönü was quiet, plain, and straitlaced. Where Atatürk was stormy, İnönü was patient. Atatürk's qualities were essential to establishing a regime; İnönü's were appropriate for consolidating one.

Atatürk's casket was placed in the throne room of Istanbul's Dolmabahce Palace as hundreds of thousands of people walked from all the city's quarters to view it. On November 17, crowds at the palace entrance became so disorderly that mounted police charged them. In the ensuing panic, a dozen people were trampled to death. Many Turks asked whether this was a sign of coming disintegration.

Two days later, the funeral ceremonies began. They were designed to close the old era and calm the nation. Six black horses pulled a gun carriage bearing Atatürk's coffin through Istanbul to the Bosporus. There it was loaded onto a Turkish cruiser for the trip across to the Asian shore. Around the ship ranged most of the Turkish navy and warships from Britain, Germany, France, the U.S.S.R., Romania, and Greece. On the Asian side, the coffin was put onto a special train that puffed slowly eastward, stopping briefly at stations lit by flares and filled with flowers and mourners.

The next morning, the coffin was met in Ankara by a delegation led by İnönü. The procession marched to the parliament building, where torches with smoky flames made the sky black with grief. Soldiers cried while İnönü proclaimed Atatürk "a heroic human being that our own nation raised." There was no religious ceremony, only the nationalist pageantry Atatürk had favored.

On the morning of the twenty-first, a company of soldiers, flanked by ten admirals and generals, pulled the wagon bearing Atatürk's remains through Ankara's streets to the Ethnographic Museum, where the body would lie until a tomb was completed. The crowd silently watched the colorful parade led by the dignified, obsolete cavalry, followed by ambassadors and small military units from nations that would soon be at war. Next came İnönü, his cabinet, military commanders, and the diplomatic corps.

Although they had buried him, the Turks would not let Atatürk die. During all his years as president, İnönü would always hear "the name 'Atatürk' on every tongue," said one contemporary politician, "as if he was still walking in Atatürk's shadow. And this shadow was getting gradually wider, longer and darker." As the international crisis rose around them, Turks would comment, "Ah, Atatürk, what are we going to do without you?" The government had extended the mourning and ceremonies for as long as possible. Yet with Atatürk dead, İnönü bore the burden of saving the country in its time of danger. And what perilous days these would be!

3 | Intimations of Catastrophe

You don't need a guide to a village you can see.
—Turkish proverb

The competition between the Allies and Germany brought a struggle between them for Turkey's allegiance. As the Nazis took over one country after another, all Europe was engulfed in war and German armies rolled closer and closer to Istanbul.

The Germans occupied Czechoslovakia in March 1939 and transformed it on the Nazi pattern. Business executives, journalists, politicians, and officials were courted, bribed, and given special privileges in exchange for collaboration. Those who refused to cooperate were arrested, tortured, and shipped to concentration camps. The ethnic German and part of the Slovak minorities formed a fifth column. Newspapers and radio stations were seized or censored. Tens of thousands of refugees fled.

One night soon after the Germans entered Prague, a young leftist Hungarian correspondent named George Paloczi-Horvath sat mournfully drinking with two British friends in that city's fashionable Embassy Nightclub. Cigarette smoke filled the room. A German major eyed the three men and finally swayed drunkenly over to their tiny table. He sat down and told them how ashamed he was to be involved in the brutal rape of Czechoslovakia.

Why, asked Paloczi-Horvath, didn't the Germans themselves stop Hitler? The major pounded the table. "Do you know what it means to live under terrorism? Do you know what it feels like to live in a police state? You are kids; you don't know the half of it," he lamented. "It's not only a question of courage. Resistance just leads to a quick arrest. To resist is generally nothing but committing an isolated suicide." German officers bowed to Hitler's seemingly magical charisma and a system which seemed to lead them to one victory after another.

Paloczi-Horvath and an equally anti-Nazi Danish colleague then made a mutual assistance pact: "If Hitler occupies my country first," said the Dane, "I will come to Budapest and stay with you. If the Germans grab Hungary, you can come live with me in Copenhagen." "And what," interrupted an older French writer sitting between them, "if he occupies both?" Exactly one year later, after war had begun, the German army would march into Denmark. Paloczi-Horvath heard the news in Istanbul's Park Hotel. The following year, as the Hungarian government joined the Axis, Paloczi-Horvath was in Budapest and had to grab the last train out to escape being imprisoned. He fled to neutral Istanbul and joined British intelligence to continue the fight.

But in the spring and summer days of 1939, Roncalli was still struggling to sustain his hope for peace. On a trip home to Rome, he saw the Fascist regime repress liberal Catholics and host Hitler amidst pomp, hundreds of swastika flags, and cheering crowds. Yet, Roncalli maintained in one of his Istanbul sermons, "History ebbs and flows. The designs of the Lord, not human plans shape [it]." Istanbul itself had seen many empires vanish without a trace, and the same fate, Roncalli hinted, was in store for Hitler and Mussolini. All would turn out well. "I don't believe we will have a war," Roncalli wrote in April 1939. A few days later, Mussolini invaded Albania and signed a formal alliance with Hitler. Roncalli was one of the last optimists left in Europe.

The Turkish leaders were more realistic. "Arms and munitions factories are engaged in feverish activity," said Foreign Minister Şükrü Saracoğlu in July 1939. "Diplomatic conversations have a sort of warlike character; newspapers, the radio and news agencies create an atmosphere of war." Europe was not yet at war, but everyone knew that a titanic battle was imminent.

The Turks thought that their resources and strategic location put them on Hitler's list of countries to be conquered. Dr. Joseph Goebbels, the brilliantly effective German propaganda minister, flew into Istanbul for a visit. On the way, his plane took a detour over Turkish military installations south of the city. When Goebbels landed at Istanbul's Yesilkoy Airport, he was met not only by a German welcoming party but also by a flock of Emniyet officials who seized all the pictures taken of Turkey's key army bases.

Belatedly, Britain and France girded themselves against Hitler's divide-and-conquer strategy, beginning a frantic race against Berlin and Rome for influence throughout east and southeast Europe. Britain unsuccessfully urged that countries in the Balkans region—Turkey, Greece, Bulgaria, Romania, Yugoslavia, and Hungary—form a defensive alliance against German expansion. In the summer of 1939 Britain and France agreed to aid Turkey if it was attacked.

As soon as he heard this news, German Ambassador Franz von Papen rushed to the Foreign Ministry and proposed a German-Turkish pact. His orders were to prevent Turkey's alignment with Germany's enemies. If the Allies obtained the use of Turkey's resources and strategic position, Foreign Minister Joachim von Ribbentrop told him, Germany would lose the coming war. Berlin knew, having broken Ankara's diplomatic code, that Turkey would be passive as long as the Axis did not attack the Balkans. But this was precisely what Hitler and his friend Mussolini intended to do. Von Papen must ensure that Turkey remain neutral even after conquest of that region began.

He used threats as well as promises. "What are you going to do," von Papen warned the Turks, "without modern weapons in the coming battle? Istanbul and all your cities will be destroyed. . . . Stay neutral!" The wily ambassador exploited the Turks' great fear. They had worked twenty years to overcome the last war's devastation. Foreign Minister Saracoğlu had just told parliament, "No victory could give us what . . . years of peace have bestowed upon us, and no responsible man could lightly let these magnificent achievements disappear in the flames of an armed struggle." Now the Turks feared that their efforts would literally be turned to ashes in a few weeks.

There were other factors working in the Germans' favor as well. Fear of German power made the Balkan States more willing to appease Hitler. Many leaders in east and central Europe thought Germany was an invincible force they had to propitiate or join. Newspapers and politicians were often for sale. Romania was a crumbling state in which corruption had become an art form. Yugoslavia was a patchwork of mutually resentful ethnic groups. Greece suffered under an unpopular dictator.

In addition, rivalries inhibited cooperation among the small countries. Territorial disputes among them gave some regimes an incentive to align themselves with Berlin. Germany's defeated World War I allies, Hungary and Bulgaria, had suffered in the peace settlement and were as eager as Hitler to revise existing frontiers at their neighbors' expense. Some Balkan elites saw Germany as a shield against the U.S.S.R.; local fascist movements collaborated enthusiastically with it.

The difficulty of accomplishing anything in this part of the world had long led frustrated diplomats to use the word "Balkan" to describe impossibly entangled feuds. Nonetheless, in the summer of 1939, a Balkan defense pact, which would convince Germany that aggression was futile, seemed the only way to avoid war. Grigore Gafencu, Romania's pro-British foreign minister, wrote, "Ankara seemed to be at the center of the efforts being made throughout the world to bar the road to war." Diplomats congregated there in June 1939 for a final attempt to save peace. A gala ball was held at the Ankara Palace, the city's grandest hotel. Limousines pulled up the drive and the great men emerged, dressed somberly and identically but representing every political hue. President İnönü and Foreign Minister Saracoğlu shook each arrival's hand as the guests filed into the banquet hall, where a giant portrait of Atatürk was the sole decoration. Incongruously, in one corner, a jazz orchestra played the latest tunes.

All eyes were on von Papen as he entered the room, surrounded by his retinue and proudly wearing two medals awarded him by the Turks in World War I. Everyone knew that von Papen was determined to block any Balkan alliance, but diplomatic politeness prevailed. Saracoğlu introduced him to everyone, and von Papen immediately took aside Gafencu, the guest of honor.

"I congratulate you on the work for peace you are carrying on here," von Papen said as he shook the Romanian's hand. "Minds must be calmed. For my part, that is what I am trying to do here and, above all, in my own country. We don't want war." He added, with a meaningful smile: "War is a misfortune I should like to spare the regime which governs Germany at the moment. You doubtless understand my solicitude for the regime. I have more reason than anyone to wish that the little experiment now being tried by my country will not cause too many disappointments."

As always, von Papen was trying to give the impression that he was the Third Reich's true architect and that this paternity meant he still held great power. Simultaneously, he portrayed himself as a moderate who, if everyone only cooperated with him, could restrain, and eventually replace, Hitler.

No German and perhaps no one outside Germany, however, more thoroughly misunderstood and underestimated Hitler than did von Papen. The British and French were naive about Hitler's fanaticism and his military might. Before Hitler seized power, German Communists had stupidly attacked anti-Nazi moderates under the slogan "After Hitler, us!" But von Papen's slogan seemed to be "After Hitler, me!" Some anti-Nazis shared von Papen's illusion. If Hitler was a mad little ex-corporal, it seemed logical that someone like von Papen must be pulling the strings.

Von Papen's greatest asset was his considerable charm. Goebbels called him "the best horse in our stable." Roncalli liked von Papen and thought him a good Catholic. Von Papen's personal popularity enraged opponents of Hitler who thought it particularly detestable that someone so cultured, suave, and polite—the personification of a European aristocrat—would be such a willing and effective collaborator of the Nazi regime.

Born in 1879, von Papen attended military schools, became a cavalry officer, and joined the army's elite general staff in 1913. At the start of World War I, he was sent as a military attaché to Washington, where he organized a ring of agents to sabotage U.S. shipyards and munitions' factories.

In 1915, von Papen sent home a big shipment of secret U.S. military plans as well as documents for use in blackmailing American politicians. He chose the apparently safe method of using as a courier a neutral U.S. citizen traveling on a neutral Dutch ship. But the secretary who wrapped the package was a Czech nationalist agent working for British intelligence. Tipped off by the Czechs, the British stopped the ship, discovered the purloined documents, and gave them wide publicity. The item that most outraged the American public was a passage in one of von Papen's letters to his wife ridiculing "those idiotic Yankees." Washington angrily demanded von Papen's recall.

Despite this amateurish failure to subvert America, von Papen's adventures there made him a hero in Germany. After service on the western front, he joined the German military mission to Istanbul in 1917. There he met İnönü, fought the British, and was interned when the Turks surrendered in 1918. After the war, von Papen returned to Germany and went into politics as a member of the Catholic Center party. Again, ambition misled him. Von Papen betrayed his own party, which opposed alliance with the extreme right. To stop some last-minute effort to block his appointment as chancellor in 1932, von Papen falsely told his own party leader—a priest, no less—that he would not accept the post. The enraged priest later labeled von Papen a "Judas," a not insignificant insult in Catholic circles.

During von Papen's six months as chancellor, Germany was facing economic collapse, growing polarization, and street violence. Von Papen's defection further divided moderates and allowed Hitler's power to grow. To win Nazi backing for his cabinet, von Papen ended a ban on Hitler's private army. Weakening the already tottering republic, he purged democratic-minded civil servants. When Hitler came to power in January 1933 with von Papen's help, the Nazi leader made von Papen his vice-chancellor.

Once more, von Papen miscalculated, thinking he could outmaneuver the Nazis. He made a speech urging Hitler to allow a multiparty state and grant more liberties. Hitler was infuriated and considered having him killed. Instead, the Nazis murdered the assistant who wrote the speech. Von Papen became ambassador to Austria, where he earned his reprieve by helping subvert that country's independence, bringing it under Hitler's control in 1938.

With this achievement under his belt, von Papen was named ambassador to Turkey in April 1939. The Turks agreed only reluctantly, since von Papen's diplomatic record encompassed the attempted subversion of one neutral country and the destruction of another. These precedents of duplicity boded ill for Turkey. "It would have been difficult for the German government to hit upon a more unpopular nominee," wrote British Ambassador Hughe Knatchbull-Hugessen in a secret evaluation of his rival. Yet von Papen defused his hosts' initial misgivings through the kind of charm he used on Gafencu that warm summer night at the Ankara Palace Hotel.

After speaking with von Papen, Gafencu went to the Bulgarian ambassador. The two men moved to a quiet corner. The orchestra was now playing dance tunes. Young diplomats did their duty by asking ambassadors' wives to dance while their husbands talked business.

Would Bulgaria, asked Gafencu, join a Balkan alliance?

That all depended, responded his interlocutor, on whether Britain would agree to rearrange the map. If Bulgaria was to get Tzaribrod and part of Macedonia from Yugoslavia, Thrace from Greece, and Dobruja from Romania, then it might cooperate. What did Gafencu think of his plan?

British Ambassador Sir Hughe Knatchbull-Hugessen was trying to eavesdrop but could not hear every word. When the conversation ended, Sir Hughe accompanied Gafencu to the buffet table, where mounds of delicacies had been ravaged by the jostling crowd. "Well," he asked, "did you come to an understanding?"

"Beyond all expectations," Gafencu replied sarcastically.

"You have allowed him to hope for the return of southern Dobruja?"

"If only that were all! I have given up everything," Gafencu laughed bitterly, "Tzaribrod, Macedonia, western Thrace. . . ."

"What?" exclaimed Sir Hughe in consternation. "He has again asked for everything?"

"Everything. That is only a beginning. Appetite grows with the feeding." Bulgaria's ridiculous demands could not be met. The Balkan States' greed and ambitions could not be overcome, Gafencu complained. Balkan politics had done von Papen's work for him. Leaving Gafencu, Knatchbull-Hugessen made the best of a good party and danced the first tango.

Since arriving in Turkey in March 1939, Knatchbull-Hugessen had also learned the impossibility of assembling an alliance of the small states. "We could do little more," he later wrote, "than stand by and watch the flood sweep away . . . the bulwark we had struggled to build."

If von Papen appeared to fit a Teutonic stereotype, Knatchbull-Hugessen seemed the caricature of a British diplomat. A product of

Eton and Oxford, he was the grandson of a great Conservative politician and the son of a cabinet minister. The very grandeur of his name seemed designed to be garnished with the title of ambassador. He looked the part as well: straight-postured, prim, thin, and well dressed. The manner in which an ambassador sat in his car was at that time as important as his appearance on horseback was a century earlier—and it embodied the national character of the country he represented. Knatchbull-Hugessen was aristocratically poised in his long limousine with uniformed chauffeur and footman. The Soviet ambassador, in contrast, sat beside his chauffeur in a husky sedan. The U.S. ambassador drove his own Chevrolet.

Knatchbull-Hugessen was a renowned dinner companion with a large repertoire of anecdotes. He was a talented painter and enjoyed good food, classical music, and eloquent speeches. Everyone liked the good-natured "Knatchy," who, far from being pompous, even wrote satirical poems about himself. The diplomatic life, he once explained, "is inevitably a series of uprootings, changes of surroundings, conditions, climate, land, modes of living and general outlook—a kind of gilded vagabondage." But behind the kind words about him was always the hint that Knatchbull-Hugessen was more charming than brilliant.

Despite Knatchbull-Hugessen's sympathy, Gafencu made no progress on a Balkan alliance that night at the Ankara Palace. Traveling on to Greece, Gafencu knew that peace was doomed. Arriving in Athens, he pointed to the Parthenon high above the city. "Does not this temple, by its perfect proportions, express the idea of the unity of Europe, inheritor of the most brilliant civilization ever known; and does it not give, with its magnificent but mournful ruins, a solemn warning to all those who would again blight our common heritage?" But this solemn warning was ignored. Soon, most of Europe would be in ruins.

Failing to spark unity among its smaller neighbors, Turkey turned to the Soviets. But the Russians were only interested in obtaining direct control over the Bosporus. Moscow made it clear that Russia would not help Turkey if Germany attacked. Having moved closer to Hitler, Soviet dictator Joseph Stalin viewed the Anglo-French-Turkish alliance as an obstacle to his own ambitions for the Bosporus.

In fact, the Soviets were about to launch their own dramatic initiative. At 1 p.m. on August 22, 1939, two huge German Focke-Wulf

Condor planes landed at Moscow airport. Foreign Minister von Ribbentrop came down the stairs to be greeted by a Soviet military band playing the Nazi anthem. That afternoon, the German and Soviet foreign ministers initialed a treaty of alliance. The next day, the astounding news was announced to a world that had already seemed jaded by the previous months' tumultuous events. Ostensibly a nonaggression pact, the accord included a secret plan to invade and partition Poland and to coordinate the two dictators' claims in the Balkans and Turkey. Ankara was badly shaken; Foreign Minister Saracoğlu was exhausted and demoralized. The Nazis and Italians, said President İnönü, were "eagerly awaiting an opportunity to attack Turkey."

He did not know the worst. When the Germans and Soviets settled down for secret, detailed discussions, Moscow listed among its goals military control of the Bosporus, rule over Turkey's strategic northeastern cities of Kars and Ardahan, and ultimately rule over eastern Turkey and Iran. If his demands were met, Stalin hinted, he would join the Axis and push Turkey, willingly or otherwise, in the same direction. But the Germans refused to make concessions because Hitler, already thinking about attacking his Soviet ally, wanted to wait until victory gave him a stronger hand.

With shock waves from the Soviet-German pact still echoing, Hitler invaded Poland on September 1. Stalin grabbed its eastern part. Britain and France declared war on Germany. World War II had begun. Von Papen heard the news on the radio and stepped into the embassy's garden. It was, he told his secretary, the "worst crime and . . . greatest madness. Germany can never win this war. Nothing will be left but ruins."

For the next six years, Gafencu mourned, "war, with massacre and destruction in its train, tore the peoples asunder, while vile passions ravaged individual men, racked their bodies, and killed their spirit. Catastrophe filled the whole world, crushing everything and leaving its imprint on every mind."

Facing a united front of the U.S.S.R. and Germany, their two greatest enemies, the Turks quickly signed a treaty of alliance with Britain and France. "Turkey has virtually entered the war," complained Moscow, blaming the Allies—not Germany—for raising tensions in the Balkans. A *Pravda* editorial carried a menacing warning: "Turkey's independence . . . is now seriously threatened." The Russians mobilized forces on the border and withdrew industrial advisers from Turkey. To convince Turkey that it must bow to German pressure, von Papen had the *Pravda* editorial translated and mailed to hundreds of Turkish notables. When 23,000 people were killed in an earthquake in eastern Turkey, German broadcasts called the disaster divine retribution for Ankara's ties to Britain and France.

Instead of caving in, Turkey retaliated by secretly allowing French reconnaissance flights to go over its territory so they could photograph the U.S.S.R.'s Baku oil fields that were fueling the German war machine. The police raided the pro-Nazi Teutonia Club in Istanbul and monitored German spy rings surveying transport and industrial facilities for possible sabotage. Dozens of German technicians and engineers were fired from naval bases, factories, coalfields, and the Golden Horn's shipyards. Two Bulgarian priests, one a former army officer, were deported after they were caught mapping Turkish border defenses.

Meanwhile, Germany was conquering Poland with astonishing speed. Just before the end, the Polish government tried to save its gold reserves to finance future resistance. The treasure was sent out of shattered Warsaw at night—as bombed-out buildings burned brightly—on three trains clattering over the barely passable tracks to Romania. The shipments crossed the border just a few hours before German planes knocked out the railroad.

The Romanians, eager not to offend the victorious Germans, insisted that the gold quickly leave their country. Since the Germans had intended to hijack the shipment in Romania, this haste unintentionally foiled their plan. Instead, the shipment was rushed to the Black Sea port of Constanza and shipped out on a British tanker.

Warsaw ordered its ambassador to Turkey, Michael Sokolnicki, to send the gold to the government-in-exile in London. On September 17, the British tanker arrived in Istanbul. The mighty French battleship *Jean Barth* stood offshore waiting to take the gold, but Turkish authorities would not let the ship dock in Istanbul. If they allowed the French warship into the port a precedent would be set and the Germans and Soviets could demand equal treatment.

On September 18, Sokolnicki went to the Turkish Foreign Ministry for advice. It gave him two choices: Britain and France could give the gold to Turkey as a loan and then reimburse the Poles, or the gold could be sent by train to French-ruled Syria. Just then, a Polish embassy clerk arrived with the news that a British merchant ship had come into Istanbul to take the gold. But Sokolnicki decided that German submarines might send the bullion to the bottom of the Mediterranean. He chose the rail route.

A new complication arose the following day. Turkish law set freight charges at ½ percent of a cargo's value, and the railways demanded payment in advance. Little credit would be extended to a Polish government-in-exile composed of refugees. No time could be lost; the Polish community was full of rumors that Turkey was about to side with Germany. So Sokolnicki jumped into his limousine and sped to the elite Anatolia Club to ask the powerful Turkish diplomat Numan Menemencioglu to ensure the shipment's security and lower the charge.

The price was set by law and could not be reduced, Menemencioglu replied. "But certainly, my friend, you know how things are done in this part of the world! Lower the gold's declared value to, say, $10 million and then persuade the French to pay the railroad's $50,000 bill."

Now Sokolnicki rushed to the French embassy to ask Paris for money. Unable to wait any longer, he ordered that the gold be loaded at Istanbul's Haydarpasha Station and sent east on the next morning's train. Someone suggested that enough gold to pay the freight could be taken off the train as it passed through Ankara. Ensuring delivery of the entire reserves, however, was his sacred trust, and Sokolnicki refused to touch them.

His wife provided a solution: "Why don't you ask Walker?" As branch director of Socony-Vacuum Oil in Turkey, Archibald Walker would have enough cash on hand. He was an outspoken anti-fascist and one of the most popular men in Istanbul. By chance, Walker was visiting Ankara that day.

The ambassador rushed over to Walker's room in the Ankara Palace. Sokolnicki explained the predicament, and the American immediately agreed to find the money. A few hours later, Walker arrived at the ambassador's office carrying a battered briefcase containing $50,000. Sokolnicki raced off to transfer the funds, and the train rolled out of Istanbul as scheduled. The gold safely reached Syria and was sent on to London, where it financed the Polish government-in-exile during the war. Walker was repaid and had thoroughly enjoyed his first experience with intrigue. He would later become the first Office of Strategic Services (OSS) man in Istanbul.

If the Poles were dazed by their country's collapse in two weeks, the Turks were equally shocked at the Nazis' rapid conquest and innovative use of massed tanks and aerial bombing. Assuming Turkey might soon be attacked, the government mobilized reservists and started making gas masks. The screech of air-raid sirens was heard in Istanbul. The Turkish government asked London and Paris to supply planes, ships, and anti-aircraft guns, but factories there were too busy making weapons for their own countries.

To promote self-reliance, the Turkish government declared emergency measures banning the export of coal or food. To avoid panic or hoarding, Istanbul's governor insisted that Turkey had enough wheat, olive oil, sugar, and other food to avoid the famines of the World War I era. The public was still frightened, however, and prices rose quickly. "Here in [Istanbul] there is an alarming dearth of foodstuffs of all kinds," Roncalli wrote on Christmas day 1939. "We hope there won't be an attack, but many think it won't be long in coming." Since the Vatican was neutral, Roncalli saw no contradiction between organizing relief for Polish refugees and socializing with von Papen, whose wife arranged the flowers and sometimes swept the floors in Roncalli's chapel.

Von Papen was already sending peace feelers through every available channel. He urged the neutral American, Dutch, and Vatican ambassadors to seek a political settlement, asking, "Otherwise what awaits us? Only barbarism and Communism."

"You may think I have taken leave of my senses," Ambassador Knatchbull-Hugessen wrote the British Foreign Office, but, he explained, von Papen was really trying "to play some conspicuous role" in ending the war. London told the ambassador to say secret talks were useless. The Allies' aim was to eliminate "Hitler and his gang," not negotiate with them.

What were von Papen's motives? Sometimes he hinted at an attempt to overthrow the führer; at other times he boasted of his influence and claimed to be acting for Hitler. Sokolnicki thought von Papen was merely posing as peacemaker in order "to be considered the 'moderate.' " When a German attack through Holland and Belgium was rumored, von Papen swore on a Bible to his Dutch counterpart that he would never let it happen.

Hitler needed some time to digest his Polish conquest. There was little fighting in the early months of 1940, and people began to speak of a "phony war." But in the spring, Germany occupied Denmark and Norway and then launched a devastating offensive through Holland, Belgium, and France. The French army was shattered. Paris fell on June 14, and the government surrendered eight days later. The remnants of Britain's army were evacuated from France or captured at Dunkerque. Like a vulture, Mussolini joined the war as Germany's ally. By the end of June, Hitler was master of Europe from the English Channel to the foot of the Balkans. German diplomats in Istanbul celebrated these triumphs, but not all Germans in Turkey were of the same opinion.

Alexander Rustow was glad to be in Istanbul in June 1940. Otherwise, he would have been dead or in a concentration camp. Instead, he was enjoying a magnificent view of the Bosporus from his study and the opportunity to teach freely.

The Rustow family tree included many military leaders. A great uncle deserted the Prussian army during the failed 1848 democratic revolution and took refuge in Switzerland. He corresponded with a fellow refugee named Karl Marx and became the first academic military historian. Alexander Rustow broke with his ancestors' professional military—if not their independent-minded—tradition. He chose scholarly pursuits and wrote a doctoral dissertation on a classic Greek paradox: "Epimenides the Cretan says, All Cretans always lie: True or False." Rustow's friends would live that paradox in Hitler's era by striving to remain cultured, democratic-minded Germans at a time when Germany seemed synonymous with bestial dictatorship.

After a radical activist phase in the turbulent period following Germany's defeat in World War I, Rustow became a civil servant. He worked on plans to nationalize the coal industry and limit cartels. But bureaucratic measures seemed ineffectual in view of the challenge to the Weimar republic from Nazi and Communist extremism and economic instability. Rustow decided he must enter politics and assemble a front of Socialists, liberals, businesspeople, and conservatives to keep Hitler out of power. Istanbul would not be the first place Rustow and von Papen crossed swords. While Rustow was trying to assemble a coalition government to keep Hitler out of power, von Papen was deeply embroiled in the maneuvers that made Hitler Germany's ruler.

Consequently, Rustow was high on the Nazi's list of intended victims. When the Gestapo searched his suburban Berlin home, Rustow knew it was his last chance to leave Germany. Along with Jews and other anti-Nazis, he needed an escape route. By fortunate coincidence, at that very moment Turkey was modernizing its universities and decided to hire German professors. About 120 refugee teachers, doctors, lawyers, artists, scientists, and laboratory workers—including Rustow—were brought to Istanbul University. A smaller number went to Ankara.

Thus, the German community in Istanbul was split. The diplomats and many old residents sided with Hitler; the refugees were passionately anti-Nazi. Pro-Nazis controlled the German school and the Teutonia and journalists' clubs. The pastor of the Lutheran church prayed for Hitler and German victory.

Most of the refugee families lived in Bebek, a wooded suburb whose cool summer breezes had once attracted sultans and their harems and now appealed to Turkish officials and foreign diplomats. Despite their complaints, these refugee families knew how fortunate they were. They could even safely visit Germany, though the passports of the Jews among them were finally revoked in 1940. The academic refugees brought to Istanbul a German cosmopolitan culture that no longer existed in the cities they had left. Among them were some of Germany's most talented people. For his son's surprise birthday party, Rustow organized a literary debate among exiled professors who had been renowned in Germany.

Rustow and others continued the anti-Hitler struggle by acting as a bridge between Allied intelligence and the German resistance. Yet they also continued more academic pursuits, and their university lectures were well attended. Some Turkish colleagues were jealous, but students were thrilled to be hearing Europe's most modern ideas from some of their most articulate, imaginative exponents. Ernst Reuter, former Socialist mayor of Marburg and future mayor of West Berlin, taught urban planning. Albert Einstein was invited but went to Princeton instead. At Istanbul University, emigrants directed nine of the twelve institutes in the medical faculty and six of the seventeen clinics. Other refugees built new institutions. Paul Hindemith was a founder of Ankara's Conservatory of Music; others revolutionized Turkish theater, ballet, and opera. Refugee advisers helped set up a social security system; architects designed public projects.

Erich Auerbach, a World War I hero, was fired from his German university post in 1936. He went to Istanbul and there wrote *Mimesis*, one of the definitive works of Western literary criticism. Auerbach found some of the books he needed in Roncalli's library, and the two men became friends.

Karl Menges, a specialist on Turkic studies and the former secretary of the Prussian Academy of Sciences, had visited the U.S.S.R. so often that Emniyet suspected he was a Russian spy. Nevertheless, Menges's university superiors valued his services enough to destroy several letters from Columbia University offering him a job before they finally let him go. His son Constantine—named after their city of refuge—grew up to become a staff member of Ronald Reagan's National Security Council and a key architect of its Central America policy.

If the Turkish police were unsure about Karl Menges's loyalties, other countries were even more uncertain about where Turkey stood. Some German, British, and U.S. intelligence reports claimed Turks were pro-German; others insisted they were pro-Ally. Within Turkey, there were lobbies for both sides. İnönü and Saracoğlu still felt that— as in World War I—the British would finally triumph, but some officers and politicians disagreed. In the Foreign Ministry's corridors, officials asked, "What is İnönü waiting for? What does he still hope for from the friendship and alliance with England? Why doesn't he come to an agreement with Germany? This hesitant foreign policy is going to be the death of us." In the end, however, everyone agreed that anything other than neutrality would be suicidal.

German victories confirmed this consensus. As Hitler's armies closed on Paris, the Turkish government declared a state of emergency and partly evacuated Istanbul. It mobilized 500,000 men. Coastal batteries began practice firing, and a handful of antiaircraft guns were deployed near Istanbul. "We do not run after adversaries," noted a Turkish leader, "but no one can guarantee that one day adversaries will not run after us!"

Tirelessly and skillfully, von Papen exploited Germany's increased power. In the summer of 1940, he was the most popular diplomat in Turkey. Social invitations from the German embassy were avidly sought;

Ankara and Berlin signed a large trade agreement. German agents arrived daily by trains to Istanbul.

Victories made the Germans arrogant; Hitler's demand for results made them careless. When von Papen went too far, the Turks showed they would not submit. The Germans had captured French documents revealing Turkey's behind-the-scenes cooperation with the Allies. The German embassy launched a covert campaign to have Foreign Minister Saracoğlu removed. This type of interference showed the worst misreading of Turkish character. "The Turkey of today is not the dead and rotten Ottoman Empire," said one angry politician. Berlin's attack only reinforced popular support for the Turkish government's policy.

The struggle between the Germans and the Allies for the support of Turkish newspapers was particularly intense. Von Papen approached one of the most influential publishers, the rotund Yunus Nadi of *Cumhuriyet*—who was also a member of parliament and owner of real estate, mines, and ranches. The German government made him richer by granting his businesses special commercial privileges. German refugees and Allied diplomats called him "Yunus Nazi."

Some days, *Cumhuriyet* was balanced, but it often argued that invincible Germany was too strong to oppose. It occasionally published anti-Semitic articles, most unusual in Turkey. On July 30, the newspaper ran an editorial written by Nadi's son and editor: "German power reigns in Europe. The European states must face this reality and determine their path in accordance with it." Germany neither endangered other peoples nor sought world domination, the article added, and Turkey must reach an understanding with Hitler. Other newspapers attacked these statements as "defeatist."

A few days later, Nadi saw President İnönü at Ankara's railroad station. When Nadi said hello, İnönü cut him short in a loud, angry voice, "What is this I am hearing about your taking German money? Why are you opposing our national policy? If this keeps up we must consider expelling you from the party."

"But, İsmet Pasha, I assure you it is not true!" a cowed Nadi answered.

"I hope not, too," shot back İnönü, "but this is what they say. Let it be known that I won't tolerate this." For good measure, the newspaper was shut down for several weeks.

Such behavior encouraged British optimism about Turkey's willingness to resist German seduction. "I have always maintained that the country is solidly behind us and behind its government," Knatchbull-Hugessen wrote.

The British embassy and Knatchbull-Hugessen's residence were just 300 yards from Foreign Minister Saracoğlu's house on Ankara's fashionable Cankaya Hill. Both offered a splendid view to the north across the city's valley to the mountains on which clouds' shadows drifted lazily. The early morning mist filled the basin until the sun cut through, revealing the ancient citadel's walls and tower. Knatchbull-Hugessen often took his walking stick, told his guard that he needed no company, and strolled to enjoy nature. Frequently, he ended his walk at Saracoğlu's house. He and the foreign minister would sit together on the veranda drinking cup after cup of strong, sweet Turkish coffee.

No two men had more opposite backgrounds. Saracoğlu, son of a poor village saddlemaker, had been a scholarship student. In government, he proved himself a good administrator, while his skill at folk dancing and love of nightlife endeared him to then President Atatürk. Nervous energy lay behind his dignified politeness and brisk businesslike manner.

One day, Knatchbull-Hugessen heard through intelligence sources that Saracoğlu was seriously considering an offer from von Papen to break with the Allies in exchange for territorial gains. The British ambassador refused to believe it. He took his limousine—flag flying from its hood—straight down Atatürk Boulevard so that everyone would see Great Britain's presence displayed.

As the worried Knatchbull-Hugessen entered the foreign minister's office, Saracoğlu stood up behind his large desk. Had von Papen at last succeeded, and was everything lost? Saracoğlu looked so grave that Knatchbull-Hugessen began to think the foreign minister had been swayed by the offer. But then Saracoğlu smiled, "Oh, what he offered me was not enough, I must have Scotland as well!"

Events in the autumn of 1940 showed that Germany would not have Scotland to give away. Britain weathered the greatest invasion threat since the Spanish Armada. The courage of Royal Air Force pilots beat the Germans in the air and helped make this what Churchill called England's "finest hour."

Knatchbull-Hugessen felt a bit guilty that duty placed him in safety while London was bombed each night. "The letters we are getting now from London," he wrote a friend at the Foreign Office, "show what a perfectly filthy time you have all been having. I feel that sometimes we don't fully realize the conditions in which you are working, but I must say I do admire the way you manage to keep up with the work in spite of it all." His colleague replied that things were not so bad. At the invasion scare's peak a man had boarded a train and told of an attempted enemy landing at Hastings.

"Where did you hear that?" asked another passenger.

"From a porter," came the reply.

"Then he must have been a very old porter still thinking about William the Conquerer's invasion there in 1066."

But many people thought Britain would now accept the inevitable and seek peace even without a German invasion. Von Papen explained that Hitler merely wanted to "rearrange the Balkans" a bit. On August 12, 1940, Roncalli met von Papen, who had just returned from Berlin. The German ambassador claimed that Hitler was "more calm and reflective . . . than he had ever seemed before." He had no intention of annihilating England and did not want to invade it, von Papen said, but such unpleasant steps would be necessary unless Churchill gave in to Hitler.

If the Catholic church cooperated in this peace endeavor, von Papen continued, the Reich would grant it special privileges. The shrewd diplomat painted a pleasant picture, playing on Roncalli's patriotism and ambitions. If Italy dominated the Middle East, he said, Roncalli, an Italian and representative of the Vatican in Rome, would be far more important.

Roncalli may have been innocent, but he was not totally naive. He thought von Papen "a sincere and a good Catholic" but felt von Papen's idea of moderating Hitler was only a daydream "in view of the raging Nazi spirit which has subverted not only every treaty but the religious tradition of Germany as well."

Reading Roncalli's report on the conversation, the Vatican's secretary of state still thought him gullible about German aims, noting, "This fellow has understood nothing." But Roncalli was also gathering his own information. He heard from two escaped Polish Jews traveling to Palestine about what was really happening in Germany's empire.

Roncalli was further dismayed when Italy invaded Greece in October 1940 and his own nephew was killed in the fighting.

Istanbul had become a grim place. There were now nightly blackouts, and Roncalli had to cancel Christmas midnight mass. Most men of military age were away in the army. The largely deserted city seemed as musty as a closed museum. As part of his health regimen, the perennially dieting Roncalli took long walks around the city. He walked to an old Greek monastery, vandalized by the crusaders in 1204, and said his prayers amidst the ruins.

4 | At the Court of Spies

The Sultan became fond of eating eggplant. Week after week, his courtier praised the many fine qualities of the eggplant. But, after a time, the Sultan tired of that dish, and his courtier began to criticize it. The Sultan asked, "Why did you once praise the eggplant and now you attack it all the time?" "Sire," replied the man, "I am your courtier, not the eggplant's courtier."

—sixteenth-century Turkish story

With a speed almost equal to that of the *Orient Express*, the German war machine raced toward Istanbul. First Czechoslovakia, then Poland had fallen. Now it would be the turn of Istanbul's front yard, the Balkans. Every development was watched from Istanbul with mounting horror and terror; each new Nazi triumph brought fresh waves of refugees pouring into the city.

The triplets of war—the might of armies, the entreaties of diplomacy, and the wiliness of intelligence—had never been so thoroughly meshed as in 1940 and 1941. Istanbul was Germany's backdoor to the Middle East and the Allies' secret passageway into occupied Europe. It became a center of espionage and intrigue for both sides. Other neutral capitals—Madrid and Lisbon, Stockholm and Berne—were also intelligence battlefields. But Istanbul was the most hotly and openly contested one.

Spying is a complex business. Information must be not only collected but also properly evaluated and used. This process is jeopardized by enemy disinformation, ambiguous signals, forgery for profit (about 200 people made their living this way in Istanbul during the war), distortion by agents eager to please superiors or avoid blame, bureaucratic rivalries, and leaders' ideology. Hitler ignored these considerations, and in the beginning, his intuition was fantastically successful. But in later years, violating the rules of intelligence proved disastrous for Germany.

German successes were due more to a sophisticated program of subversion than to any skillful use of intelligence. Berlin's minions brilliantly coordinated propaganda to spread a paralyzing terror of German might alongside soothing promises of Germany's nonaggressive intentions. They subsidized newspapers and politicians in the target countries. They infiltrated agents disguised as business executives, archaeologists, or camera-toting tourists. Local German communities were organized into Nazi and paramilitary groups. Germany bought goods at high prices and exported products at low ones to foster economic dependency. It played on regional rivalries to conquer victims one by one.

Each military triumph strengthened the Axis's appeal to opportunists or the fainthearted. As a secret U.S. intelligence study put it, "Both Axis and Allied propaganda alike hinge largely on their respective military achievements. Germany having so far scored in this field, her propaganda carries more weight than ours." Slickly produced films of German victories had a great psychological impact on audiences unaccustomed to media manipulation. In Istanbul, the German consulate provided the films for "educational purposes" to the Turkish army. The officers, eager for this glimpse of modern warfare, saw the graphic portrayal of Poland's and France's fate as a foretaste of what might happen to Turkey if it entered the war.

These techniques also, however, put the Turks on guard against German interference in their internal affairs. The regular police arrested suspicious aliens; military intelligence watched the frontiers. Foiling foreign spies was the job of Emniyet.

Its agents staked out, shadowed, and politely interrogated foreign intelligence operatives and military attachés. All foreigners had to carry *tezkeres*, internal passports listing their travels and personal history. Dossiers were kept on every alien. Reporters and printers were registered. The Emniyet recruited informants from concierges in buildings where foreigners lived and among embassy secretaries, clerks, guards, and translators by appealing to their fear, patriotism, or cupidity. A merchant claimed he knew that every employee of the Ankara Palace Hotel, from cook to manager, was an informer: "They're all wearing the shoes I sold to the Emniyet!"

This network yielded much information about foreign espionage efforts. An Istanbul electrician, for example, reported that he had been hired to install an unusual amount of wiring in a house. The police followed the trail to a radio dealer and caught him sending secret messages to Germany from his boat. On the basis of his confession, more Germans and dozens of Turks were arrested.

The Emniyet's first great triumph, though, was partly a matter of luck. In April 1940, a German was caught photographing a Turkish naval installation. On hearing of the arrest, his wife went out at 2 a.m. to see one of her husband's friends; then she took poison and collapsed dead in the street. This dramatic behavior threw suspicion on the man she had rushed to inform, Hans Henning von der Osten, a well-known German archaeologist and former employee of New York's Metropolitan Museum. The arrested man's papers showed von der Osten was coordinating German espionage operations. He was arrested, interrogated, sentenced by a military court to twelve years' imprisonment, and deported.

The Germans found a clever way to limit friction with the Emniyet. All the Abwehr (the German military intelligence service) agents assigned to spy on Turkey worked for the post in Bulgaria. The Emniyet did not hesitate to arrest or expel them. But the Emniyet did not bother the Abwehr's Istanbul station personnel, who focused on the Allies and stayed out of Turkish affairs. The Abwehr's liaison man with the Turks was Wilhelm Hamburger, an Austrian-born agent under journalist cover. The Sicherheitsdienst (SD), the Abwehr's rival, which worked for the Reich Security Ministry, maintained its own contacts through Ludwig Moyzisch, nominally a commercial attaché.

Omnipresent in Istanbul, the Emniyet's eyes and ears were positively omnipotent in the countryside. Government warnings about foreign infiltrators made peasants so suspicious that they would take up axes, scythes, and old shotguns to capture traveling diplomats; the peasants would set them free only after the diplomats spent several hours proving their innocence.

A touring American professor saw how mistrust of foreigners turned everyone into a police informant. Rotund and blond, with a mustache and goatee, he appeared to be German. At a hotel, a Turkish air force lieutenant spat at him and had to be restrained by fellow officers. As he arrived in each town, the police would take him directly from the train platform to their office for questioning: "Where did you get these documents? Obviously you are not an American. These are false papers. How do you explain the fact that you were heard speaking German on the train yesterday?" Only with great difficulty did he persuade them that he was not a spy. In the end, they would express pleasure that an American was taking the trouble to acquaint himself firsthand with their country. He would then walk just a few blocks into town, where a crowd of boys shouting "*Alleman!*" ("German!") would surround him and herd him right back to the police station.

Although an alert citizenry protected the interior, technical backwardness made the state's secret communications vulnerable. The Germans had broken the Turkish diplomatic code, and reports on the messages were regularly submitted to Hitler. Foreign Minister von Ribbentrop did not dare give Hitler bad news; the führer ignored anything that contradicted his own views. Still, this information was valuable. Turkish messages became one of Germany's most important intelligence sources, particularly on Soviet affairs. The intercepted and decoded reports included dispatches from Turkish military attachés in Moscow who were touring the front, descriptions of new weapons displayed at parades, the effect of German bombing raids, and the arrival of U.S. aid. Turkish dispatches from London provided the Germans with some information on Allied summit conferences.

A 1941 incident illustrates the complexities inherent in this kind of spying. In Istanbul, von Papen's Iraqi counterpart told him that the British could read high-level Italian dispatches. German code breakers were asked if this might be true. "Of course," they replied, "we've been doing it for years." But how could Berlin alert Rome to the danger without admitting its own espionage? Hitler told Mussolini a cover story: "Information from Ankara led us to try our hand at decrypting a radiogram from the Rome-Baghdad traffic, and we have just succeeded." To the Germans' surprise, Italy kept employing the vulnerable code. The Italians wanted these messages to be discovered in order to control what their enemies and allies believed. Italy's foreign minister explained in his diary, "In the future, the Germans will read what I *want* them to read."

Despite some successes, however, German intelligence was undermined by competition between Admiral Wilhelm Canaris's Abwehr and the SD—the foreign intelligence unit of Reinhard Heydrich's Security Ministry. The Abwehr looked down on the SD as incompetent; the SD saw the Abwehr as ideologically unreliable. The antagonism was symbolized by the contrasting backgrounds and personalities of their leaders.

The prematurely gray-haired Canaris, his face weather-beaten from service at sea, was a respected naval officer; the younger Heydrich had been dismissed from the navy for dishonorable conduct. Heydrich, the embodiment of Nazi brutality and fanaticism, was noted for his sense of sadism; Canaris, for his sense of humor. Heydrich served under Canaris in the 1920s and alternated between trying to destroy the admiral and seeking to win his acceptance. Canaris was a conservative nationalist who had little love for the Hitler regime and sheltered anti-Nazis in the Abwehr's ranks. Before the war, Canaris used back channels, sometimes through the Vatican, to warn the British of Hitler's aggressive intentions.

Canaris had joined the German navy at the age of 18. During World War I, his cruiser was scuttled off Chile to avoid capture by the British. Canaris escaped and made his way back to Germany. In recognition of his skill and initiative, he was sent on an intelligence mission to Spain, where he recruited seamen to provide the German U-boats with information on Allied shipping. He also befriended a young Spanish officer named Francisco Franco. Caught by the French while trying to return to Germany disguised as a monk, Canaris was released because of poor health, went back to Spain, and was safely evacuated by a German submarine.

After several naval commands in the 1920s and 1930s, he became the Abwehr's chief in 1934 and built the tiny agency into an organization of 15,000 people. It gathered and analyzed reports from military attachés, agents under diplomatic or nonofficial cover, and local ("V-men") informants.

As his Istanbul representative, Canaris chose Captain Paul Leverkuehn. Born in Lubeck in July 1893, Leverkuehn was a frail, bald, bespectacled man, chronically moody and nervous. But he was an industrious worker with a quick mind and extensive international experience including past service in Iran and Turkey.

Leverkuehn's political credentials were, however, questionable by Nazi standards, and Hitler later called him "a typical Canaris man," a characterization not meant as a compliment. His law office at 7 Pariser Platz in Berlin was in the same building as that of his friend Helmuth von Moltke, whose circle of friends was the backbone of the anti-Hitler underground. Leverkuehn's own background was conspicuously cosmopolitan. He studied law in Edinburgh and worked in Washington and New York, where he met fellow lawyer William Donovan, who later headed the OSS.

Eventually, the Nazi SD's distrust of the Abwehr and its minions in Istanbul would prove well founded. But Leverkuehn and his colleagues did perform valuable services for Germany against four targets: the Balkans, the U.S.S.R., Turkey itself, and the Middle East. Beginning with three empty rooms and a desk, file cabinet, and typewriter, Leverkuehn soon built up a formidable network of agents.

Anyone dropping in at the Park Hotel restaurant or bar any evening between 1940 and 1942 would have witnessed the results of Leverkuehn's work. Every evening, Leverkuehn's agents assembled there; the mixed cast comprised pro-Axis characters including Germans, Austrians, Hungarians, Arabs, Japanese, Turks, Iranians, an exiled Egyptian prince, and a half-dozen Scandinavian and Swiss hangers-on. Through the hotel's front windows one could see the huge swastika flag atop the German consulate; ships carrying the same banner cruised under the balconies facing the Bosporus.

Some of the agents were tough guys who knew how to get things done in back alleys. One of them so often bragged about his espionage exploits in Iraq that he was nicknamed "Kovacs of Baghdad." Although living in the Tokatliyan Hotel, he spent a lot of time at the Park Hotel meeting with colleagues and Arab agents. The Emniyet finally decided that Kovacs was spying on Turkey and should be deported. One of its officers baited the Nazi agent by saying, "We have discovered that you are Jewish." Kovacs panicked, thinking his bosses might believe it, and started screaming that he would telephone the German consul to get a written declaration that he was indeed an Aryan in good standing. The policeman replied: "In Germany, Goebbels decides who is a Jew and who is not, but in Turkey we decide." He was expelled to Bulgaria, where he continued his career.

Another rough character was a Turk who had been fired from a government job for allegedly selling documents to the Germans. He frequented the best restaurants and often came to the Park with German agents. Allied agents at the bar would point him out to newcomers as "a man to be avoided." Since he was a Turk, the British and Americans could not understand why he was still running around loose. The reason was probably that he kept the Emniyet informed on German activities.

Another group of Leverkuehn's agents consisted of propagandists, smoother types who tried to bribe or influence journalists and the Turkish elite. They spent every evening in nightclubs, hotels, restaurants, and bars spreading and gathering rumors. For a while, their leader was Alfred Chapeau Rouge, a tall, slender man with slightly grizzled gray hair who had served in Baghdad and Beirut and was officially listed as a vice-consul. His blonde Austrian wife was a rabid Nazi whose father was party leader in Bucharest. But the couple did not get along with von Papen. There was talk that the disfavor was because of their lavish spending at the Park and patronage of Jewish shops, but all the Germans did so. Even von Papen could be seen drinking coffee at the Haim and Mandil cafés. The real problem was that von Papen saw Chapeau Rouge as a bureaucratic empire builder challenging his authority. The ambassador forced his recall to Berlin in January 1942. Similarly, von Papen eliminated other rivals, including the local Nazi party chief who tried to establish his own intelligence network and openly insinuated that von Papen was ideologically unsound. The ambassador knew his secret peace feelers made him vulnerable to such charges.

In organizing Abwehr activities, one of Leverkuehn's most active lieutenants was young Wilhelm Hamburger, another Park Hotel resident who was nominally a newspaper correspondent. The son of a wealthy Austrian businessman who was also an influential Nazi, Hamburger was responsible for several Arab spy rings and for smuggling goods to Germany past the Allied economic blockade. Among his frequent companions were Istanbul merchants who made big profits by selling goods to Germany. After dinner at the Park, Hamburger and colleagues would hold court in a small lounge next to the dining room, meeting agents to receive their reports.

Below Leverkuehn and Hamburger extended networks of thugs and tipsters that included Persians, Arabs, Turks, and Russian émigrés who bought information from seamen and dockworkers. They followed Hamburger's orders in smuggling guns and gold to Arab or Iranian plotters, helping German agents infiltrate the Middle East, and watching Allied officials.

The Abwehr also employed polished people, particularly beautiful women, who could move in elite and diplomatic circles. One of this group was Wilheminna Vargasy. She made a specialty of cultivating American and British men, never missing a cocktail party. Some found her ordinary, but others thought her charming and very sexy. Knowing she might be a German agent did not stop them from talking and flirting with her. She was blonde, with blue eyes, and spoke Hungarian, English, French, Russian, and Bulgarian with ease, as well as some Greek and Turkish. For a while, she worked for the American Associated Press correspondent despite Istanbul gossip claiming she had previously lived with a French general in Syria, photographing his papers and correspondence.

Her Axis connections were easy to spot. On her frequent visits to Bulgaria, Vargasy—traveling aboard a German military plane or in a first-class train compartment—was always seen off by German consulate officials. Once, when she had trouble obtaining a new visa from Hungary's consul in Sofia, the German legation told the official to do as she wished. She also had a weak head for alcohol and sometimes made pro-Nazi and anti-British statements when drinking too much. After the Turkish police arrested and strip-searched her, she was thrown out by the Hotel Londra and had to take an apartment in the Pera district. British intelligence was particularly upset when it discovered she was having an affair with an American intelligence officer.

The Abwehr also had several dozen agents among Hungarian bargirls from the joints around Taksim Square and scores of part-time helpers among the hundreds of Germans in Turkey. Operations were financed by selling dollars and smuggled gold on the black market. Bribed railroad workers ran contraband across the border into Syria. In Istanbul, money was passed to agents at the Novotni and Abdullah's restaurants, the Abwehr-subsidized Elli's Bar, and the Taksim Casino.

Leverkuehn's first and most loyal recruit was Paula Koch, sometimes sensationalized as the Mata Hari of the Second World War. In fact, she was a rather sober gray-haired lady, 56-years-old in 1940. She grew up in Aleppo, Syria, and was a highly praised nurse with the German army during World War I. In later years, she lived in Brazil and Indonesia. Returning to the Middle East for the Abwehr, she made effective use of her long acquaintance with leading Arab families.

Most Abwehr efforts in Turkey early in the war were devoted to subversion and espionage in the Middle East. The objective was to gather intelligence on Allied military forces in the region and to stir the Arabs and Persians to revolt against the British and French authorities there. England ruled in Palestine and Jordan, exercised enormous influence in the nominally independent states of Egypt and Iraq, and controlled Iran's oil fields. France reigned in Lebanon and Syria.

Koch and Hamburger set up efficient Abwehr courier systems connecting Berlin and the Balkans with Istanbul and Istanbul with the Arab world. They recruited members of dissident political groups, sailors, shipowners, and railroad workers to carry letters, instructions to agents, and propaganda into the Middle East and to bring back intelligence reports. During the earlier years of the war, material was sometimes delivered from Arab boats directly to German submarines.

But the most enduring communications link was through the Armenian nationalist party, the Dashnaks. Joseph and Lucy Ayvazian, owners of a resort hotel in southeast Turkey, were the network's key figures. He had been orphaned and raised by Koch's family as her stepbrother, so he was totally loyal to the female German agent. The hotel made an ideal meeting place and post office for the Abwehr. It was only natural for buyers from the Austro-Turk Tobacco Company, all of them Abwehr men, to stop at the Ayvazians' hotel. Twice a year, a large shipment of money arrived from Berlin and was distributed to the Arab world through this chain. Intelligence from Arab agents was sent to Aleppo in northern Syria; from there, two bribed customs' officials passed the reports to the driver of a bus that daily crossed the Turkish-Syrian border. Lucy herself often traveled between Istanbul and Syria. Scores of Dashnak members in a half-dozen countries were involved in the ring.

A related chain comprised Arab mercantile families who, in Middle Eastern style, had one relative in every port of call. The Ayvazians worked closely with the Barbour family. Farid Barbour lived in the Turkish port city of İyskenderun; cousin George owned a wine shop in Beirut; and another relative, Alexandre Azar, was a lemon exporter in

Tripoli, Lebanon. These commercial interests allowed them to travel and ship material between various countries.

A Turkish diplomat in Ankara put messages for German agents in his country's diplomatic pouch. They were delivered to a rightist official in Turkey's Beirut consulate who distributed them. Every opportunity was exploited, from opium smugglers carrying messages to Arab agents crossing borders as Moslem pilgrims visiting holy sites. A dozen different porters and trainmen on the *Taurus Express* between Istanbul and Syria also carried Abwehr messages, gathered gossip, and sometimes stole travelers' papers. Transport workers in Iraq managed a covert branchline operation into that country. The Palestinian Arab nationalist leader Fawzi al-Kawukji was particularly active in this work.

While most Arab politicians had bowed to London and sought its support, many of them resented this situation. When war had seemed imminent in the late 1930s, the British had tried to appease the Arabs by limiting Jewish immigration to Palestine and offering to ensure that Palestine would become an Arab-ruled state. This policy effectively blocked the Jews' escape from Hitler's empire and its gas chambers. Despite these British concessions, Palestinian Arab leader Amin al-Husseini rejected any compromise and led an armed revolt to expel both the British and the Jews.

Husseini's followers, Iraqi militants, and Egyptian radicals collaborated with Hitler because they shared his anti-British, anti-Semitic views and held what Arab historian George Antonius called "a certain degree of undisguised admiration of Nazi achievements and power." They also believed in strong leadership, militarism, extreme nationalism, and contempt for Western democracy. Germany's unity and strength was taken as a model by many in the Arab world.

The rulers of Egypt and Saudi Arabia sought to keep a foot in each camp so that they could benefit no matter which side won. They were conspiring with the Germans while demanding British concessions on the basis of their alleged support. In 1939, for example, King Abdul-Aziz ibn Saud of Saudi Arabia unsuccessfully asked the Germans to arm and finance Husseini's rebellion in exchange for Saudi help.

After Italy invaded Egypt in 1940, Hitler took the region more seriously. He developed a grand strategy for total conquest: one German pincer would cut through the Balkans and U.S.S.R. toward Iran and its oil fields, eventually meeting another advance through Egypt and the Middle East. German occupation of France also gave Hitler control over French-ruled Syria and Lebanon. When Germany and its friends appeared the likely victors, previously pro-British Arab moderates scrambled to join them. But the resentful radical nationalists fended them off, refusing to share the booty.

Pro-Axis ideas flourished particularly in Iraq, then the leading Arab oil producer, where nationalists considered their country destined to lead the Arab world and resented continuing British influence. Iraqi Prime Minister Rashid al-Gailani and a group of colonels called the "Golden Square" were powerful allies for the Germans. The presence of the Palestinian Arab leader, Husseini, in Baghdad was a bonus for the Germans. He had fled Palestine to escape arrest for his terrorist activities. Through von Papen, Husseini obtained Berlin's subsidies beginning in March 1940. He became the main German agent in Baghdad, assisted secretly by the chief of Iraqi intelligence.

The Abwehr planned to arm the Iraqi rebels with weapons seized from the French in Syria. Other arms would be smuggled through Turkey in deceptively labeled crates. When all was ready, the Iraqi army would occupy the Royal Air Force base at Habbaniya, destroy oil pipelines, and expel the British. Husseini would then be installed as leader of Palestine to wipe out the Jews there.

When the British forced Prime Minister Gailani to resign, his pro-German supporters staged a coup to return him to power in April 1941. Some 9000 Iraqi troops surrounded the British base. To aid the uprising, the Germans sent a Heinkel-111 fighter-bomber squadron, 750 tons of arms and ammunition, and a military advisory team, which reached Damascus on May 12. The airlift was ordered to wait there for instructions from Baghdad. The Iraqi army, however, mistakenly shot down the arriving German liaison officer's plane, and German bombing raids against the British base failed due to poor coordination with Iraqi ground forces.

A quickly assembled British military column rushed across the desert from Amman toward Baghdad, defeating the Iraqi insurgents, and reaching the outskirts of the capital on May 30. Gailani and Husseini fled, respectively, to Turkey and Iran. But before the British could gain control of Baghdad, Gailani's supporters launched a pogrom in Baghdad's Jewish quarter, massacring at least 180 people, injuring 1000 more, and looting thousands of homes and businesses.

In contrast to the many Arabs who professed pro-Axis attitudes, the Zionists were virtually the democratic world's sole allies in the Middle East. When war broke out, David Hacohen, director of the Jewish trade union's construction firm in Palestine, contacted British intelligence on behalf of the Zionist movement. Hacohen, whose business in Lebanon, Syria, and Iraq gave him many contacts, agreed to organize a network of twenty to thirty Jewish agents in Arab countries to watch pro-Axis activities and gather information. A small radio station was established at his house in Haifa for broadcasting to the Balkans. A British-run sabotage training school was set up in a nearby hotel. British troops, assisted by soldiers from the Jewish self-defense forces—including Moshe Dayan, who lost an eye in the action—invaded Syria and Lebanon on June 8, capturing Damascus three weeks later.

As the British forces advanced, German agents and their Arab allies fled to Turkey, where most of them were interned by the neutral Turks. Leverkuehn subsidized the escapees and in September 1941 organized a conference of Arab nationalist leaders in Turkey. The Germans decided to send Gailani and Husseini to Berlin, where they could advise the Nazi government. Some pro-German Arabs would remain in Istanbul to maintain contacts with underground movements, collect intelligence, and await the day when German troops would arrive on their borders.

Husseini, who had fled from Iraq to Tehran, was disguised as the Italian ambassador's footman; he eventually left, along with the rest of the embassy staff, when Iran broke relations with Italy. Smuggling Gailani from Turkey to Germany was a more difficult endeavor. Leverkuehn thought about shipping him to Bulgaria in a packing case left in the consulate's basement from prewar German archaeological expeditions, but then he switched to another plan.

When a seven-member German press delegation arrived in Turkey, the Germans informed their hosts that an eighth man, Herr Wackernagel, had come with the delegation to Istanbul but was too ill to accompany the others on their tour. The night before the group was to go home, Gailani arrived at the German consulate after sneaking away from a dental appointment. A German doctor wrapped him in bandages like a mumps patient, and the next morning he was taken to the airport. The acuity of the Turkish delegation on hand to say farewell was dimmed by hangovers from the previous evening's party. They wished the sick man a quick recovery. Gailani was soon enplaned for Germany.

Berlin's espionage efforts in Iran were threatening enough to persuade the British and Soviets to take over that country in 1941. Iran was the source of much of Britain's oil and also sat astride a major supply route for the U.S.S.R. Captain Bruno Schulze-Holthus, Abwehr chief in Tabrīz, went underground, protected by pro-German Iranian nationalists. At one time, he hid in a brothel. He left there one cold night disguised as a mullah, with a henna-dyed beard, dark silk trousers, and Persian clothes, walking along Shapur Street north to the main road and the city's outskirts. His contact, the chief German agent in Iran, told him that one of the shah's top generals, Fazlollah Zahedi, promised that "a great percentage of the Persian Army is ready to rise at a signal from us." But there was no way to communicate this news to Berlin. Schulze-Holthus's wife, the only German available, was sent on the long, dangerous journey across the mountains by donkey and finally reached Istanbul, where she reported to Leverkuehn.

Zahedi did not keep his promise. To avoid capture, Schulze-Holthus took refuge with the Bakhtiari tribes. The British, fearing he might sabotage the vital railroad carrying military supplies from Persian Gulf ports to the Soviet Union, chased him for several months until the tribesmen tired of the game and sold him to the British.

Despite setbacks in the Arab world and Iran, the Germans stepped up propaganda and made plans to install Husseini and Gailani, both handsomely subsidized, as heads of puppet governments in Palestine and Iraq. Currency was printed and uniforms manufactured for the projected Iraqi regime. The two men and their retinues competed for German recognition as the Arab world's leader, bickering over spoils that never materialized. Their German supervisors also took sides, and the two factions spent the rest of the war engaged in petty plots against each other.

Meanwhile, the British acted energetically to arrest most of Berlin's remaining contacts in Arab countries. In Egypt, British authorities threatened to depose King Farouk unless he removed his prime minister, who was receiving secret German subsidies, and his army chief of staff, who had given maps of the British defenses to the Italians. In a humiliation Egyptian nationalists would long remember, Farouk gave in. The British disarmed and demobilized Egypt's unreliable army.

Many Egyptians saw the war as, in the words of a young pro-German officer named Anwar al-Sadat, "a foreign conflict in which we had no interest." When Germany's Afrika Corps advanced into Egypt, the king, leading politicians, and army officers prepared to welcome the troops. "Great Britain stood alone," Sadat wrote. "Her weakness in the Middle East was apparent to everyone," and her military position in the war "had become untenable."

Demonstrators in Cairo streets shouted for a German victory. But the British defeated Rommel at El Alamein on October 19, 1942, and he was forced to retreat. U.S. landings in Morocco and Algeria trapped him between British and American forces. The German invasion of the Middle East, which at one time seemed unstoppable, was at an end.

Far from being hurt by their collaboration with Germany, however, some of Berlin's ex-agents went on to important postwar careers. Ayatollah Abdel Qassem Kashani, detained for pro-German activities, became leader of the Iranian anti-shah movement of the 1950s that was a forerunner for Ayatollah Khomeini. General Zahedi staged a 1953 pro-shah coup and became a pillar of that regime. Husseini returned as leader of the Palestinian Arabs and unsuccessfully continued his efforts to wipe out the Jews. Fawzi al-Kawukji, the most important Palestinian Arab military commander of the 1948 war, was one of Husseini's men in Berlin. Yasser Arafat was a relative of the latter and took the former as one of his role models. Nasser and Sadat came to rule Egypt; the collaborationist Baath party came to rule Syria and Iraq—the latter's president, Saddam Hussein, was raised by an uncle who was active in the anti-British revolt.

While the Abwehr's Istanbul-based Middle East efforts failed, the Nazis were simultaneously conducting far more successful operations in the Balkans. All those lands had been ruled from Istanbul before World War I. Now the same area would fall to a foreign empire threatening Istanbul's security.

5 | The Last Springtime

Hajji Baba was on his hands and knees outside his house looking for something. His neighbors joined the search. One asked, "What did you lose?" "A gold coin," Hajji Baba replied. "Where did you lose it?" "In the house, but the light is better for searching out here."
—Turkish folktale

Czechoslovakia and Poland had fallen to the Nazis. But Hungary, Romania, Bulgaria, and Greece and all the rugged Balkan mountain ranges still stood between Istanbul and the Germans. During 1940 and 1941, however, the German war machine moved closer to Istanbul. The countries that had seemed the city's shield—Hungary, Bulgaria, Yugoslavia, and Greece—caught on fire and melted away. Every event in that process was watched from Istanbul with mounting horror and terror, each new Nazi triumph brought thousands of refugees pouring into the city. In the fate of those captive peoples and bombed-out cities, Istanbul's citizens foresaw their own seemingly inescapable future.

The Turks were basing their own decision of which side to take on whether the Allies were able to block Germany's advance eastward. Some of them were inspired by London's insistence that it would never surrender or compromise with Hitler. They heard the BBC proclaim, "There can be no mistake about the position of the British Empire [whose] resistance to the efforts of Germany to dominate the world will continue."

But others were more influenced or frightened by what happened to their neighbors, and the spring of 1940 was the last happy season most of the Balkan countries would see for many years. Their fortunes would soon be smashed, their independence destroyed, and many of their people murdered or made refugees. As the Turks looked on with trepidation, one of modern history's great tragedies unfolded, bringing German troops within a few dozen miles of Istanbul.

"It seemed the sun had never shone with such warm, life-giving profusion," American journalist Leland Stowe wrote in 1940. "The war in the west seemed very remote, like the fading blurred outline of an ugly dream."

In Budapest and Bucharest, Sofia and Belgrade, there was laughter, music, wine, and food in great supply that springtime. In Budapest, from 5 to 7 every afternoon, people paraded up and down the Corso along the Danube. The cafés were crowded with onlookers drinking Colombian coffee and small glasses of Tokay wine. There was much clicking of heels and kissing of hands as young officers in fancy uniforms flirted with pretty women. The parade included servant girls wearing country-style embroidered blouses and full skirts, visiting gentry with high boots and hats sprouting pheasant feather plumes, businessmen in expensive suits, underpaid but proud government bureaucrats, students wearing visored caps and carrying briefcases over their shoulders—all promenading and watching the sun set across the Danube over the beautiful old city's hills. At dusk, strings of lights appeared along both shores and across the Danube bridges.

The parliament building was one of the most spectacular landmarks. "We have everything one could want in the way of a parliament building," Hungarians said, "except a parliament. That structure houses a trained seal act." Hungary was a kingless monarchy ruled by an admiral—Miklós Horthy, a 70-year-old relic of the vanished Austro-Hungarian empire—without a seacoast.

Many of the patrons in the cafés facing the parliament building were from among Budapest's 300,000 Jews, a community that had made a tremendous contribution to the country's cultural, intellectual, and commercial life. But nationalist parties resented the group's prosperity, liberalism, and mere existence. The Germans subsidized the green-shirted, Nazi-imitating Arrow Cross. Rightist leader Bela Imredy successfully sponsored anti-Semitic laws but then had to resign when it was discovered he had a Jewish grandmother. The way Imredy brought his own downfall symbolized the self-destructive nature of Hungarian and Romanian anti-Semitism. When Jews were forced out of business, Germans bought their assets, further undermining these nations' independence.

Similarly, the extremist nationalism that pushed Hungary and Romania into the Axis camp resulted in the loss of both countries' independence. Hungary hated Romania for having taken its province of Transylvania after World War I. Romania reciprocated that sentiment. A Budapest barber pretended to spit when he mentioned the Romanians, noted an American writer, and a Bucharest barber actually did spit when he spoke of the Hungarians. Both states competed for Berlin's support; while Hungary drifted toward German domination, Romania stumbled in the same direction. The Germans manipulated both countries. "The time has now come to make it perfectly plain," one German diplomat said of the Balkans, "our wishes alone count."

If anything, Romania's capital, Bucharest, was more joyous than Budapest in 1940. Hundreds of lighthearted people strolled in the parks, on fashionable boulevards, and in the Jewish quarter's narrow streets, past the palace, the mansion of the king's mistress, and the churches. "Indecent as it probably sounds," an American journalist later wrote, people had a good time in Bucharest that spring as the world crumbled around them.

The sun shone with bright Mediterranean intensity. At noon people flocked to eat hot little mushroom pastries at Dragomir Niculescu or cheap caviar (sold by the pound) and fresh-from-the-oven white bread at Luchian down the street. Romanian lunches lasted from noon to 5 p.m. Dinner was often eaten as late as 1 a.m. at Capsa, central Europe's best restaurant. Patrons dined on sturgeon, goose liver, shish kebab, veal, pilafs, and sweet pastries. Afterward, in carriages drawn by beribboned horses, they took romantic rides along boulevards of sweet-scented lime trees. The shop windows displayed luxuries; the air was filled with the stirring music of Gypsy orchestras. Weekends were spent in the mountains or at the Black Sea beaches. Like the *Titanic*, Bucharest went down with lights blazing and bands playing.

Corruption and incompetence helped sink it. "I had heard about Romania," wrote British journalist and intelligence agent David Walker, "but had never believed what I had been told." Lampooned as "Ruritania" in such contemporary films as the Marx brothers' *Duck Soup*, Romania had become a symbol for corrupt, incompetent government. Walker spent three days rescuing his trunk from customs by buying presents and rounds of *tsuica*—the local plum brandy, potent enough to fuel a car—for twenty officials.

Everything required a bribe. One foreigner, angry that a taxi driver was taking him around in circles, ordered the driver to stop near a policeman. He gave the cop a small tip to admonish the cabbie. The policeman gazed stupefied at the coin and then, smiling broadly, clubbed the driver senseless. The passenger had paid too much for a mere lecture.

The corruption was typified in a Romanian story in which courtiers explained the system to a new king by passing around a piece of ice. After it had gone around the entire circle, an aristocrat put the remaining, melted ice in the king's hands: "You see, Your Highness? So with the handling of Rumanian funds. Everybody touched the ice and passed it on to the next man. Nobody took anything yet nothing remains."

The currency black market was rampant. Customs men and railroad workers warned people entering the country not to change money outside of banks; then they offered their own rates. An *Orient Express* dining-car steward was so excited at one large financial transaction that he had the train stopped at a station while he discussed the appropriate rate with his partners, the sleeping-car porter and the engineer. One could live like a millionaire on $100 a month by exchanging dollars on the black market. Fifty cents bought enough Romanian currency to rent a suite at the Athenee Palace, Bucharest's best hotel. A full dinner with caviar and lobster cost the equivalent of a quarter; English wool suits cut by King Carol's tailor cost $10.

King Carol, known unaffectionately as "Carol the Cad," systematically robbed his subjects; the corruption of his mistress, Magda Lupescu, made Imelda Marcos appear austere by comparison. Carol's castle surpassed Hollywood in flashy bad taste. The entrance hall featured a 20-foot-high picture of Carol. Portraits of heroically posed soldiers, all with Carol's face, lined the walls. The first floor was a copy of the Versailles Palace's Hall of Mirrors; the exterior was an imitation of London's Buckingham Palace.

Carol's imaginative money-making schemes financed it all. He and his cronies owned the factory making uniforms for civil servants, and they periodically changed the required designs to promote sales. Shopkeepers were forced to contribute to the building of border fortifications, though no defenses were ever constructed. The king knocked down beautiful historic houses to expand his palace. Carol's behavior set the national standard.

"Compared with Bucharest," a journalist wrote, "even Paris was a prude." Sheltered young Britons and Americans were shocked, then seduced, by the city's vanity and heated erotic atmosphere. Love affairs were abundant; narcissism was the order of the day. Army officers, though forbidden to wear corsets in 1939, still sometimes varnished their fingernails. A policeman directing autos at the city's main intersection ignored traffic jams while admiring himself in a hand mirror. Extremes of wealth and poverty far exceeded anything the newcomers had seen before. Peasant women, feet wrapped in torn-up burlap sacks, swept manure from the streets with crude twig brooms. Ragged peasants roamed down avenues lined with modern ten-story buildings whose elevators often broke down.

This city was the unwilling host for an espionage war between the British and Germans. The Athenee Palace Hotel was the main stage. "More real drama went on within the walls of that white stone building than was ever imagined in Hollywood," one journalist wrote. The little bearded tobacco merchant reading a Greek newspaper in the corner worked for British intelligence; the well-dressed, pretty, dark-eyed woman sitting at the bar reported to the French. German agents mustered every morning and began their rounds by 8:30. Bartenders sold rumors to everyone. The Swiss manager stayed neutral. A dozen languages and accents wafted through the lobby. Tipsters sometimes furnished transcripts of telephone conversations made by the king's own wiretaps. Everyone ignored the official signs posted in cafés: "Discussion of politics is forbidden." Archie Gibson, the quietest and shyest of the foreign correspondents, directed British intelligence in Romania. He was so low-key, a colleague commented, that his most extreme flamboyant act would be to wear a slightly brighter tie on the day Germany surrendered.

Romania itself suffered one disaster after another. In June 1940 the

Soviets demanded that Romania give up Bessarabia, its northern province. Hitler supported Stalin, rejecting Carol's plea for help. Carol ordered three days of mourning and then surrendered. Hundreds of thousands of Romanians became penniless refugees. The government did nothing to help them but paid Carol for his lost royal estates.

Desperate to appease Germany's growing power, the king appointed a collaborationist cabinet which renounced British guarantees, throwing Romania on Germany's mercy. Hitler, however, considered Hungary a more important ally and awarded Romanian Transylvania to it in July. The blows continued. In August, Carol yielded southern Dobruja at Bulgaria's demand after selling his late mother's favorite estate there. Following an old custom, the late queen had willed that her heart be buried at that villa. Thus, Romanians could accurately say that Carol had even "sold his mother's heart." It was the last straw.

In September, the thoroughly discredited king abdicated and fled with his money and mistress. General "Red Dog" Antonescu became dictator, acceding to a steady increase in German influence and anti-Semitism. Antonescu and his cabinet applauded enthusiastically an anti-Semitic play, *Bloodsucker of the Villages*, at the National Theater. In October 1940, German soldiers began entering Romania under the guise of a military training mission which, within six months, included 200,000 instructors. German money, military victories, and subversion allowed Berlin to control the situation. In November, Hungary joined the Axis and Romania followed suit.

War came to the Balkans from an unexpected direction. Confident of easy victory, Mussolini invaded Greece from his foothold in Albania in October 1940. Lacking proper winter uniforms, the Greeks were decimated by frostbite, and there were thousands of amputations. But to everyone's surprise, the Greeks stopped the invading troops and then drove back the better-armed Italians through the rugged mountains. Advancing into Albania, Greek soldiers came upon an Italian sign proclaiming "Nothing can stop the Italian army!" A Greek had added at the bottom "From retreating!"

Hungary, Romania, and Bulgaria were becoming virtual German satellites; Greece was fighting for its life. The Turks were shocked by these developments. Von Papen returned from Berlin to turn his charm on İnönü: "I know, Mr. President, what misgivings affect you and your country at this time. . . . You may have little faith in diplomatic as-surances, but I stand here as a man who loves Turkey as his second home, and who has had the honor of being your comrade-in-arms. As long as I occupy this post, I undertake that my country will not break the peace with yours." İnönü smiled and shook hands. He may not have believed von Papen, but there was little he could do about it.

The Balkans' fate was settled at a meeting between Soviet Foreign Minister Vyacheslav Molotov and Hitler in Berlin. On November 12, 1940, the crowd at Berlin's railroad station saw a curious sight. For Molotov's arrival, a Nazi band played the Communist "Internationale" amid rows of hammer-and-sickle flags. German Foreign Minister von Ribbentrop boasted, "No power on earth can alter the fact that the beginning of the end has now come for the British Empire."

Both Germany and the U.S.S.R. wanted to rule in the Balkans. The Soviets, Molotov explained, wanted bases near Istanbul and control of the Bosporus. Germany should help get them if Turkey refused. Hitler replied coolly, and with an almost humorous legalism, given his usual behavior: The international treaty governing the strait could only be revised if the British and French consented. In later years, Hitler and von Ribbentrop would often remind the Turks of Moscow's demands as evidence of the U.S.S.R.'s aggressive intentions against Turkey.

But if Germany was going to clash with Russia, the Soviets would stop supplying Hitler with petroleum. Thus, German control of Ro-mania's Ploesti oil fields was a necessity. They lay along the foot of the Carpathian Mountains, where the substance oozed to the surface in small pools and stuck to hikers' shoes. One pipeline led to the Black Sea port of Constanza, though only neutral Turkey could still use that submarine-plagued sea route. The Germans transported Romanian oil on railroads already overloaded with freight and troop trains or by barge up the Danube River. The Danube, however, was frozen for three months in winter and the rapids of the Iron Gate cliffs could be passed by only one boat at a time steered by an experienced helmsman.

The British tried every possible way to reduce Germany's oil supply. They bought Romania's output at premium prices. River pilots were offered full pay in exchange for staying home. Oil trains to Germany were sabotaged; British planes bombed Regensburg, the German Dan-ube port where barges were unloaded. British intelligence chartered 150 barges and tankers to keep them from working for the Germans, and half of these vessels eventually slipped through to Istanbul.

During 1940 and 1941, the British and Germans fought a secret war over Romanian oil. The former planned to destroy the oil fields or block the Iron Gate rapids with sunken ships if Romania seemed on the verge of falling under German control; the latter implemented countermeasures. Bribed Romanian intelligence officials turned a blind eye to British sabotage efforts while simultaneously letting the Abwehr place plainclothes soldiers from the crack Brandenburg Regiment as watchmen for every train, tanker, port, and oil installation.

Germany gradually won the upper hand. It persuaded Romania to fire British advisers in the oil fields and then to nationalize the producing companies. In July 1940, the Romanians began arresting, beating, and expelling British residents who were accused of sabotage.

The British were slow and indecisive. They had originally planned to send a strike force through Turkey to blow up the oil fields. After months of planning, the Royal Engineers' Fifty-fourth Field Company came to Turkey from its base in Egypt in the summer of 1940. The Emniyet, worried that Germany might one day use Romanian oil to fuel an invasion of Turkey, helped the British. The Turks camouflaged the British troops as the "Number 1 Road Construction Party" in a quiet area near Istanbul. When the British embassy in Bucharest radioed that the moment for action had arrived, the men were to rush back and board a waiting ship kept loaded with their equipment and explosives.

Less than four weeks after sending the team, however, the British military command recalled it to Egypt. The British embassy in Bucharest angrily decried this retreat "at the precise moment of crisis," but the generals judged that insufficient Romanian cooperation—despite a large sum earmarked for bribes—would doom the plan. There were also ethical qualms against what would have been an attack on a nonbelligerent state.

British dithering also blocked another operation. At British request, David Hacohen and Tuvia Arazi of the Haganah, the Jewish self-defense forces in Palestine, traveled to Bucharest to survey the situation. They offered a daring scheme for sabotaging the oil fields and carrying out guerrilla warfare against the Germans. Eight hundred trained Haganah men would exchange places with Romanian Jews, who would be saved by being sent to Palestine. The soldiers would hide their weapons until ordered to carry out sabotage missions. The British first encouraged this idea but then vetoed it as too risky.

Only when it was already too late did the British make a serious effort to block the Iron Gate rapids. In April 1941, a flotilla of tugboats and barges loaded with dynamite sailed toward the Danube's narrowest point. They were to be sunk as obstacles, and their crews, disguised Royal Navy sailors, would make their way to safety as best they could. These well-fed, clean-cut Englishmen did not quite resemble the rough Balkan types who usually sailed these boats, but Romanian authorities promised that the ships would not be searched when they stopped at a river port to refuel. Nonetheless, the boats were inspected and their mission uncovered. The Abwehr had known of the plan all along through its Romanian informants and had arranged to expose it in a manner designed to maximize London's embarrassment.

The number of German agents in Romania rose daily. They were far superior to the dumb, arrogant martinets portrayed in American movies. Many of them posed as camera-toting tourists or journalists and spent their time wining and dining influential people. German purchasing agents descended like locusts, buying up so much food that the country was reduced to rationing. One of the most effective German agents, a beautiful blonde "agricultural reporter" who occupied a third-floor suite at the Athenee Palace, specialized in charming and seducing cabinet ministers. The local Gestapo chief openly subverted the government. When Romanian police raided his apartment and found it full of machine guns, rifles, and hand grenades, he faced them down by coolly claiming to be the local representative of the Krupp arms company. These items were merely his samples. The police apologized.

The badly outnumbered and outspent British could not compete. To keep up morale, they resorted to such pranks as kidnapping the doorman at a Bucharest restaurant where a visiting German minister was giving a luncheon for politicians. The British-installed replacement told arriving guests that the meeting was canceled. The Nazi speaker arrived to find an empty hall. Another time, British residents of the Athenee Palace arose before dawn to mix up all the Germans' boots and shoes left in the corridors for polishing by the hotel staff. Coming down for breakfast, the perpetrators enjoyed the ensuing confusion.

One of British intelligence's best informants on the German military buildup was a midget who insisted on a peculiar rendezvous. "There will be news for you on Wednesday," he told the British agent Walker. "I shall go to the Turkish baths at eight in the evening. Please join me there." The prospect of sitting naked amid the hot steam meant that paper and pencil would obviously be out of place. Walker would have to memorize the numbers and types of incoming German munitions. But the midget would accept no other locale. The police, he claimed, "might put wires in your bedroom, sit at the next table in a restaurant, open your safe and your mail, listen to your phone calls, interrogate your mistress, suborn your wife, denounce your mother, even arrest you: but they never, never, never followed you into a Turkish bath."

It was hard to know who could be trusted and who might be an enemy spy. One day, a British journalist was boarding the Danube ferry from Bulgaria to Romania when he saw armed Bulgarian police drag a thin, pale young man onto the dock. "He must leave Bulgaria," said their officer.

"He cannot enter Romania," replied the ferry captain. "He has no visa." The boy cried that he was fleeing from the Nazis, pleading, "Don't let them kill me!"

"No visa, no entry," said the captain, ordering the gangplank raised. Just then, a passing German oil barge flying the swastika flag sounded its loud horn. As everyone else turned around to look at the boat, the journalist saw the "anti-Nazi" boy reflexively raise his arm in the Hitler salute.

The ease with which Germany captured Romanian politics, commerce, and oil wells provoked much British self-criticism. "As has happened before in this war," the British correspondent and intelligence agent David Walker wrote, "we let the Germans be too quick for us: and we were too genteel in our own behavior. . . . We surrendered to German hands, without firing a shot or [blowing up] an oil well, a zone absolutely vital to the enemy conduct of the war." British diplomats continued their languid ways, pinning their hopes on the decadent elite rather than on the peasant and labor opposition groups to block German influence and stop Romania from becoming Hitler's ally and oil supplier.

The Germans were more adept at sponsoring political movements, including the Fascist Iron Guard, whose peculiarities reflected Romania's bizarre theatricality. The founder of this extremist nationalist group was not even a genuine Romanian but the son of a Polish immigrant. The Iron Guard swore to destroy all Jewish, liberal, foreign, Communist, and French influence in Romania. Influenced by Hollywood films about gangsters and the Ku Klux Klan, it engaged in elaborate ceremonies and oaths.

When the Guard tried to overturn Carol's regime in 1940, its leader and a dozen of his lieutenants were arrested and executed. After the king fled and Antonescu came to power, Iron Guard leaders persuaded the Romanian Orthodox church to canonize its martyrs as saints. The Guard marked the occasion by launching a three-day reign of terror, murdering 500 Jews and liberals.

While the Nazis were ideologically closer to the Iron Guard, they considered Antonescu the ruler best able to guarantee the continued flow of Romanian oil and food to Germany. In January 1941, the Iron Guard launched a coup against Antonescu and another bloody pogrom against Bucharest's Jews. About 660 Jews were murdered, most of them killed and mutilated in the city slaughterhouse. Hundreds of people died in street battles. But the Germans backed Antonescu as he crushed the Iron Guard. "Air raid sirens screamed, church bells tolled for the dead, synagogues burned, tanks rumbled up the fine boulevards, and the provincial broadcasting stations seemed to change hands hourly," wrote David Walker. When an earthquake devastated the city soon afterward, it seemed as if the end of the world had come.

Most of the British had already left for Istanbul to organize an intelligence base there. The Athenee Palace was full of German officers. German planes roared overhead. The Germans' antiaircraft emplacements protected the oil fields; their technicians ran the railroad. Walker hung on to the last, commuting between Athens, Belgrade, and Sofia on the only available airline, Germany's Lufthansa. "The Nazi pilot seemed so amused to have an enemy Englishman aboard that he said, 'Ticket please!' in perfect English," Walker told a friend.

At last, Romania had been turned into a virtual German colony and military base for prosecuting the war. On February 10, 1941, the British embassy held a press conference to announce that England was breaking relations with Romania and closing down its mission there.

The Romanian censor refused to let reporters send any story about the break in relations. "But," they complained, "we've just come from an official British briefing!" The censor replied, "That is no proof that it is true."

Nonetheless, British and other Allied citizens were ordered to leave at 10:30 p.m., a half hour after curfew to discourage any popular demonstration of support. "But for piteous appeals for visas from hundreds of Jews, who besieged the Legation until the bitter end," a British diplomat wrote, "the withdrawal was completed without incident." German and Romanian troops lined all approaches to the Bucharest railroad station. At Constanza, six German tanks stood by the depot to ensure that no passenger strayed. The Allied civilians boarded a Turkish ship for the journey across the Black Sea to Istanbul. Curious German troops watched at the dock. As the ship pulled out, the soldiers shouted defiance and sang martial songs.

"The last time I saw Bucharest," recorded an American correspondent, "it was much more a city of fear than a city of pleasure." As Walker left Bucharest en route to Bulgaria, he looked down from the plane window and saw a long German military convoy headed in the same direction.

Bulgaria was Hitler's next target, and it was well on the way to becoming another German base. German "tourists" crossing from Romania on the Danube ferry calmly opened their suitcases at Bulgarian customs to show the uniforms and revolvers packed inside. Germans, openly giving Nazi salutes in the lobbies, made up 90 percent of the guests in Sofia hotels in February 1941.

The large, well-staffed German Tourist Agency never sold a ticket. Railroad cars arrived daily with German weapons for the Bulgarian army and were packed with Bulgarian food for the return trip. A Bulgarian housewife told an American journalist: "We have no butter and no vegetable oil nowadays. We're lucky to get even seven ounces of sugar a week—and this in a rich farming country like Bulgaria. The Germans take everything. Well, we've seized territory from Romania. Now we have to pay for it!"

Like Hungary, Bulgaria was driven into the Axis camp by its ambitions and territorial claims against Romania, Yugoslavia, and Greece. King Boris complained, "My army is pro-German, my wife is Italian, my people are pro-Russian." The peasants admired Russia and referred to the country that had helped liberate them from Ottoman rule as "Uncle Ivan." The ruling generals and officials, impressed by German power, were convinced that resistance was futile and collaboration would be profitable.

The Abwehr tried to sabotage Bulgarian-Allied trade by mixing explosives resembling lumps of coal into fuel sold at Bulgarian ports. On one occasion, a British freighter in Bulgaria's port of Varna rejected the poor-quality coal. An Italian freighter was then loaded with it as horrified Abwehr agents watched. The Germans bought it back at a premium.

Bulgaria also became a German reconnaissance base against Turkey. The Abwehr rebuilt a small ship to pose as a coastal freighter for photographing the Turkish coast. Buffeted by the Black Sea's rough February weather, the boat finally came up alongside Turkey's defenses. It was heading back to the open sea when Turkish soldiers on shore opened fire. Several men fell wounded as the ship fled. The Abwehr's photos showed details of new fortifications but the expedition also proved that the Turks were too alert to be fooled. Aerial spying was easier. A German photo-reconnaissance squadron stationed in Bulgaria made successful flights over the U.S.S.R., Turkey, and Syria.

The U.S. envoy to Bulgaria was the remarkable George Earle. Heir to a great sugar fortune, scion of a family that arrived on the *Mayflower*, a descendant of Benjamin Franklin, and graduate of a leading prep school, Earle rebelled against all these traditions. He dropped out of Harvard to become a naval officer, aviator, polo player, and tireless self-promoter. Politics was a logical next step. He abandoned his father's Republican loyalties for the Democrats and became an early supporter of Franklin Roosevelt's candidacy in 1932. President Roosevelt was ever after grateful. In 1935, Earle was elected the first Democratic governor of Pennsylvania in forty-five years. There was even talk of a run for the White House, but Earle's flamboyance and heavy drinking, as well as charges of corruption, led to the defeat of his 1938 Senate bid. Roosevelt then appointed him U.S. ambassador to Bulgaria.

Although this seemed a safely obscure post, Earle was never one to keep a low profile. He welcomed journalists to his office, which was filled with cages of songbirds. Throwing his enormous cowboy hat on the desk next to a beautifully crafted chess set, Earle settled in for long talks, punctuated by visits to his big liquor cabinet. He often showed reporters his latest secret dispatches. When not the product of Earle's overactive imagination, these messages consisted mostly of warmed-over newspaper stories.

But life around Earle was never dull. At any moment, his pet cheetah might bound into the office to terrify visitors. "Earle and his cheetah suffered from the same sort of problem," one of his guests wrote. "The cheetah was really a good-natured beast, but, when she placed paws on your shoulder and began to purr, you could not be sure that she was not about to bite your ear off. So with George Earle."

Some correspondents liked the man's accessibility and lack of stuffiness; others were put off by his crude, domineering nature. The Sofia prostitutes complained that he was stingy. But Earle did everything possible to help the British and block the Germans.

In February 1941, Earle hosted a man who had similar objectives. William "Wild Bill" Donovan was a successful New York lawyer who had commanded the famous "Fighting Sixty-Ninth" Regiment in World War I. Roosevelt would soon make him director of the OSS, the new U.S. civilian intelligence agency. To get a firsthand look at the war and to rally support for the British, Donovan embarked on a long trip through Europe. He conveyed Roosevelt's message that, as a Turkish newspaper put it, "the United States is determined to remain to the end at England's side and render the latter's defeat impossible; and that the United States will assist all countries who may resist aggression." The Bulgarians gave Donovan a polite but cool reception. The Germans were far closer and better armed than the Americans.

Donovan was made to look foolish when Earle took him to Maxim's Nightclub and a German-sponsored pickpocket lifted his wallet. A week later, Earle went back to Maxim's and set off an incident publicized around the world. The day began when he invited the United Press and Associated Press correspondents to see his confidential cables. The two reporters spent an hour looking at dispatches which did not contain anything they did not already know.

"Okay, boys," said Earle, "I've done a favor for you, now you have to do one for me. I have a big problem. I've sent my wife home. I have a Bulgarian mistress aged about twenty but last week I was in Budapest where I fell in love with a seventeen-year-old Hungarian girl. And I invited her to come to Sofia and move in with me. But the problem is I have to get rid of the Bulgarian girl. Tonight I have a simultaneous date with the two girls, so the five of us will go out on the town." Each woman would think that the other was dating one of the journalists, a ploy Earle hoped would fool them both and avoid publicity.

All went well until the women went to the powder room at the same time and compared notes. Neither was willing to give up her sugar daddy—an appropriate title, given Earle's sugar fortune. They sat on either side of Earle and competitively pawed him. Earle, realizing his dilemma, got progressively drunker.

At an adjoining table sat an elderly, distinguished-looking German businessman celebrating his wife's birthday. The waiters brought them a cake. Earle jumped to his feet. "Look at those god-damned Nazis," he said. The German asked the orchestra leader to play a Viennese waltz. Enraged, the 220-pound Earle picked up a whiskey bottle and broke it over the man's head. The orchestra stopped and everyone gaped in surprise for a moment. Then a half-dozen burly German "tourists" came rushing over to attack Earle.

The two reporters who had accompanied Earle, Robert St. John and Hugo Speck, acting as loyal American citizens, rushed Earle back to the manager's office and barricaded the door. A melee broke out. Screaming women hid under the tables, glasses were overturned, and the Germans tried to break down the door to get at Earle.

Suddenly, a huge Bulgarian appeared from the crowd. He stood in front of the office door and literally tossed off Germans as fast as they came. Asked later why he had come to Earle's defense, the Bulgarian replied that he knew Earle was very rich. He was a shoemaker and thought the ambassador might commission a couple of pairs of shoes. Although the man had put himself in great danger, Earle never gave him any reward.

Finally, the police arrived and broke up the fighting. The correspondents poured cold water over Earle, trying to sober him. He demanded to be taken to the embassy, where he called up his typist and dictated a cable: "I have this night been the victim of a brutal physical assault," he said. According to Earle's version, he was minding his own business. The club was full, the drinks were flowing, and everyone was having a good time. The orchestra was playing "Tipperary," the marching song that had become a pro-British anthem. An arrogant German officer stood up and demanded that it play a German waltz instead. When Earle objected, the German "threw a champagne bottle which just missed my head. [I] retaliated by injuring his features." A group of enraged Germans then attacked the plucky American, and blows were exchanged until the police arrived. "It was hot while it lasted," concluded Earle, "and I still think 'Tipperary' is a swell tune. [The] incident was regrettable but I saw no other course. . . . I was very glad that I had two well-known American newspapermen with me who knew that in my account I spoke the truth."

He showed the cable to Speck and St. John. "I want you to read this before you send your dispatches," Earle told them, "because this is the official version of what happened. If you report anything conflicting I will have to disclose that you were both intoxicated."

St. John and Speck left the office. It was around 4 a.m. St. John asked, "What are you going to do?"

"I've always thought of retiring to a farm so I think I'll cable Earle's version."

"I already have a farm," said St. John.

"If you cable what really happened it's going to be two to one."

St. John went back to his hotel and considered how he could reconcile journalistic integrity with Earle's threat. Finally, he came up with a solution. Last night, he wrote, there was an altercation at a nightclub in which George Earle and a German businessman were injured. There are two versions of what happened. . . .

The skirmish made headlines around the world. Earle received many congratulatory messages. Members of Congress who knew about Earle's drinking habits demanded his withdrawal. Roosevelt laughed off the incident, dubbing it "the Balkan Battle of the Bottles."

But the serious news from Bulgaria was that the Germans were taking over and the British were being forced out. On February 24, a British employee of the Passport Control Office—the cover bureau for British intelligence—disappeared en route from Sofia to Istanbul on the *Orient Express*. He had been kidnapped and tortured by the Bulgarians, who later staged an anti-British show trial with the employee as chief defendant. The Passport Control Office in Sofia and a British consulate were also burglarized.

On March 1 Bulgaria followed Hungary and Romania into the Axis. "It makes me ashamed of the human race," mourned Earle. The next day was Bulgaria's annual independence day celebration. The king stood in the reviewing stand saluting his troops. As soon as the parade ended, German tanks rolled into Sofia and occupied strategic intersections. Hundreds of U.S.-built trucks full of German infantry passed through Sofia. German tourists and businessmen appeared in their uniforms; German Junker-52 fighter-bombers roared over Sofia from their new bases. As the British diplomats prepared to evacuate still another capital, the British Press Bureau received a crate from London containing 400 copies of a booklet entitled "How to Recognize German and Italian Aircraft."

The Germans made only one concession. The Bulgaria-Turkey border was a wild, desolate area through which ran Ankara's only rail links to Europe. The snow-tipped mountains marched ridge after ridge beyond the Struma River's narrow gorge, the scene of desperate fighting during World War I. If the Germans dug in there, the Turks could not hope to dislodge them from that perfect jumping-off point for an invasion. Turkey warned that it would go to war unless the German army stayed 30 miles from the frontier. Hitler agreed in order to maintain good relations with Turkey, but this was the only part of Bulgaria where his legions did not appear.

As the British again departed, David Walker, posing as a Bulgarian reporter, stayed for a few days in Sofia to interview German soldiers. Again, he was the last Briton aboard a sinking country. When he finally left on a train to Yugoslavia, he shared a compartment with a young, drunken German agent who thought Walker was pro-Nazi because he was reading a German magazine. The man's gossip provided Walker with a great deal of useful information about German plans.

Now it was Bulgaria's turn to be brutalized. Anti-Nazis were arrested and tortured. British intelligence smuggled out the leader of the Peasant party in a large packing case purportedly containing embassy archives. He took 2 pounds of butter and some oranges to eat, as well as a long-nosed Luger automatic to resist capture. A British agent accompanied the van carrying the crate. At the Bulgaria-Turkey border, Bulgarian guards complained that the truck had no papers proving diplomatic status. They insisted on searching it. The British official spent seven hours persuading them to let the van go. More than thirty hours after leaving Sofia, the little convoy drove into the garden of the British consulate in Istanbul at 4:30 a.m. The Bulgarian politician sprang from his crate like the blackbirds from the pie. Only after briefing the British for over five hours did he consent to rest.

The liberal Bulgarian journalist Michael Padev had a more difficult time. He was arrested and questioned by Germans convinced that Ambassador Earle was a master spy directing all U.S. espionage in the Balkans. Released after spending several months in a prison camp, Padev and a friend sought to escape by sea to Istanbul. But the man who sold them a boat tried blackmail; when they refused his demands, he sent an anonymous letter to the police denouncing them. A friendly officer warned Padev in time.

Determined to escape Bulgaria, the two men traveled from village to village disguised as road laborers, working their way closer and closer to the Turkish border through areas full of German troops. An old peasant promised to take them the last few miles on a secret mountain path but became ill and then refused, saying the frontier guard had been reinforced.

Looking for a way through on their own, Padev and his companion finally came to the last village, split by the Maritsa River forming the border. They could see Turkey beyond rows of deep trenches, observation posts, and gun emplacements. That evening, Padev ran into a Bulgarian officer he had known as a student in Paris. Recognized, Padev feared all was lost, but the lieutenant instead invited the two men to his room.

"It's my duty to report you," he said. But instead the officer urged them to return to Sofia. Only forged documents would get them across. "It's not a frontier, it's a front," he told them. He had seen Jewish refugees expelled from Romania and Bulgaria but refused entry into Turkey for lack of a visa. Trapped in no-man's-land, they died of hunger or exposure. No one had gotten through in the last few months. So the two men turned back in sight of their goal and returned to Sofia, where they spent three months buying false papers through a diplomat from a German satellite state. This time they went back to the border by train, posing as meat merchants selling to the Germans.

As a precaution against attack, the Turks had wrecked the railroad bridges over the Maritsa. Padev and his friend had to cross the frontier, with other travelers, by car. It took them a half-hour to clear the Bulgarian border post. Now they had to face a Gestapo checkpoint knowing their names and pictures were in German files. For two hours they waited in the car while guards marched back and forth in front of them. Suddenly, a German official with a military escort approached and shouted, "Arrest him!" Padev waited to be dragged away. Instead, the Germans seized another man, a Polish officer who had escaped from a prisoner-of-war camp only to be recaptured a few feet from freedom.

Finally, Padev and his friend walked across no-man's-land onto Turkish territory. An Italian official who had crossed with them came up to the pale Padev and said, "You don't seem quite yourself. Have you got a temperature?" Padev's compatriot wheeled around and growled, "It's none of your business you Fascist swine." They were safe.

The British diplomatic staff took a more comfortable but ultimately more hazardous route to Istanbul. After the break in relations, the staff members left Sofia by train on the morning of March 11. Earle came to see them off. Germans wandered freely up and down the platform amid the unguarded baggage. The porters loaded two unclaimed suitcases onto the train. As the train bumped toward the Turkish border, Stanley Embury, son of an air attaché, and David De Bethel, a code clerk, took the bags into their compartment and went up and down the corridors trying to find their owner. Finally, they opened the cases to see if there were any clues. One contained two large radio batteries, newspapers, and a metal plate; the other held toiletries, a shirt, and a sweater with a battery wrapped inside it. The men shrugged and put the cases aside. Everything could be sorted out in Istanbul.

On disembarking at Istanbul around 9 a.m., Embury took the smaller case with him in his taxi. He went to the Pera Palace Hotel with most of the other staff members. A porter carried the suitcase through the door and placed it with the other bags near a column on the right of the lobby's staircase. Most of the diplomats had just gone up to their rooms when there was a flash of light and an explosion from the direction of the suitcases. People ran from their rooms shouting that the Germans had come. The whole neighborhood shook and windows were broken in all directions. The first floor of the hotel was in shambles, with furniture blown across the lobby; the elevator collapsed, its cable cut. Six people were dead, and another twenty-five had been injured. The Pera Palace never fully recovered from the damage to its lobby or reputation.

Hysteria spread throughout the city. When the news reached his hotel, De Bethel remembered his own mysterious suitcase, raced to his room, took the bag outside, and flung it over a cliff. When recovered later, it was found to contain a larger time bomb whose German-made mechanism had been stopped by the force of its fall.

At the time, many people thought the Pera Palace explosion signaled that war was about to come to Turkey. But Hitler had other victims in mind before striking at Turkey. German troops lined the borders of Greece and Yugoslavia. And there was another clue to German intentions. Just before he left Romania, St. John managed to sneak a look at a little black book that all the German soldiers in Bucharest seemed to be studying: the German army edition of a work entitled *Introductory Russian*.

6 | The Front Line Comes to Istanbul

The horse kicks, the donkey kicks, the mule gets kicked.
—Turkish proverb

A single question dominated everyone's mind in the spring of 1941: Where would Hitler move next—eastward against Turkey and the Middle East or westward against England? No one in Istanbul knew for certain. *Cumhuriyet*, Istanbul's leading newspaper, editorialized: "One thing he will not do is stand still. . . . For Germany, a long drawn-out war means defeat. Hitler's real target is the British empire so he will not come toward Turkey." British Ambassador Knatchbull-Hugessen was sure that Germany would be cautious in the Balkans because an offensive there "would inevitably bring Russo-German rivalry to a head." But this was precisely Hitler's plan: to secure the Balkans before attacking his Soviet ally.

Turkey's state-owned radio optimistically announced that the government "has taken all defensive precautions." The border with Bulgaria was "like a steel fortress. Whoever attacks it will be shattered." More soberly, British intelligence estimated that a German offensive could take Istanbul in forty-eight hours. Even German-backed *Cumhuriyet* was starting to worry about a Nazi attack on Turkey, whining: "If Germany has a quarrel with England, let them go to England to settle it. England is not in the Balkans."

With Hungary, Romania, and Bulgaria all in the Axis camp, "the danger has reached our very borders," commented the speaker of the Turkish parliament. The march of German troops into Bulgaria accelerated hoarding and air-raid drills in Istanbul. Every school was given an emergency evacuation plan; museum treasures were sent for safe-keeping to the countryside; and the government offered to pay the fare for any resident leaving Istanbul. Evacuees filled every bus, train, and boat east.

Turkish morale might have been even lower if people had taken more notice of a *Cumhuriyet* article on February 21, 1941, which revealed the world's best-kept secret. It noted that both the Allies and the Axis powers "are hard at work on the uranium bomb. One bomb will level an entire city." But Istanbul's many wooden houses made it vulnerable enough to ordinary bombs. A single air raid could turn the whole city into an inferno. The British and U.S. embassies advised their citizens to leave the country altogether. More men were drafted into the army. The Greeks, Jews, and Armenians among them were assigned to unarmed road-building crews in the interior.

In response to the crisis, von Papen brought his son to Turkey so that he would not be drafted into the German army. He warned German residents against panic and forbade them to leave. They were instructed to send home food packages, circumventing a Turkish anti-famine law allowing only the export of vegetables. One German wrote a thank-you letter—which the British intercepted and gave to the Emniyet—to a relative in Istanbul: "I got your parcel with delight and thoroughly enjoyed the contents, only I do not understand why you wrote to ask if I enjoyed the peas when all the cans were filled with the most glorious lard, which to us was like rain in the Sahara."

The Turks were neutral, but Germany's proximity made them increasingly nervous. They invited British delegations to discuss joint defense and assured them that Turkey would fight if its own territory or Greece was attacked. When British Minister of State Anthony Eden visited Ankara, the usually undemonstrative Turks greeted him with a rare spontaneous demonstration. After meeting Turkish leaders, Eden was given a grand send-off at the Ankara station for his return to England through the Middle East. But after his train puffed slowly eastward for 15 miles, it halted at a little station until late at night. As the city slept, the locomotive pulled back onto the main line and headed west through

Ankara at top speed to Istanbul. Eden then made a secret trip to Athens, encouraging the Greeks by promising them British military aid in the event of a German attack.

With Hungary, Romania, and Bulgaria already on his side, Hitler now demanded that Yugoslavia join the Axis. On March 25, the Yugoslav government agreed. Convinced that Yugoslavia's fate was sealed, the journalists packed their bags for the next story; the British diplomats started burning documents and preparing suitcases for the next evacuation. But the atmosphere in Belgrade was passionately anti-German. Thousands of people sported British flag pins in their lapels. English speakers were stopped on the streets and praised for being enemies of the Nazis. Gypsy orchestras played "Tipperary" over and over as diners stood and sang at the top of their lungs. Then the bands played nationalist tunes.

In quiet corners of Belgrade and in their Istanbul headquarters, British intelligence men met Yugoslavs who opposed appeasement and planned a coup. Students staged sit-down strikes, tore up pictures of Hitler, and denounced their own rulers as traitors. The police refused to intervene against them. At 2:30 a.m. on March 27, army tanks and thousands of air force soldiers in blue uniforms surrounded the royal palace, ministers' houses, and police stations. The patriotic officers installed a government that rejected the Axis pact.

For a few days, Belgrade rejoiced. The country was full of rumors that huge numbers of British soldiers were coming to its aid. Tens of thousands of proud, tough peasants, unfamiliar with the power of the German war machine against even courageous men, joined the army and bragged about defeating the Germans. Crowds gathered in the Terazia, Belgrade's main square, to chant, *"Bolye rat, nego pakt!"*— "Better war than the pact."

New York Times correspondent Ray Brock wrote that it was "the most . . . heartfelt demonstration of pure joy and thanksgiving" he had ever seen. "Up the street 30,000 voices rose in the war song. The song was taken up by a troop of cavalry starting its way through the multitude and the riders paused only to accept handfuls of mimosa from the crowds and tuck the bouquets into their bridles. . . . The rising and falling chorus of voices filled all Belgrade throughout the day and into the night as new thousands poured into the streets."

This time, it was the German diplomats who were forced to board trains leaving the country. A Yugoslav officer explained: "Perhaps what we have done is a great folly. Many of us will certainly have to die. But at least Serbia has kept her honor and has shown her teeth to the jackal."

Hitler was determined to make Yugoslavia pay the price for resisting. At 4:30 a.m. on Easter Sunday, April 6, German Foreign Minister von Ribbentrop made a ranting radio speech. Unable to hear clearly through the static, the American journalist Robert St. John, then in Belgrade, asked his assistant to translate. The man was so excited he could hardly speak. "War! War! War is here, St. John," he yelled into the receiver. "War, I tell you. Hitler . . . tells his army to march against Yugoslavia. Against Greece. . . . My God it is awful!"

At that moment, the air-raid sirens went off. Most of Belgrade's 300,000 people were still sleeping, unaware of any declaration of war. Those awakening assumed it was merely a drill and did not get up. Rushing to file a story, St. John found a taxi. A Yugoslav air force officer was wildly gesturing in the middle of the street. "For God's sake, for Serbia's sake," he shouted, "you must take me to headquarters." He jumped into the cab and explained that thirty-two German bombers, taking off as von Ribbentrop was speaking, had just crossed the frontier.

Reaching the Serpski Kral Hotel, St. John looked out the window through field glasses. The roar of planes grew louder and louder. Puffs of ineffectual antiaircraft fire blossomed in the sky. German planes bombed government buildings as the ground shook and the hotel shuddered. Flying low, they bombed at will, and the noise of their dives mingled with the explosions. There were 200 to 300 bodies in Terazia Square alone; Kalamegdan Park was full of the dead. Ironically, the German embassy was among the buildings wrecked; St. John's hotel slowly burned to the ground as the journalists evacuated it. Dazed people fled into the countryside. German planes hovered like vultures. The bombing continued until Thursday and wrecked a quarter of the city. As many as 20,000 civilians were killed.

Bulgaria and Hungary were now dragged into the war as German troops used them as a base for invading Yugoslavia and Greece. The collaborationist Bulgarian government seized territory from both victims. Hungarian Premier Pál Teleki committed suicide over his country's dishonorable betrayal of Yugoslavia. People in Budapest, bewildered by their country's entry into the war, wept openly on the buses. A performance of *Fidelio*, Beethoven's great opera condemning tyranny, was canceled at the Budapest opera house. Across the blue Danube drove German trucks, tanks, and armored cars rolling southward.

Yugoslav officials, foreign diplomats, refugees, and journalists fled Belgrade by car to escape the approaching Germans. Hundreds of people seeking gasoline and food would converge on a provincial town and then bolt at the cry "The Germans are coming!" Cars broke down on narrow mountain roads; friends and families became separated. German bombers roared overhead at treetop height. Rumors and Yugoslav radio propaganda spoke of victories by Yugoslav armies that no longer existed. When Yugoslavia surrendered on April 17, five British and American journalists, landlubbers all, escaped by sailing a tiny fishing boat down the coast to Greece, only to be chased by the Germans invading there.

Meanwhile, the Greeks, who had defeated the Italian invaders, were again fighting courageously against hopeless odds. A company of soldiers ordered to hold the strategic Rupel Heights at all costs revived the spirit of Thermopylae. They stopped a massive German attack for thirty-six hours, held mass, blew up their own escape routes, and fought until they were wiped out. A small British expeditionary force, made up of the few soldiers and pilots England could spare, arrived in Greece and was wildly cheered in the Athens streets, but it could not stem the tidal wave. Within three weeks, the swastika flag was raised over the Parthenon in Athens. From Bulgarian and Romanian ports German ships sailed past Istanbul carrying occupation troops to Greece's islands, some only a few miles from the Turkish shore. Refugees poured into Turkey from Yugoslavia and Greece, often traveling the last few miles by rowboat.

"Speedy and great successes in the Balkans," wrote an anti-Nazi German diplomat in his diary. "The army is an incredibly brilliant instrument with all the stronger characteristics of the German people, and filled with absolute self-confidence. It is tragic! With this magnificent instrument the destruction of Europe is being accomplished to perfection."

The badly shaken Turks went back on their word. They had assured Britain they would go to war if Germany and Bulgaria attacked Yugoslavia or Greece. Now Ankara did nothing. Almost all its neighbors were in German hands or had become German allies. Von Papen warned that if Turkey went to war against Germany, Hitler's friend Stalin would attack it.

Istanbul was clearly threatened. German troops were only 40 miles from the approaches to the strait and controlled the sea routes north and south of the city. "We have been assured the Germans have no designs on us," said one newspaper, but Berlin had said the same thing to Greece and Yugoslavia. A reporter wrote that Istanbul was the only European city that retained strong nerves. But they were stretched to the limit.

As Belgrade was being leveled and Greece was facing conquest, a British military attaché wrote home from Istanbul about the peaceful, prosperous atmosphere there: "Every garden has a red Judas tree in it, and it's a wonderful sight: even across the Bosphorus the Asiatic side is a blaze of red silhouetted against the black cypress trees of the vast cemeteries." He had just hosted a very successful cocktail party with mussels fried in batter, caviar, tiny lobster patties, and plenty to drink. Yet he thought this idyll would not last. Once the Germans rested a bit, he predicted, "a smashing attack will be staged on Turkey. . . . I think we have at least a month. . . . I listened to Churchill's broadcast last night, which didn't hold out much comfort. I don't mean that I have the slightest doubt about the ultimate end, but it does look a hell of a way off."

Cumhuriyet's military correspondent asked the question on everyone's mind: What would Germany do next? Unless Moscow entered the war on its side, Germany must attack the Soviet Union. Otherwise, the United States and the U.S.S.R. might join England, and all three could ally against Germany as they had done in World War I. To avoid this, Hitler had to strike at them separately.

In this spirit of divide and conquer, a smiling von Papen returned from Berlin to Istanbul. "I come as a dove of peace, bearing an olive branch," he told everyone. "I assure you that you can all spend the summer pleasantly at the beaches." Having already made nonaggression pacts with Moscow and London, Ankara now signed one with Berlin on June 18, 1941.

Three days later, von Papen was awakened in the middle of the night by a message from Berlin. Hitler had turned east seeking still more conquests: he had launched a massive invasion of the U.S.S.R. The next day, Churchill proclaimed an alliance with the Soviets. Together they would fight against Hitler.

With the Germans to the west, war to the north, unstable neighbors to the south and east, and their ships under periodic attack on the Black Sea and Mediterranean, the Turks were surrounded by battle. Despite public bravado, they knew their army was thirty years out of date. It lacked armor and airplanes, antiaircraft guns and transport. Seeing the Balkans' quick collapse, Turkish leaders congratulated themselves on having maintained neutrality and escaping a similar fate. Even so, Germany could now blockade Turkey's Aegean coast and the Bosporus. Von Papen might demand that Turkey renounce its alliance with Britain.

On August 1, Knatchbull-Hugessen wrote the Foreign Office: "My own very strong conviction . . . is that . . . the Turks can be counted on to resist—even, like the Greeks, to the point of national self-immolation—any head-on challenge to their independence and national integrity . . . but what I fear is the possibility of their buckling under some lateral strain such as the conviction or even the suspicion that their allies and friends (including ourselves) do not believe in them and might therefore let them down or at any rate give them less whole-hearted support than they are likely to need."

The opening of a new front where the Germans might advance against insufficient Allied resources would only further demoralize the anti-Hitler forces. The Germans themselves had already explored the idea of striking east from Bulgaria and Greece into Turkey and Iran. This advance would allow flanking attacks on the U.S.S.R. from the south and on the Middle East from the north. Leverkuehn had already reconnoitered Iran and found a mountain road that could be used to attack from the rear and destroy the Baku oil fields. But the German high command knew it could not invade Turkey and the U.S.S.R. at the same time.

Yet if Hitler's choice made the Turks safe from attack, at least unless the U.S.S.R. collapsed, Germany's offensive against Russia made its intelligence work in Turkey all the more important. Canaris himself visited Istanbul in disguise to assess the possibilities. New agents arrived daily and easily obtained good cover credentials. One day a leader of the Czech refugee community asked the U.S. ambassador to meet a recently arrived refugee. The man came to the embassy bearing a card, which read "Dr. Ivan Spitka, Doctor of Philosophy, Journalist-Correspondent of the Danzig Press Agency." He had lost his papers, Spitka explained, but now had a passport from Czech Ambassador Hanak and was planning to go on to the Netherlands East Indies by way of Iraq and India. Would the American diplomat be so kind as to pen a letter to the U.S. consul in Bombay verifying his credentials? The ambassador agreed.

About three months later, Spitka was jailed in Bombay as a suspected German agent. This time, the American ambassador called Hanak directly. Hanak immediately told him that it "is properly suspected that Mr. Spitka is a German spy. . . . He never presented himself at my office in Istanbul to ask for a Czech passport." The appalled American thanked Hanak and added, "It is something of a shock to me to realize that, although unwittingly, and seemingly with no actually tragic results, I contributed towards facilitating the movements of someone whom, on investigation, you consider to be an enemy agent." Americans were still learning about the extent of duplicity in the world.

For the British, Istanbul became the crucial base for their Balkan intelligence operations. Retreating before the German tide, they set up or aided resistance groups in the occupied countries. Archibald Gibson, the mild-mannered *London Times* correspondent and Bucharest head of MI-6, Britain's intelligence-gathering agency, joined his brother Harold, former head of MI-6's Czech station, who was now running its Istanbul operations. Harold had first worked in the city for MI-6 during the 1920s. The Russian-born Gibsons had intermarried with old British Istanbul families like the Lefontaines and Whittalls. Harold Lefontaine was Harold Gibson's predecessor as MI-6 station chief; a Whittall was MI-6 liaison with the "friends," as Zionist intelligence was called. "There were so many Whittalls around," said a British diplomat, "one could hardly go into the embassy corridor without tripping over one." Gardyne de Chastelain, who had run sabotage operations in Romania, now headed the Istanbul office of the Special Operations Executive (SOE), the British intelligence group responsible for conducting guerrilla warfare behind enemy lines.

Evacuated British officials worked to spark resistance by the Yugoslavs, Greeks, and Albanians. Wilfred Stirling, who fought with Lawrence of Arabia during World War I and later trained Albania's gendarmerie, was the SOE man charged with organizing Albanian resistance. He formed a committee of Albanian politicians and organized partisan bands. One of their leaders was the illiterate populist chieftain Abas Agha Kupi. "Will you English fight on?" Kupi asked.

"I give you my word we will," Stirling replied.

"Thank God," Kupi smiled, and he added, "May your life be prolonged!"

The SOE's Istanbul office was in a beautiful eighteenth-century house with a spacious garden. From his office window, Stirling could look down and see von Papen sitting in the German consulate's garden. The British agent had a big safe for storing codes, telegrams, and the gold coins that were espionage's medium of exchange. One agent called it "the stables" because the gold coins kept there, which carried a picture of Saint George on horseback, were popularly known as Britain's "cavalry."

While the SOE organized resistance and sabotage, MI-6's task was to reach people behind German lines and to gather intelligence. The agency had radio contact with two opposition leaders in Romania and Greece, couriers traveling to Yugoslavia, and underground railroads established by the Czechs and Poles. But it was difficult to smuggle in more radio transmitters, since those available weighed 40 pounds and filled a big suitcase.

One of British intelligence's main assets was the breaking of German codes. As always, though, it was analysis and not raw data that determined this work's value. There was much material, for example, on the German buildup in the Balkans, but British intelligence assessments failed to predict the German attack on Greece and Yugoslavia. As the official history of British intelligence concluded, "In the warnings a few items were remarkably accurate anticipations of German plans, but they were accompanied by many exaggerated and conflicting rumors."

From June 1941 on, the British decrypted Abwehr signals from Turkey and later both Abwehr and SD communications in the Balkans and North Africa. By 1942, they were reading 3000 messages a week despite the Germans' improved ciphers and security. Still, these communications were so filled with code names, obscure references, and garbled or indecipherable code groups that even "breaking" a code usually provided only hints as to what the Germans were doing.

Thus, for intelligence from occupied east and central Europe, the British were dependent on the Polish, Zionist, and Czech services in Istanbul. The Czechs were double refugees, first from their own homeland in 1939 and then in 1941 from posts in Poland and the Balkans, where they had been running underground activities. Forced to flee again from the Germans, the Czech military intelligence officers converged on Istanbul, traveling on British, Romanian, Polish, and Yugoslav passports. They lived in boardinghouses on Istiklal Boulevard and worked in the same building in which British intelligence had its offices. One Czech agent, a German staff captain, was London's best source on enemy troop movements until he was arrested and executed by the Gestapo; another, recruited years earlier, was now Hungary's intelligence chief.

But the most effective intelligence collectors were not high officials or diplomats but railroad workers. Riding throughout Europe, hauling military trains and passing all the munitions factories, they saw German troop movements and potential bombing targets. In addition to their own observations, engineers, conductors, and brakemen heard news from friends traveling other routes. They needed no bulky radios, because their jobs regularly took them to Istanbul. Sleeping-car porters worked for both sides, smuggling money, documents, and information across borders. Jewish refugees arriving in Istanbul were another important source of intelligence. New arrivals were interviewed by Czech and Zionist agents for news from the occupied countries. These contacts and data were passed on to the British.

Through such sources, the Czechs obtained one of the war's greatest intelligence scoops when railwaymen reported the massive German buildup in eastern Poland that signaled an impending invasion of the U.S.S.R. Stalin foolishly ignored the warnings of the Czech government-in-exile, but the experience taught him to respect Czech intelligence.

The Czechs' first operation had been helping their airmen and soldiers escape from the occupied homeland to reach their exile army in the Middle East. Thousands of men were sent through Poland before the war closed that route and the Soviets imprisoned 1500 Czech soldiers caught in eastern Poland. After the Germans invaded Russia, the Czechs insisted that the Russians release these soldiers so that they could rejoin the common fight against Hitler.

The Soviets finally let the internees' senior officer, Lieutenant Colonel Ludvík Svoboda, come to Istanbul and arrange to transport the rest of the men there. After sending several groups through Turkey, the Czech government-in-exile and Stalin agreed to organize a Czech army division in the U.S.S.R. In early 1942, Czech intelligence officers, accompanied by Svoboda, left Istanbul for Moscow to coordinate operations on the eastern front.

The NKVD, Stalin's intelligence service, stole Svoboda's diary containing embarrassing material and then pressured or bribed him into becoming a Soviet agent. After the war, he collaborated with the Russians and helped deliver his country to Moscow's control. Years later, the U.S.S.R. made him president of a satellite Czechoslovakia. The same regime, however, accused the patriotic Czech intelligence officers, who had performed so heroically during the war, of having been British spies. They were imprisoned or driven into exile.

But during the war, the NKVD asked the Czechs in Istanbul to be their intermediaries with other Allied intelligence services and advisers on organizing anti-German sabotage. This channel was the basis for Moscow's demand that the Czechs help assassinate von Papen. On other occasions, with permission from their government, the Czechs acted as intermediaries between the British and the Russians. Many clandestine meetings were held at mosques, where the Europeans could pose as tourists. Once, a British SOE man arrived at the Süleymaniye Mosque too early—just before his Soviet counterpart left their Czech go-between. Under orders to have no direct contact with his capitalistic ally, the Russian could only give a little bow in the SOE agent's direction as a signal of comradeship.

Meanwhile, the Vatican remained neutral; Roncalli, its emissary in neutral Turkey, maintained links with both sides. "Here we are still out of the war," he wrote from Istanbul to relatives assuring them of his safety. "What more can one ask?" But Roncalli's pacifism did not mean passivity. Greece was under his jurisdiction, and he visited it eight times in 1941 alone with a visa from von Papen and a pass allowing him to use German planes. His humanitarian mission there included relief work and visits to Italian troops, German wounded, and British prisoners of war.

"The signs of foreign domination are everywhere: from the Acropolis and from the best-known monuments flutter reminders of defeat and national humiliation," Roncalli noted in Athens. The German requisition of food, the war damage, a British blockade to deny goods to the enemy, and the lost 1941 crop had produced a terrible famine. The usual colorful crowd filled Athens' broad sunlit avenues, but the faces were those of people just returned from a funeral. Women fainted in the streets from hunger. Stores had no goods; factories lacking raw materials closed. Power plants shut down and people burned pinecones to stay warm. As hundreds died of starvation in Athens, a group of Greeks asked Roncalli for help. He made a quick dash to Rome to see the Pope, and the Vatican sent aid to Greece.

A man quite different from Roncalli was also involved in relief efforts: Saffet Tozan, a wealthy Turkish adventurer, information merchant, and arms smuggler. Tozan felt "sick to see the hunger [in Athens]—and he's a pretty tough guy," wrote an American friend. "It's amazing how he manages to travel around so freely and stand in well (apparently) with both sides."

Tozan had started public life as an idealist, and only in his disappointment did he become a colorful character on the shady side of the law. He had grown up in the Ottoman elite, whose tradition was defined by the motto "In the service of faith and state." Its members trained for careers in the army, government bureaucracy, and the mosque. Trade and commerce was for the non-Islamic minorities; gentlemen's wealth came from land. Ottoman aristocrats combined European sophistication with their own historic culture: the wives wore Paris fashions under Islamic garb; their houses were filled with heavy, ornate "Louis Farouk" furniture.

During the Ottoman empire's last years before 1914, the decadent regime was clearly on the verge of collapse. Those seeking to save the empire were divided between the Young Turks, who favored a strong nationalist government, and the Decentralists, who wanted a constitutional monarchy. As a leader of the latter group, Tozan was imprisoned by the Ottomans and later by the victorious Young Turks. But in Ottoman times, money and family could accomplish anything. Complaining about their quarters, Tozan and his friends were moved to a resort hotel. Still dissatisfied with the food, the inmates pooled their resources, bought the hotel, and hired a new chef.

The decentralizers thus enjoyed good cuisine, but they lost all the political battles. After the republic came to power in the 1920s, Tozan was still disgruntled. He entertained a stream of visitors in his Istanbul home with its big classical portico, beautiful rose garden, and fine view of the Bosporus. Yet he always feared that the government might take everything away from him. As a reminder, a photo of the prison where he had been jailed adorned the wall of his study, with an "x" marking his cell's window. Short, portly, and gray-haired, Tozan had a light-hearted demeanor that hid his disappointment with a country and century in which he was an anachronism. He talked incessantly of the good old days, sometimes swinging a large battle mace he kept on his desk for exercise.

Defeated in politics, Tozan turned to money-making with a vengeance. Physically, he may have resembled a Sidney Greenstreet character, but psychologically Tozan was a cynical idealist, *Casablanca's* Rick in Istanbul. He ran guns for the Spanish Republicans during the civil war. He did business with French and British intelligence and with the Germans as well. He had many Arab friends but also helped smuggle Jews from Romania to Palestine. No one knew his labyrinthine interests. Wartime Istanbul was the ideal environment for his operations. "I am not a man of honor," he told a friend, but he made himself useful to everyone.

Whether for idealism or financial reward, Tozan accepted an assignment to be the first British agent sent into Hungary. He was caught in April 1943 and was sentenced to twelve years' imprisonment. Ironically, the regime that Tozan hated saved him: the Turkish government secretly demanded that he be released or they would stop all intelligence cooperation with Berlin. The Germans complied. He returned to Istanbul and went on to Syria to report to the British. So suspicious were the British about his sudden release—Ankara obviously could not reveal the real reason for it—that they assumed he had become a double agent. The British held Tozan in an internment camp for several months. After the war, they apologized by awarding Tozan the Order of the British Empire. The Greeks gave him a Cross of St. George.

While Tozan was a master conspirator, the Americans tried to avoid being dragged into others' plots. The Polish resistance had to cross a half-dozen borders to help the underground at home. In August 1941, the Poles tried to use the American Bucharest YMCA director, James Brown, as a link in this chain. Brown feared that the welfare and educational work of his organization would be compromised by any involvement in intelligence activities. He refused to accept delivery of a package brought by a Polish courier and insisted it be taken to the U.S. embassy. Suspicions were confirmed when the package was shown to contain letters to Polish and Romanian contacts, wads of dollars, cipher tables, and code groups and directions for using them.

If the Romanian police had found this material in Brown's possession, he would have been in serious trouble. In fact, a few weeks later he was arrested and charged with espionage, but the embassy got him out within forty-eight hours. "These dispersed activities are exceedingly dangerous, amount to nothing anyway, and we desire to have nothing whatsoever to do with them," wrote the U.S. ambassador to Romania with a diplomat's typical distaste of espionage. America was also still a neutral country.

This was only the beginning of problems for the YMCA director. After twenty-one years in Romania, Brown reluctantly decided in November 1941 that he must leave, but he refused to go until he could find someone to take over his relief activities for the 3500 Polish refugees still there. The Chilean diplomat who represented Polish interests in Bucharest had just been caught embezzling relief funds. Friends in Romanian intelligence warned Brown that the Gestapo, which was suspicious about all Americans, had him under close surveillance. But Brown stayed at his post until some Romanians agreed to help the impoverished Poles.

Brown and his wife managed to get out of Bucharest on December 11, and they arrived in Sofia at 10 a.m. the next morning. The U.S. ambassador, George Earle, picked them up at the railroad station but conveyed bad news: Romania had just declared war on the United States, and Bulgaria's parliament would meet in two hours to consider the same notion. "Take the noon train for Turkey," Earle advised, since they would probably be allowed to cross the frontier no matter what happened. The train reached the border at 9:30 p.m. but the Browns had missed the evening bus and had to spend the night in a filthy room near the station. No bus left the next day. At 5 p.m., a well-dressed

German civilian came up to the American couple. He explained that the Browns' passports were not in order and that James Brown was now Germany's first American prisoner of the war.

Brown and his wife were held in a German hotel and then forced to return to Romania in German custody. Thus, five days after leaving, they were back in Bucharest. At the Splendid Park Hotel, they were questioned by a well-dressed Gestapo man, about 55 years old, with thin iron-gray hair and piercing blue eyes. Speaking fluent English in a bullying manner, he asked how they had left Romania without the Gestapo's knowledge. Brown said their visas had come through proper Romanian channels. The secret policeman accused Brown of being a spy. The Gestapo, he emphasized, had "ways and means to extract information."

For the next two and a half hours, two Romanian-speaking Gestapo officers searched each item in the Browns' suitcases but found nothing compromising. A German officer then ordered that Mrs. Brown be placed in a run-down hotel and that Brown himself be taken "somewhere else." Brown complained so vigorously that his wife was returned to their old home.

Brown was taken to a secret military prison on Bucharest's outskirts; it was run by the Romanians but controlled by the Germans. For six days, he was kept in a small, dark cell with an iron bunk and a small table. He was given two daily meals of only black bread, water, and a little thin soup. A guard carrying a machine gun escorted him to the toilet twice a day.

At 10:30 p.m. on December 19, Brown was taken down a long corridor to a small room. The Gestapo officer entered and told Brown that the Gestapo had been watching Brown for a long time and had enough evidence to convict him as a spy. Unless Brown confessed, the Germans would be compelled to resort to "other methods" to make him do so.

The first charge was that a Thanksgiving party at Brown's home was really a political meeting. The Germans wanted to know the names of the Romanians and Americans present, their views on the war, and their plans to smuggle Romanian politicians out of the country. When Brown answered honestly that he knew nothing about such matters, he was called a liar.

The interrogator then inquired about one of Brown's friends, an

Argentinian diplomat, of whom the Germans were suspicious. Brown replied, "He believes that the Nazis are a group of tyrannical, cruel and barbaric bastards and they will never win this war."

"That's what we want to hear," said the German, "tell us more." Asked his own view of the war, Brown replied that it was obvious since he was imprisoned in a German dungeon. "Your answer is not definite enough for me. Express yourself more specifically and in detail," retorted the Gestapo man. Brown explained that he shared the Argentinian's attitude.

The interrogation ended at 2:45 a.m. Since the Gestapo was not satisfied with the responses, Brown was taken by two Germans to another room. A thick iron bar was embedded in the cement walls near the ceiling, and attached to it were two strong ropes, each ending in a slipknot. From the side door, a man entered carrying a rubber truncheon. Brown was forced to stand on a stool, a noose was slipped over each wrist, and the stool was kicked out from under his feet. As Brown swung in the air, the man hit him with the bat on his back and kidneys; then the man twisted each arm as much as he could. After this treatment, Brown was forced to sit on a chair while his toenails were slowly pushed up, causing agonizing pain but leaving no marks. The interrogator seemed to enjoy the show.

Finally, at about 5 a.m., the Romanian guard returned Brown to his cell. The next morning he was again questioned for three hours about alleged contacts with British intelligence. Unbeknownst to him, influential Romanian friends were aware of the arrest and appealed to their government for Brown's release. On Christmas eve, without a word of explanation, he was let go; several days later the Browns were allowed to leave Romania. Brown concluded, "We now appreciate more than ever before that freedom is the most priceless possession in the world."

While the Browns were passing through Sofia again, the U.S. ambassador there, George Earle, had his hands full. A mob of 300 pro-German Bulgarians, protesting U.S. support for the Allies, attacked the U.S. embassy and shattered all its windows. Earle picked up his Winchester rifle and started for the front door, intending to fire at them. This time, the impetuous ambassador would have a real fight on his hands. One of his Bulgarian messengers, a man Earle's size, tackled him. They were rolling on the floor when a smaller servant ran in to escape the mob. The messenger told his colleague to hold Earle's feet. The other man refused, insisting, "It is not allowed to hold an ambassador's feet!"

"Then seize his hands! Hold his head! Just fall on him!" the messenger shouted. The two Bulgarians managed to pin down the enraged Earle to stop him from getting them all massacred.

Mounted police finally arrived and dispersed the mob. At midnight, an embarrassed King Boris visited Earle. He pushed at the broken glass on the floor with his foot. "I want to offer my profound regrets and apologies," said His Highness. "I am surprised, but I am relieved to see you are alive." Boris continued in the same gloomy vein, "Ashes to ashes, dust to dust, if the bombs don't get us, the Gestapo must!"

Earle himself left Sofia at the end of 1941 but not before a final adventure. One night, Earle later recalled, he was in bed reading a book. "It was very quiet. I heard a noise at the door and . . . I saw the door handle move, then it stopped."

A little later, it happened again. "Someone was trying to get in my room, and I remembered the King's admonition to be very careful at night. I called out, 'Who is it?' and the handle quit moving." Earle picked up his gun, went quietly to the door, and jerked it open. The hall was empty.

He returned to bed, but the door handle began to move a third time. "I put two bullets just above the lock," Earle said. "And then I yanked the door open." He still saw nothing. As Earle stood there, gun in hand, wondering what was happening, the handle shook again, the walls joined in, and plaster began falling from the ceiling. It was the beginning of Sofia's worst earthquake in modern history.

7 | The Story Pursues the Journalists

> The Sultan disguised himself as a beggar. A peasant invited him into his hut to drink wine. After one cup, the Sultan said, "I am really a prince." After a second, he added, "I am really the Sultan." "No more!" cried the peasant snatching away the wine jug. "Another drink and you will claim to be Allah!"
>
> —Ottoman tale

Foreign correspondents darted from capital to capital in 1940 and 1941, ever southward and eastward, until Turkey was the only place still unoccupied by the Germans. From Prague to Paris, from Budapest to Bucharest, from Sofia to Belgrade and Athens, they followed the story of Nazi advance and Allied retreat until they, too, were caught up in the fighting. With communications broken down, they filed no more stories for several weeks. It was hard enough just to evade the blitzkrieg and make their way, weary but alive, to Istanbul.

When Athens fell, C. L. Sulzberger of *The New York Times* hopped a boat to the island of Chios where, along with two Greek cabinet ministers and a former mayor, he bought a seat on a departing rowboat moments before a German garrison arrived. Two fishermen took them the short distance to the Turkish coast. Sulzberger made his way to Ankara and began reporting again. He wrote about Germany's grip on the Balkans, its invasion of the U.S.S.R., and its expected attack on Turkey.

The correspondents worked frantically to scoop each other. They dictated dispatches by telephone to Switzerland until they found a faster system. At 2 a.m., when Turkey's government radio stopped broadcasting, journalists were allowed to transmit their own stories direct to New York. Sulzberger had left behind his Greek fiancée, Marina, in Athens and whimsically started to add personal messages to her. On her birthday, as Marina and her family sat gloomily around the radio, they heard Sulzberger's voice suddenly emerge from the static. She sent him word that she was listening and gave him a simple code so that he could, in a one-way fashion, communicate with her.

After several months, the Germans gave her permission to leave Greece. Then a deaf old Greek officer who was a family friend came with a special request. Would Marina carry an important message for Allied headquarters in Cairo? He told her: "I cannot be held responsible if these papers are discovered on you. Certainly, and quite properly, you will be shot." She had only two days to memorize detailed documents reporting on German military bases so that she would not have to take the papers with her. Helped by her mother and grandmother, Marina paced back and forth on the bearskin rug, studying the materials as if they were school lessons.

At last, carrying the one suitcase permitted, Marina took the Lufthansa flight to Sofia, passing through German military and Gestapo checks in Greece and then through Bulgarian and Gestapo inspections. She took the train to Istanbul and was again questioned at the border, but her bag was not opened. When she reached the safety of Istanbul, Marina unpacked her bag and fainted: she had absentmindedly put the documents in the suitcase. Some time later, her brother, who was in Cairo with the Greek exile forces, saw intelligence reports on an air-raid carried out "according to target data provided by Marina Lada."

During their time in the Balkans, the American journalists had learned how to circumvent government authorities, outwit police, and play hide-and-seek with censors. When calling in stories over Romania's bugged telephone lines, Robert St. John of the Associated Press referred to King Carol as "Boy Scout," his mistress as "Glamor Girl," Hitler as "Oscar" or "That Man," and the German ambassador as "the Monkey." Bucharest itself was called "Eden."

Editors at home did not care how difficult it was to send the news; they demanded scoops. If the competition got the story first, a correspondent received a complaining cable from his boss asking how this had happened. "That little word 'how,' " explained St. John, "was the difficult one to answer." It meant: "How long will it be before you get on top of the story? How long do you think you can hold your job if this sort of thing continues? Receiving [such] a cable was like being awakened from a pleasant dream with a glass of ice water in the face."

The job of foreign correspondent attracted swashbuckling types and taught them cynicism and toughness. Yet their experience with German tyranny also made them feel personally involved in the titanic struggle. Cecil Brown of CBS arrived in Belgrade just in time to flee the German attack. After three weeks on the run, he reached Ankara and was immediately scheduled for a nine-minute broadcast, his longest ever, on what had happened in Yugoslavia. Finishing the transmission over the radio at 2:30 a.m., he went to the Ankara Palace Hotel for a drink with Nezi Manyas, the popular Turkish government liaison man, and fellow CBS correspondent Winston Burdett. As soon as he entered the hotel, Brown collapsed from exhaustion and worry about losing his job, since he had been unable to send a dispatch for three weeks. A few days later, a cable from CBS arrived: SPLENDID BROADCAST. NOBLE PIECE GRAND REPORTING. EVERYONE DELIGHTED HEARING YOU. Brown felt he had fulfilled a duty in telling the story of his brave Yugoslav friends and informing the American people about the real stakes in Europe.

After the excitement of being in the midst of full-scale war, the correspondents found neutral Ankara to be a bit dull. Americans taught the British to play baseball; the journalists drank at the Ankara Palace Hotel bar. Turkish vodka was so bad that the correspondents mixed it with orange juice and so—legend has it—invented the screwdriver. The official tone was set by straitlaced President İnönü, who decried the "politics of *raki*"—Turkey's potent, licorice-flavored liquor—of his predecessor, the sybaritic Atatürk. İnönü's total abstemiousness heeded the warning of a popular Turkish saying: "Two *rakis* make a man as talkative as a monkey, three make him as brave as a lion, and four make him as fierce as a tiger." A single *raki*'s effects were unknown, since no Turk ever drank just one.

Ankara was less heady than *raki*. It was hot in the summer and very cold in the winter, lacking the fertile beauty of the coast. Equidistant from everywhere, Ankara was in the midst of nowhere. Atatürk chose it as capital precisely for this reason: to be a showcase of how the interior could be developed and modernized. By 1940, 150,000 people lived there.

The city's northern flank was a rocky, conical hill called Timurlenk after the Mongol chieftain whose conquering horde had smashed the Turks at the battle of Ankara in 1403. Around its foot clustered the old city, built up over 3000 years by succeeding empires. The city's massive walls had been rebuilt in the thirteenth century, reinforced with Roman columns, Greek tombstones, and slabs bearing Arabic inscriptions. Where necessary, openings had been cut in the crumbling city walls. The wooden houses had austere exteriors and windowed balconies, following the Middle Eastern urban tradition that wealth and women be concealed. The buildings were huddled together for protection among the city's narrow, winding cobble-paved alleys and arched gateways.

In the new city, this dense network of lanes gave way to broad avenues. Any rubble seen there was from construction, not decay, and its austerity was that of modern architecture rather than that of medieval frugality. Instead of pressing against a castle's walls, Atatürk's city spread out through the valley below.

The straight, broad lines of the new avenues also had philosophical implications. A town born of conscious urban planning rather than the accretion of centuries seemed to say that life is not merely determined by fate but can follow the course humanity sets for it. Coexisting with nature does not have to mean imitating the earth and mountains—as the old buildings did—for one can copy the world's light and space as well. Streamlined in sandstone and marble, the new city represented a different kind of functionalism, subordinating materials to purpose.

The main street, Atatürk Boulevard, ran from the edge of the old town across the new city past the National Assembly, the unpretentious Ministry of Foreign Affairs, and other government buildings. Beyond lay the embassies. On the downtown side, von Papen's offices were adjoined by the ugly Soviet mission, which looked like a stranded concrete boat. When von Papen took his short walk home, he passed in quick succession the embassies of his Japanese, Italian, and Hungarian allies and those of Germany's Yugoslav and Polish conquests.

A few blocks further along, Atatürk Boulevard climbed Cankaya Hill, forming the valley's south side, where it passed the Defense, Justice, and Interior ministries and the army headquarters. The British, French, and U.S. embassies were behind them, flanking the president's palace at a small but respectful distance. President İnönü's residence was light and spacious—full of Chinese porcelain, colorful paintings, handsome rugs, and modern furniture—in contrast to the old style, crowded with heavy furnishings.

Atatürk had loved to drive down the hill to drink and dance until dawn at the Pavilion; İnönü stayed home and played bridge. His disinterest in nightclub music may have been caused by his legendary deafness, but the magnificent view from his house might also have prompted inertia. All-glass walls looked out onto rolling steppes, snow-capped mountains, and an endless blue sky. Visitors often compared the landscape to the American southwest.

Like İnönü, most Turks kept to themselves. Except for the big annual party at the presidential palace on national day, foreigners had to provide their own entertainment. They could play tennis or go horseback riding in the magnificent countryside, but gas rationing discouraged auto excursions. There were horse races in the spring and fall. Four theaters showed old films, the philharmonic orchestra performed weekly concerts, and the state opera presented *Madame Butterfly* and *Fidelio* in Turkish during its 1941–1942 season. But for those seeking a rousing good time, there was only one place to go at night: Karpic's.

Legend had it that Ivan Karpic began his restaurant at Atatürk's request so that the republic's founder could have somewhere to dine. Atatürk even held cabinet meetings there. The decor was simple; one journalist compared it to a "Kansas railroad station lunchroom." Yet Karpic's colorful clientele made it a magical place during the war years.

Karpic's assistant, Serge, darkly handsome like a film star, actually ran the place. But the bald, round-headed Karpic, with his thick accent and white coat, provided the atmosphere. He personally scooped caviar in generous dollops from a big dish, supervised the preparation of the food, proudly oversaw his shish-kebab specialty, presented flowers to the ladies, and watched to ensure that everyone was happy with everything. But he did not hesitate to criticize diners who mistreated their food by using too much salt or who danced before properly digesting his masterpieces.

Von Papen dined in one corner, with Knatchbull-Hugessen only two tables away. Seated around the room were Soviet diplomats, Japanese attachés, American journalists, Italian embassy secretaries, Swedish officers, and Romanian businesspeople. "Diplomats of opposing sides who had been poker-playing friends until war broke out," recalled one observer, "now looked through each other without a flicker of recognition."

One of Karpic's most valued customers was Foreign Minister Numan Menemencioglu. Accompanied by his mistress and entourage, Menemencioglu was in the restaurant almost every evening. He exuded the air of an old-style pasha through aristocratic boredom, detachment, and skepticism. His grandfather was the country's most famous poet, his father was an important statesman, and he himself was the state's most experienced diplomat. Plagued by illness, weakened by operations, and constantly reported as being at death's door, Menemencioglu had a tough persistency. He stayed out late, rose early, and outlived all his contemporaries.

Most of the American journalists and diplomats who came to Ankara and Karpic's were in their twenties; not long away from home, they were having their first encounter with the wider world. They talked late into the night and brooded on topics of love, war, and peace. Sulzberger and his friends bribed Karpic's Hungarian musicians to play anti-German songs. An American embassy clerk brought a clarinet and accompanied the band from his table. When music from *Carmen* was played one raucous night, some spirited Americans acted out a bullfight as waiters rushed to protect the furniture. After dinner, the journalists completed their reports and went to the radio station to send them.

One night in August 1941, *New York Times* correspondent Ray Brock showed up at the radio station at 2 a.m. demanding to broadcast a story. Another journalist was already inside, as the "on air" light above the door attested. According to his version, Brock tried to enter by turning the handle gently; according to the Turks, he was kicking and hitting the door. Nezi Manyas, a government press official who sat in the studio to ensure that reporters sent the censor-approved scripts, opened the door and began to yell at Brock; Brock insulted Manyas and threatened to punch him. The mercurial American became even angrier when he discovered that the censors had cut a paragraph from his story. The Turks threatened to call the police; NBC correspondent Martin Agronsky and another American reporter persuaded Brock to leave.

Brock was constantly getting into trouble. Even Americans thought Brock's articles exaggerated. The Ankara Palace Hotel complained that his tab went unpaid; Karpic's found he had run up an alarming bill and worried that the hard-drinking correspondent might start a brawl there. The government suspended Brock's broadcasting privileges; Brock claimed this was a German plot against him and left the country for a few weeks. He rejected U.S. embassy efforts to patch up the dispute. But one night, back at Karpic's, he came over to Manyas's table and apologized. Nobody could continue a personal quarrel at Karpic's.

Friends, foes, and opportunists were all trying to use American journalists for their own purposes. As soon as correspondents checked into Istanbul's Park Hotel, their phones started ringing endlessly as strangers peddling information called to set appointments in some hotel or out-of-the-way café.

Sulzberger, Burdett, and Agronsky scoured the embassies and diplomatic cocktail parties for news. While America was neutral, von Papen was happy to give them interviews. The British were so helpful that journalists worried about becoming conduits for their propaganda. Vichy French diplomats assured American reporters of their patriotism, promising to join the Allies when the time came. Still, an American correspondent wrote in his diary, "They go on collaborating."

The Soviets, in contrast, were often unfriendly. Russian diplomats were instructed in great detail about how to behave and whom to speak with at public functions. Watched and evaluated by the local representatives of Stalin's secret police, the NKVD, Soviet diplomats were sometimes so intimidated that they stood in the corners and avoided speaking with anyone. Leonid Naumov, nominally the Soviet press attaché, was actually an NKVD assassinations expert. When a journalist visited at the Soviet embassy, Naumov told his staff: "Downstairs is a foreign correspondent, perhaps a spy. Find out if he is a spy and if so for what agency he is working." The Soviets did not always do so well, however, when faced with real practitioners of espionage. At an embassy party marking the anniversary of the Russian Revolution, Naumov ordered a young vice-consul to spare no vodka in loosening the tongue of Istanbul's deputy police chief. Instead, the Turk outdrank the Russian, helped him to his quarters upstairs, and enjoyed a good look at the embassy's top-secret section.

The Turks were also very reserved when dealing with foreigners. An American journalist called them the "most suspicious people I've ever encountered." This trait had its humorous side. When the American photographer Margaret Bourke-White came to Turkey for *Life* magazine, customs officers doubted that the 300 flashbulbs in her luggage were all for her own use. Consequently, they wrote the bulbs' total weight in her passport to ensure that she did not sell them. Bourke-White hired two men to accompany her during the trip and paid them for each used bulb they picked up. When she left, customs officials had no complaint: the bulbs mysteriously weighed more than when she had arrived.

President İnönü, though, had his own complaints about Bourke-White. She took two hours of his time and ordered that all his furniture be moved to achieve better pictures. After all this effort, however, *Life* published only one photo. An American diplomat told Selim Sarper, the government press-office director, that the magazine was saving the other photographs for prominent display as soon as Turkey was again in the news. "Yes," Sarper replied sadly, "they will probably be used when Turkey goes into the war."

Sarper was determined, however, that the correspondents would not make that happen. After some of them went near the Soviet border without telling him, he called them into his office. "I'm furious," he said. "You had no right and should never have gone without permission. It is dangerous country and you could have been murdered. Some people don't like Americans." Then he smiled and added, "So, of course, I had you followed every minute of your trip and know everything you did."

Suspicious by nature, unused to having so many foreign correspondents, and nervous about being drawn into the war, the Turks tightened up. "Practically not a single night passes in which I am not involved in a censorship fight," noted Martin Agronsky.

In October 1941, a Turkish editor, whose views reflected government policy, wrote an editorial attacking American journalists for irresponsible sensationalism which endangered his country by angering the Germans. Germany blocked certain escape routes from Greece and canceled an exchange of wounded prisoners when newspapers carried articles about them, he complained. "Journalism is the art of learning everything . . . and announcing it without delay. [Reporters want] front-page stories under large headlines, regardless of the . . . consequences." But they had a humanitarian responsibility as well as a professional duty, he concluded. "The untimely, premature and unnecessary release of news in these ghastly times where there is a question of life or death for several nations of Europe is paid for . . . with the blood of real people."

"The authorities," a U.S. diplomat wrote, "have no experience and little understanding of the American conception of a free press, and are prone to be rather uncomprehending and crude and arbitrary in enforcing their right to prevent any journalistic activities which they consider contrary to their national interests." Selim Sarper, Press Bureau director, explained that while his office always wanted smooth relations with journalists, the police had other priorities. One case involved a young Kansas woman who worked for United Press and was expelled after erroneously reporting a Turkish military buildup along the Soviet border. The effect on Moscow was bad enough, but since her boyfriend was from the pro-German Nadi family, the Turks saw her action as a German plot to embroil Turkey in war. The woman married her fiancé and was allowed to return to Turkey in exchange for giving up her writing career.

The more congenial Agronsky also had problems. Once, after important Turkish-German economic negotiations, Agronsky concluded his broadcast with the words "In the end the chief commodity the Germans succeeded in getting from the Turks was acorns—that is nuts." After the U.S. press publicized that line, the Turks realized it was a double entendre implying they had insulted the Germans. Agronsky lost his radio privileges for a week.

The fireworks really began when Sarper went on a trip and left his deputy, Izzedin Nisbay, in charge. One of Agronsky's reports ended, "Even lumping together all the Bulgarian, Italian and German troops at the moment available near Turkey's frontiers, the Germans cannot yet muster enough forces to safely attack the Turks now or in the near future; but in spite of this, it is persistently rumored in some foreign circles here that a German attack is imminent." Shortly thereafter, a BBC broadcast quoted only the last part of Agronsky's statement, highlighting rumors of a German invasion.

On the evening of September 9, Agronsky received an urgent summons to Nisbay's office. He was kept waiting an hour before being ushered into the acting press director's presence. Manyas acted as interpreter.

"I have heard," said Nisbay, "that you are a gentleman and am certain you will cooperate in erasing the BBC's slur on Turkey's honor." Agronsky pointed out that his script cleared censorship and saw no reason for objecting to the BBC broadcast. Nisbay became excited: "I am the one to judge when my country has been insulted! I am positive that you will rectify this insult by reading a rebuttal of the BBC's statement." The harried official was having visions of Istanbul in ruins and German tanks roaring through Ankara because he had failed to stop a provocative story.

Without another word, Nisbay turned to his secretary and began to dictate what Agronsky should report over his network: "From time to time the BBC makes announcements . . . which are outright lies. . . . I protest energetically against the tendentious statements of the BBC which hasn't the right to abuse my trust or the trust of my company. . . . It is very agreeable to me to be in a country so very hospitable and one which offers us facilities better than England." Agronsky would then swear he would never "ungraciously abuse the confidence of Turkey and of Turks, who are proud . . . in this world on fire to have still kept their country intact and outside the misery of the war, at the same time as they have succeeded in keeping friendly relations with all their neighbors."

Nisbay turned back to the shocked Agronsky and added, "I am certain that you will read this as if you do not . . . I will be sure that you have conspired with the British to hurt my country. If you adopt this attitude I will know how to deal with you."

Agronsky replied that it was not considered ethical for American correspondents to read documents ghostwritten by foreign officials. Nisbay flew into a hysterical rage: "I know now that you are not a gentleman. You have insulted my country and must take the consequences. You will not be allowed to broadcast any more." He began screaming that Agronsky was in league with British propaganda to ensnare Turkey in the war.

At this point, Agronsky said he would listen no more. Nisbay shouted, "I am the master here; you will not leave this room until you have agreed to correct this terrible British lie." Then he stalked out of his own office. An embarrassed Manyas urged Agronsky to be patient: "Give me a few minutes and I will calm him down." By now it was 11 p.m. and Agronsky had dinner guests waiting at his apartment.

After fifteen minutes Manyas returned with Nisbay who was in a better mood. Nisbay again asked Agronsky to read the statement. The American again refused, and Nisbay once more became hysterical. "You are not a gentleman," he yelled. Striking himself on the forehead, he shouted, "Your action will be imprinted forever here!" Turkey was in great danger because of Agronsky and his colleagues, he ranted, pulling from his pocket an article by a retired U.S. admiral stating that Britain would have to seize the Turkish straits to prevent the Germans from capturing them. "You're responsible for this," he shouted, "and I will see to it that you are unable to make so much trouble again!"

Manyas tried to mediate. Finally, as midnight struck, Agronsky agreed to tell his office that the Turks objected to the BBC item. Nisbay's whole attitude changed. "Now you are a gentleman," he proclaimed. Manyas made the two men shake hands. "You must understand," Nisbay said, "that British propaganda twists the statements of great and famous gentlemen and correspondents like yourself to its own lying ends." As soon as he reached home, Agronsky called the U.S. embassy. It protested and was assured that Nisbay had been reprimanded. At any rate, there were no further incidents.

But the Turks did have reason to be worried about the activities of foreigners, a number of whom, including one of Agronsky's fellow American correspondents, were Soviet agents. Everyone in Ankara's small foreign colony liked Winston and Lea Burdett. He was a thin, intense, and energetic CBS correspondent. She was an anti-Fascist Italian with a hearty laugh, able to match the male journalists drink for drink.

Burdett became a foreign correspondent in a peculiar manner. As a reporter on the *Brooklyn Eagle*, he joined the U.S. Communist party in 1937. In January 1940, Burdett was contacted by his cell leader and told to meet Joseph North, a well-known Communist journalist, at his Greenwich Village apartment. "We want you to go to Finland," said North, for a special assignment "in which you can be useful to the party."

Two days later, Burdett rendezvoused with North on a Manhattan street. A third man joined them as they walked to a Union Square restaurant. He was Jacob Golos, the chief NKVD agent in the United States. Golos asked Burdett to go to Europe as a journalist to gather information for the Russians. Burdett agreed, and Golos ordered him to hand over his Communist membership card. Burdett would now work under direct Soviet discipline. Golos gave him a ticket for Stockholm.

Burdett's contact in Stockholm told him to go to Finland to cover that country, then defending itself against a Soviet invasion. When the Finns signed an armistice, Burdett decided to stay in Europe as a foreign correspondent. He traveled through Moscow to Bucharest and then Belgrade, where he met and married Lea Schiavi. She was still working for Italian magazines, but her prospects for continued employment were slim because her political views—she spat when mentioning Mussolini's name—made her unpopular with the Italian authorities.

In Belgrade, the NKVD again contacted Burdett and told him that at a certain trolley stop he would be met by a tall gentleman wearing one gray glove and carrying the other. This man gave him the names of six midlevel Yugoslav officials he should get to know, though Burdett later claimed he had made little effort to fulfill these instructions.

Burdett came to Turkey in March 1941 and stayed at the Ankara Palace Hotel. While visiting the Soviet embassy, he told a diplomat named Antonina Gaglovina about his previous work for Moscow. A few days later, a young, well-groomed Russian visited Burdett in his room and announced: "Everything is good. You can be of use to us, and your contact will be Madame Gaglovina."

Burdett's task was to write reports on Turkish politics and policies. The key issue for the Russians, as for the journalists and other diplomats in Ankara, was the meaning of Turkish neutrality. The truth was not hard to discover. The Americans and British well understood that the Turks wanted to stay out of the fighting and to tilt toward the Allies. They would carefully avoid antagonizing the Germans, and though they hated the Russians, the Turks would do nothing to provoke them either.

But to the ideologically corseted hierarchies in Berlin and Moscow, the most obvious facts were met with deep suspicion. Burdett's reports, identical to what all the correspondents were saying daily, were far more credible to the Soviets because they were secret and had been obtained by clandestine means.

Gaglovina was happy with Burdett's work, handed over during his interviews with her. She was a rather amateurish spy, though, sometimes emerging from a big embassy limousine to greet Burdett at a café where many people knew them both by sight. Apparently, no Western intelligence service ever caught on.

Burdett finally decided to break with the Soviets because of growing disillusionment with their policies. He so informed Gaglovina in March 1942. She was angry to lose a prize source. Burdett then had to rush to India to cover a story for CBS. Meanwhile, Lea decided to visit Soviet-occupied northern Iran. Her party set out in a car from Tabrīz, headquarters of the Soviet occupation army, and spent the day at a Kurdish village. On the way back, two armed Iranians stopped the car and shot Lea. The driver floored the accelerator to escape, and the car bounced down the road as the gunmen fired at it. Lea died a few minutes later.

Burdett went to Iran to investigate and found the authorities there loath to dig into a crime involving a foreign power. At first, Burdett thought she was killed by Fascists; later, he concluded the Russians were responsible, since they had full military control of the area and there were few, if any, Axis agents left in Iran. Whether Lea Burdett was killed by the NKVD in revenge for her husband's defection or because of some intelligence involvement of her own remains a mystery.

Tragic and dramatic personal experiences were teaching a generation of Americans about the world's harsh realities. They had first followed the story as detached neutrals; then they became caught up in it. As the United States entered World War II, Americans would now shape events as well as watch them.

8 | The Americans Arrive: 1942–1943

You can't carry two watermelons under one arm.
—Turkish proverb

While hostile armies paused at its borders, the icy cold winter of 1941–1942 invaded and overran Turkey. People froze to death in Ankara, where the temperature sank to below zero. By January 4, after a week of snowfall, the country was paralyzed. Hoarding and the transport system's collapse forced a steady reduction of bread rations. Fuel shortages meant that buildings were heated only two or three times a week and hot water was supplied only a few hours a day.

But such hardships were mild compared with what was happening in the neighboring countries engulfed by war or German occupation. The more Americans found out about these events, the more they felt themselves committed to the anti-Nazi cause. As President Roosevelt had said of the Nazis, "No one can tame a tiger or turn it into a charming kitten."

An American military attaché in Istanbul obtained copies of a German soldier's photos showing Romanian Jews being deported to concentration camps. Locked into boxcars without food or water for five or six days, he reported, they died during the journey. The bodies were thrown into quicklime, and the clothing was sold so there would be no evidence.

A few days later, the same American was at a dinner party at which von Papen was also present. The German ambassador made a dramatic toast. "As you know, Germany always stands for peace," he said, with his wine glass raised high. Turning to the American officer, von Papen added, "I hope America will take notice." The annoyed American looked away. "The ambassador is trying to catch your eye," said the officer's neighbor. He pretended not to hear. "The lightning has now struck on every side of Turkey," an American diplomat wrote in December 1941. "I hope it will not be our turn next!" The next day, the Japanese bombed Pearl Harbor. America was now in the war for keeps.

Still, the shivering American and British residents of still-neutral Istanbul had some consolations to accompany their New Year's toasts for 1942. Their countries were now allies in the war. After so many retreats—in France, North Africa, the Balkans, and Greece—Britain was returning to the offensive. Its intelligence forces were preparing the return to Nazi-occupied Europe. German armies deep inside Russia were suffering far more from a winter whose intensity had stopped their advance.

Hitler had originally intended to invade the U.S.S.R. in the early spring of 1941, but the campaign into Yugoslavia and Greece had delayed his attack on the Soviet Union until late June. The Germans had been unable to destroy Russian resistance before "General Winter" came to the Soviets' aid. Berlin's whole timetable was upset. Instead of preparing for the expected attack on Turkey after the snows ebbed in 1942, every available German soldier was now needed on the Russian front.

The German attack, however, made Stalin eager to have Turkey in the war to draw away German troops and open new supply routes for the U.S.S.R. He secretly ordered the killing of von Papen in February 1942 to provoke a German-Turkish conflict. But von Papen survived the murder attempt, and the Turks discovered Moscow's game. Now the Turks were even more angry and suspicious toward the U.S.S.R. Preoccupied with the invasion of the Soviet Union, and worried that Turkey might cooperate with his enemies, Hitler made a historic decision: he would not invade Turkey and would do everything possible to keep it neutral.

Over dinner in Berlin on March 31, 1942, Hitler commented, "On the political and sentimental level, there's no obstacle to an alliance between Turkey and the Reich." He was ready to guarantee the Bosporus strait's neutrality to prevent it from being used for supplying the Soviets. Pro-German Turks were invited for a tour through Hitler's domain. "Everywhere we went," one of them wrote, "we were greeted with feelings of affection mixed with respect and admiration, which Germans all feel for the Turkish nation." The delegation visited Hitler's Berchtesgaden lair, Vienna, the Ukraine, and newly captured Sevastapol on the Black Sea to inspect the German "army which has won victory on top of victory for three years." The Germans promised Turkey military equipment to compete with the U.S.-supplied, British-distributed lend-lease supplies.

With this relaxation of tension, İnönü spent the spring and summer enjoying horseraces at Ankara's Hippodrome. In June 1942, after a year's stalling, Ankara felt secure enough to reopen the railroad bridges connecting Turkey with German-occupied Greece and Bulgaria. As Stalingrad desperately fought the besieging German Sixth Army, Istanbul expanded Taksim Park. "The reason Turkey is wrapped in peace and quiet and is far from disasters," exulted Istanbul's mayor, "is that our leaders who know how to make war also know how to guard peace!" A Turkish diplomat explained: "Few people realize how very difficult Turkey's position is and how dangerous a game she has been playing. . . . Turkey has rendered her greatest service to the Allied cause by retaining her precarious neutrality." The weather took more of a toll than the war. January's snows were followed by a heat wave in June, heavy rains in October, severe storms in November, and an earthquake in December.

The only way the Allies could profit from Turkey's neutrality was to use the country as a secret base for gathering intelligence and supporting European resistance movements. These missions had to be accomplished, however, in a way that would avoid any provocation which might make the Germans attack or the Turks expel the Allies.

The British had led the way; their new ally, the United States, would now mount its own espionage effort. The Office of Strategic Services (OSS) had just been organized as America's intelligence agency. The man named to lead it, William Donovan, had learned from his earlier travels through the Balkans, Turkey, and the Middle East that the

Germans were waging a new kind of war in which covert operations and propaganda played a central role. He also came to understand that the Balkans could be the Axis's soft underbelly. Starting virtually from scratch, Donovan created an impressive, if amateur, group of espionage operators, analysts, and guerrilla fighters.

The OSS plan for the Turkey operation, "Project NET-1," argued: "Turkey offers a base of penetration into the entire enemy-occupied Southeastern Europe. From Istanbul run the only land routes into that territory, and from Izmir small boats can be operated into the Dodecanese and Aegean Islands and to the Greek mainland." The base would recruit, infiltrate, and aid "agents and groups into these territories for the purpose of organizing subversive activities of all kinds." The first step in laying a foundation for OSS operations in Turkey was taken on January 9, 1942, when a little round woman named Betty Carp boarded the *Taurus Express* at Istanbul's Haydarpasha Station. She had been invited to Washington by her old friend Allen Dulles to work for the OSS.

Carp was unquestionably the most popular person in Istanbul's foreign community. She was born there of Austro-Hungarian parents in 1898 and, at the age of 16, went to work for the U.S. embassy as a switchboard operator. Carp started accumulating hundreds of friends among shopkeepers, policemen, officials, and diplomats from a dozen countries. She found out everything the consulate needed to know, cut red tape, and accomplished tasks with almost magical speed in a society notorious for its inefficiency. As her diplomatic friends moved to new posts, Carp developed a worldwide network of acquaintances with whom she kept in touch and from whom she raised funds for charity.

Carp became so indispensable that, although officially only a reception clerk, she was given far higher responsibility. The U.S. ambassador's letter of recommendation notes the love and respect inspired by Carp's "quickness and sensitivity of perception and her amazing resourcefulness in finding practical solutions to almost any kind of a difficulty that presents itself." Carp helped everyone in Istanbul as "adviser on local customs, [philanthropist], employment agency, and spiritual adviser." She was, in short, "a remarkable personality—with a deep understanding and tolerance and love for her fellow humans of all degrees, and as nearly selfless as any man or woman I have ever known, in her complete freedom from striving for her own interests and from malice or jealousy towards others." With her usual combination of humility and practicality, Carp told her boss, "How can I personally hand such a letter to any man?" She paused, then added, "I think I will mail it to him."

Allen Dulles had been a State Department officer in Istanbul, and he became an early member of Carp's fan club. As one of the OSS's chief organizers, he urged that Carp be hired to help launch operations in the Balkans and Turkey. He explained: She "was for over twenty years in a highly confidential and important position in the American Embassy in Turkey. . . . I have known her personally since 1920 and can absolutely vouch for her. In addition to an extraordinary knowledge of the Near East and all its personalities, she speaks and writes fluently English, French, Italian, German, Greek, and Turkish."

Carp's cover story for going to Washington was that she worked for Dulles's law firm. When a State Department official teasingly asked what kind of law she would be practicing, Carp jokingly replied she would specialize in divorce cases and was willing to start with his.

Carp's voyage to America was an ordeal. From frigid Istanbul, she went through Beirut, Jerusalem, Cairo, and Khartoum. She spent three torrid days at a remote colonial outpost when engine trouble forced her plane down in central Africa. At last, Carp arrived in unbearably humid Nigeria. Rommel was on the offensive. "Wouldn't it be dreadful," a British officer asked her, "if we found Rommel sitting in Shepheard's Bar in Cairo one of these days?"

On February 12 another plane took her to Gambia, where she ran into Laurence Steinhardt, the new U.S. ambassador to Turkey, who was heading the opposite way. He had had a near escape the previous day when British antiaircraft guns fired at his plane after it failed to give the proper landing signal. He was lucky to have survived. A few hours earlier, three Vichy planes had been shot down in the airfield's vicinity.

Carp then flew via Trinidad and Bermuda to Baltimore through forty-eight hours of storms. The whole trip took over five weeks. Nevertheless, Betty immediately went to work in Washington. She wrote memo after memo on every aspect of Turkey; on American teachers, missionaries, oil and tobacco men, and journalists whom the OSS might recruit; and on Axis agents to watch. She particularly recommended

Archibald Walker, director of Socony Oil operations in Turkey, as a good prospect for the OSS. The 59-year-old Walker had served the company for thirty-five years all over the Balkans. The slim, sandy-haired executive had a ruddy complexion that showed his excitable personality. "Very erratic," Carp wrote, "very capable, very brilliant, but carries his one-track mind and independence of thought and action to the extreme." Anyone who visited the German embassy was barred from his house; he even dropped friends for listening to German music. To be denied Walker's hospitality was a real punishment, since he was among Istanbul's most popular hosts and owned one of its most beautiful homes.

Precise, elegant, and gracious, Walker was both tough and sentimental. "No sooner is some country invaded than he rushes up to [its ambassador] and offers him his home, his car, his purse." Walker was approached by the OSS and he agreed to begin gathering intelligence in Istanbul. Carp selected two young American tobacco buyers as Walker's first agents; they were to keep an eye on Axis ships traveling into Istanbul and along the Bosporus.

The OSS was also looking for Greeks or Greek-Americans who might be infiltrated back into that country. This search took Carp to some unexpected places. On a Friday evening in March 1942, she entered a dirty Greek restaurant in New York's tough waterfront section. Signs on the walls urged the leftist clientele to "Give to Russia." All the other patrons were Greek workers or merchant sailors who told Carp about their dangerous voyages carrying supplies to England through submarine-infested waters. Sitting at a corner table, Carp ordered dinner in perfect Greek, impressing everyone with her fluency. She was such a hit that everyone invited her to come the next evening for a Russian war relief rally set for 8 p.m.

The next night she arrived on time only to be told, amid much laughter, that Greeks always started everything late and nothing would happen until 10. "But, of course," her hosts explained, "if we had told people to come at 10, no one would arrive until midnight!" Finally, the restaurant was filled with 300 people in their Sunday best. They drank beer, ate Greek food, and toasted the health of Stalin, Churchill, and Roosevelt. Men unknown to the clientele were warned off. "This is an international place," growled the guard; "everyone can come in, even fascists can walk in, but fascists never walk out again."

The first speaker talked at great length, urged unity, begged everyone to think of General MacArthur and of the wonderful Red Army and to fight until America won the war. His patriotic speech then shifted tone. If the Red Army fights so bravely because its soldiers are Communists, he said, he was proud to call himself one. "Greeks! The tragic fate of your country is due to England alone! England let you down, she did not help you, she is responsible!" The Turks, too, he added, were not to be trusted. A man at Carp's table stood up to say it was impolite to attack the Turks since a distinguished guest from Istanbul, Carp, was present. Another Greek yelled at her, "We want to know: Is Turkey biding her time or is she going to work with the Axis? New Turks—old Turks—they are all the same." At such gatherings, however, Carp began to recruit Greeks for the OSS, and some of these people would find themselves operating from Turkey a few months later.

In addition to working with the Greeks, Carp's job involved meeting Soviet officials visiting the United States and writing accounts of Moscow's views. One of her key contacts was an old Istanbul friend who was now secretary to the Soviet ambassador in Washington. As early as March 1943, Carp noted that the Soviets intended to establish "a protective ring of friendly neighboring states" on their borders after the war.

Impressed by Carp's skill, Dulles wanted her to join him in Switzerland at the end of the war, but she decided to return to her old job in Istanbul. William Donovan, chief of the OSS, personally sponsored her application for U.S. citizenship. In August 1953, a State Department bureaucrat decided to fire Carp as part of a payroll cutback. Allen Dulles, at that time the CIA's director, stormed into a meeting on the matter, pounded on the table, and stated in no uncertain terms that firing Betty Carp would be a "national disgrace" and would seriously impair U.S. security. She was quickly reinstated.

Assembling an intelligence service required a variety of skills and personalities. Betty Carp, the well-connected observer, analyzed political developments and found people to recruit. Archibald Walker was an energetic man of action who excelled at initiating projects. But the OSS's weakness, as events in Istanbul would show, was that it lacked experienced intelligence operatives.

This period not only marked the birth of U.S. intelligence but also was a turning point in the style and scope of U.S. diplomacy. The old-school methods of polished gentlemen, elegant conversation, and a narrow focus on high statecraft no longer sufficed in a topsy-turvy world. American representatives abroad now also had to deal with a new set of issues: economic competition, espionage, propaganda, intelligence gathering, and public relations. U.S. responsibilities required a broader, more active foreign policy. New types and larger numbers of people were needed to carry out these activities.

In 1939, the U.S. Ankara embassy and Istanbul consulate housed only an ambassador, three diplomats, and a couple of military attachés. Two years later, there were eleven diplomats, twenty-one clerks, a large military detachment, and representatives of many new agencies created to deal with wartime exigencies. The Office of War Information (OWI) rented a large building on Istiklal Boulevard and employed twenty Americans and a hundred local people. One of its main projects was a news service for the Turkish press. The Foreign Economic Administration, Board of Economic Warfare, and U.S. Commercial Corporation decided which local companies to embargo for trading with the enemy and supplied U.S. goods to maintain Turkish morale and loyalty. They also bought up chrome, acorns (used for tanning hides), wool, hazelnuts, and even chests of opium for medicinal use to keep these goods out of German hands. Most of these products were stored in warehouses during the war and sold at discounts thereafter. But one could never tell what might turn out to be important for the German war effort. The Allies later discovered, for example, that Germany used high-quality Turkish cotton to make counterfeit British banknotes for paying its espionage agents in Turkey and elsewhere.

The Lend-Lease office provided military aid to meet the Turks' demand for defensive equipment, though much of it rusted on Turkish army bases. A Soviet diplomat complained, "The Americans are giving you Turks lots of weapons."

"But the Americans are giving you a lot more," answered a Turkish official.

"Yes," responded the Russian, "but we use them."

The State Department was hard-pressed to maintain its supremacy over these new wartime agencies and to adjust to the changing demands of diplomacy. Laurence Steinhardt, who came to Ankara as U.S. ambassador in early 1942, was an appropriate symbol and manager for this new era of change. He was a clever lawyer—active, energetic, analytical, sometimes abrasive—who would never accept the old-school diplomatic maxim warning against excessive zeal. He was truly American in his brisk self-assurance, jocular manner, and matter-of-fact problem-solving approach. Steinhardt's appearance—tall, handsome, graceful, and distinguished looking—made him look like an American ambassador from central casting. The Turks liked his directness.

At first, British ambassador Knatchbull-Hugessen thought Steinhardt too vigorous and cocksure, "inclined to take the line that he can get things done where no one else can. . . . He loses sight of everything else . . . blurred by the bright vision of his own personality." As a New Deal Democrat, Steinhardt also spoke the new language of liberalism, sometimes criticizing Britain's imperial attitude. As a representative of America's new international activism, he voiced a buoyant, sometimes arrogant, self-confidence. "We won the last war for you by throwing our money and our soldiers into the struggle," he told British guests at a dinner party. "We are going to win this war for you but with a difference." The United States and the U.S.S.R. were going to be the world's principal powers; Europeans must face up to "how important a part America is going to play in your lives."

The new American ambassador had another attribute for which he was disliked by some British and State Department officials: he was Jewish. As an activist in Democratic politics, Steinhardt had been a strong Roosevelt supporter and the president successively made him U.S. minister to Sweden and then to Peru. Before these appointments, only three Jews had served as U.S. ambassadors, all to Turkey during Ottoman times.

When Steinhardt became ambassador to the U.S.S.R. in 1939, Nazi newspapers and American anti-Semites attacked him. He was in Moscow when World War II began with the German invasion of Poland. Thousands of Jews and Poles fled eastward into lands occupied by the Soviet army. Polish-American and American Jewish organizations bombarded the State Department with letters asking that the refugees be helped to reach safety in the United States. The State Department and Assistant Secretary of State Breckinridge Long, who oversaw visa and immigration affairs, were most unsympathetic. Long saw himself as a protective shield against waves of uncouth, subversive immigrants, and he ensured that legal restrictions were observed to the last punctuation mark. Those who had barely escaped the Germans with their lives were required to furnish detailed documentary proof of their background, citizenship, education, and professional credentials.

The only way to aid a significant number of refugees, Jewish leaders realized, was by going directly to the White House. Roosevelt issued a special order reducing the power of legalistic U.S. consuls to deny visas and easing requirements for refugees designated as "well-known intellectuals or labor leaders." Long was determined to reverse this decision, arguing that the refugees might be Russian or German agents.

Tragically, Steinhardt supplied the ammunition Long needed. Steinhardt's background made him both sympathetic toward these refugees and worried about admitting them to the United States. Members of the wealthy New York German-Jewish elite to which Steinhardt belonged passionately wanted to be accepted by the upper-crust society that often sought to exclude them. Their own out-group status made them sensitive toward social justice, but the group's desire to imitate a snobbish social elite made its members nervous about anything that might cast aspersions on or threaten their own status. Some of them feared that the large-scale immigration of poor eastern European Jews could increase anti-Semitism. These attitudes shaped Steinhardt's insecurities.

Writing from Moscow, Steinhardt stressed the need for caution in admitting refugees. The vast majority of them, he said, did not qualify even for visitors' visas or for the president's special program. "Thus far," he claimed, "not a single well-known intellectual or labor leader has made an appearance at the Embassy unless a high school geography teacher is to be regarded as a well-known intellectual and anyone performing manual labor is to be regarded as a labor leader."

Many of the refugees, he continued, had been politically active in the Zionist Labor party, the Jewish Socialist Bund, and the Jewish Joint Distribution Committee. Incredibly, he warned that these people were "professional political agitators . . . who might well transplant their entire political organization to the United States." The pro-refugee organizations, Steinhardt concluded, "are obviously more interested in finding a haven for these unfortunates than they are in safeguarding the welfare of the United States in the most critical period of its history. I still regard admission to the United States as a privilege, not a right."

Long rushed the telegram to Roosevelt, who agreed to tighten regulations. Steinhardt's arguments were ridiculous. The Zionist and Bundist officials were anti-Nazi and anti-Communist. Their organizations had long-established American branches and posed no possible threat to U.S. security. Most of the refugees who were refused a safe haven in the United States were later killed when they fell into German hands.

In similar circumstances, a Japanese consul in Lithuania, Sempo Sugihara, was saving 4000 Jews by giving them visas. When France fell a year later, Portugal's consul in Bordeaux, Aristides de Sousa Mendes, rescued several thousand more by the same method. No British or American diplomat followed their example.

When Steinhardt briefly returned to America before taking up his new post in Turkey, Zionist and other Jewish groups urged him to do more to help refugees. Steinhardt told the Zionist leader Emanuel Neumann that he was still very sympathetic but that he had to protect his own position as a diplomat.

Steinhardt found himself in another potentially hostile situation in Turkey. Turkish leaders had mixed feelings about the appointment of a Jew as U.S. ambassador. Atatürk had asked Roosevelt in 1933 not to make a practice of doing so. When informed of Steinhardt's appointment in 1942, the Turkish foreign minister commented that this was "very sad news."

The Turkish government admitted Jewish refugees only when it was sure they would quickly pass through to Palestine. The story of the ship *Struma* personifies the cowardice, prejudice, and bureaucratic meanness of so many nations whose actions complemented or even collaborated with Nazi genocide against Europe's Jews.

Desperate to escape from occupied Romania, 769 Jewish refugees —including 300 children and 200 women—crowded aboard the little *Struma*, an aged ship whose usual capacity was 100 passengers. Just before its departure on December 12, 1941, Romanian officials came on board and seized the passengers' money, jewels, some supplies, and even copper cooking pots. Three hours after leaving, the ship's engine broke down. A tugboat came in response to the *Struma*'s SOS, but the Romanians demanded that repairs be made on the spot rather than bringing the *Struma* back to harbor. The tug escorted the *Struma* to the Romanian territorial limit to ensure that the ship did not return or tarry. The engines failed several times more until the *Struma* was towed by a Turkish tugboat into Istanbul on the night of December 16.

The rusting, overcrowded hulk—decks crowded with exhausted, frightened people—was moored opposite the busy Tophane ferry landing. The Turkish police, fearing the passengers might try to remain in the country, insisted they stay on board. The captain was allowed ashore only to arrange for repairs. When Turkish officials demanded that all bills be paid in hard currency, Walker, the Istanbul representative of an American company, stepped in and provided the necessary dollars.

The passengers wanted to go to Palestine. But since the British government refused to grant them visas, the Turks would not allow them to land or to continue their journey safely by train. Forced out of Istanbul harbor, overcrowded and unseaworthy, the *Struma* drifted off course. After further wanderings and sufferings—and despite the fact that it flew a neutral flag—it was sunk by a Soviet submarine. There were no survivors.

The institutional battles for control of U.S. foreign policy, State Department anti-Semitism, Steinhardt's personal situation, and the Turkish attitude toward minorities all came together in one issue. In June 1943, George V. Allen, director of the State Department's Division of Middle East Affairs, wrote Steinhardt a "personal and confidential" letter on a "matter of considerable delicacy." Allen continued, "My remarks result from the sincerest desire not only to perform my job as best I can but equally from the warm friendship which I feel for you and your interests." The implication that Steinhardt's career depended on his heeding Allen's demands would loom throughout their correspondence in an unsettling manner.

Allen thought there were too many "American officials of the Jewish race" in Turkey. German propaganda, he warned, was trying to inflame Arabs and Moslems with the threat that "the United States intends to turn over all of the Near East to the Jews after the war." Berlin sought to exploit the fact that three U.S. agencies in Turkey—the embassy, Lend-Lease, and OWI—were headed by Jews.

Allen said he considered Steinhardt to be a successful ambassador and "loyal American through and through." Although the State Department was "most loath to raise the question of a person's race or religion in considering him for an appointment abroad," Allen wanted to ensure that no more Jews would be sent to Turkey and that some of those there would be transferred. Unless pending appointments were headed off, "irreparable harm may be done not only to you personally but to broad American interests."

Responding to Allen's urgings, Steinhardt wrote Secretary of State Cordell Hull that Turkish leaders "do not harbor any anti-Semitic feelings" but might blame him for the presence of more Jewish officials, thus weakening his influence and damaging U.S.-Turkish relations. His argument is not persuasive, however, since no one claimed that the Turks had pressed the matter, no untoward incident ever took place, and Steinhardt admitted that all the Jewish officials had good relations with the Turks. Objections might have just as easily been raised against American Christian officials in Turkey, several of whom were former missionaries with strong ties to the Greek and Armenian communities.

Steinhardt's real animus was aimed at the directors of the OWI in Turkey, Robert Parker and his deputy Hal Lehrman. Steinhardt's remarks on Lehrman read like the old German-Jewish elite's classic prejudice toward new immigrants. "As you know," Steinhardt wrote Allen, "a single individual can frequently draw attention to a situation of this kind by his conduct just as the diners in a restaurant are made conscious of the presence of a Jew by his loud or rowdy conduct or bad manners, whereas prior to his entry there may have been a dozen well-behaved Jews . . . of whose identity . . . the other diners were not conscious."

The ambassador's antagonism also reflected the local skirmishes in the State Department's bureaucratic battles with the OWI and other wartime agencies. Steinhardt was angered by OWI-Istanbul's size and independent behavior; the personalities and mission of the OWI officials inclined them toward a higher profile than Steinhardt liked. Their job was to affect Turkish public opinion and to gather information using newspapers and radio broadcasts from the German-occupied lands. Parker, the head of the OWI in Turkey, was a veteran foreign correspondent whose years of circumventing officials and outsmarting censorship in the Balkans made him view embassy methods as too stuffy and slow. The colorful, audacious foreign correspondent and the cautious, disciplined diplomat were almost inevitably rivals.

Since the Germans distributed news stories and periodicals, Parker was determined that the OWI would provide more and better ones, including prized copies of *Life* and *Vogue*. The magazines, explained an OWI report, were "like gold. We keep them in the old bank vaults in the office basement under lock and key, use them sparingly for bribery, giving them to politicians' wives and well-known dressmakers."

Despite his animosity to the OWI, even Steinhardt became involved in cultural battles. When a famous German pianist came to Ankara to play with the national symphony orchestra, the United States countered with a soprano, unfortunately one with no known reputation. Steinhardt scheduled a reception before her recital. The woman refused to come, complaining cigarette smoke might affect her voice. Steinhardt scolded her, "What do you mean? This is war!"

The OWI did better with art forms that were American specialties. It leased a theater in Istanbul to show war-oriented Hollywood films and newsreels. The promoters had to be careful, since showing propaganda pictures to Turkish citizens was illegal and foreign propaganda was supposedly barred from Turkey. But the Turks were desperate to see the movies. A customs official let OWI material pass without opening a box. "We're glad to help the Americans," he explained, "but I would like to bring my wife and daughter to your cinema." Free passage of OWI pamphlets was exchanged for three season tickets. A night watchman threatened to arrest an OWI man unless he got a ticket.

The psychological impact on audiences was tremendous. After seeing *Edge of Darkness*, a film about resistance in Norway which OWI impresarios worried might be too melodramatic, a Norwegian refugee came up, eyes red from weeping, and asked, "Have my people really suffered so much?" Pulling herself together, she added proudly, "You see what we Norwegians are!" A Greek gentleman, throwing his arms about in fine Homeric gestures, said, "This might have happened in Greece, too. You must show this picture many times so that people in Turkey will really understand what is happening."

But these successes took place amid the OWI's own disorganization, infighting, and tendency to ignore embassy directives. "It's a madhouse," one Turkish employee commented. An OWI official wrote home, "The chronicle of the past few months is a very sad one, full of betrayals, politics, jealousies and skulking in dark corners."

On Thanksgiving day 1942, Parker returned from the American community's picnic to pick up his mail. The embassy mailroom was locked, so Parker took the simple expedient of kicking in the door. This was the last straw for Steinhardt. He spent the next several months making sure Parker was recalled and barred from returning to Turkey in any capacity.

Remembering the earlier strictures on the number of Jews working for the U.S. embassy, Steinhardt complained that the OWI office was packed with minorities, including a "large number of Levantine Jews." The OWI payroll, however, contained relatively few Jewish names compared to the number of Greek, Armenian, and Slavic ones. There were sound reasons for employing people from all these groups. Since the OWI's job was to survey Balkan developments and translate materials, it needed people proficient in not only English but also such languages as Turkish, Bulgarian, Hungarian, and Romanian. Jewish refugees from the occupied countries were fluent in these languages and had an up-to-date knowledge of conditions in those areas. Jewish journalists purged from the official Turkish press agency for suspected Allied sympathies could find work only with the OWI.

There were several other conflicts between Steinhardt and the colorful OWI staff, including the controversy over George Littmann, a wealthy Romanian who had owned his country's most fashionable resort. Littmann lived in a luxurious Park Hotel suite, wore a monocle, and always appeared with a beautiful woman on his arm. A friend described him years later as resembling Rodney Dangerfield in the role of a European aristocrat.

Before joining the OWI, Littmann had worked for British intelligence, but he fell out with his superiors. The British claimed Littmann tried to sell visas to other Romanian refugees, and they even hinted he might be an enemy spy. When an OWI official pointed out to a British intelligence man that everyone in Littmann's family was a refugee and that his son was a Royal Air Force pilot, the Briton replied, "Those are the worst kind."

Littmann's contacts with Romanian officials were useful in smuggling anti-Nazi leaflets and initiating covert contacts with Romania's leaders. But some of these activities were not cleared with the proper authorities in the embassy, and in the summer of 1943, Steinhardt ordered the OWI to fire Littmann immediately. The OWI protested, which only made Steinhardt angrier, before it finally complied.

Security was a chronic problem. The British, Turks, or OSS periodically claimed that one or another OWI employee was an enemy agent. While one Turkish OWI employee was found to be a German agent, the OWI claimed that most of those accused were innocent: one employee simply had the same name as a Bulgarian agent; another, a Greek, was ordered ousted because his father was pro-fascist though even the Greek embassy insisted that the man himself had a spotless record. The OSS went so far as to complain that the OWI had discomfited the Turks by accidently uncovering an Emniyet agent in its office.

While the OWI officials were quite unorthodox by State Department standards, the same could be said about Steinhardt himself and his deputy, Robert Kelly. Kelly, 48 years old in 1942, came from a poor Boston family but worked his way through Harvard, where he studied Russian and became fascinated with that country. As a military attaché in Latvia, he reported on the early years of Lenin's regime. He joined the State Department and was chief of its Division of East European Affairs between 1926 and 1937. Kelly trained the department's first Russian specialists, many of whom would later become ambassadors and architects of U.S. foreign policy. The tall, corpulent, impeccably dressed Kelly was a fixture among the State Department's Washington barons, though his scholarly, even monkish, demeanor kept him an outsider.

In 1937, Kelly's career suffered a fatal setback. Convinced that the U.S.S.R. would inevitably continue to foment revolution and subversion, Kelly criticized Roosevelt's policy of improving relations. He was forced from his post and exiled to Turkey, where he stayed until his retirement in 1945. Embittered, Kelly became more of a loner and his quarter-century of experience was wasted at a time when expertise on the Soviets was desperately needed. The Russians, he would tell anyone who listened, were still as nationalist and expansionist as they had been in czarist times. The German invasion was a matter of "two thieves falling out." These were unpopular sentiments during the war.

The growing U.S. establishment in Turkey outran its accommodations. Steinhardt lived on the second floor of the Ankara embassy; Kelly's apartment and office were on the first floor. During the day, the ambassador's dining room was used as an office. Steinhardt's mostly young staff worked long, hard hours and sought diversion whenever possible. One of them suggested that Ankara's coat of arms should bear crossed cocktail glasses.

There was, however, no luxury. Living costs were high. An apartment rented for $175 a month, suits cost $100, and shoes were $22, astronomical prices in those days. Given these expenses, Americans faced a great temptation to take their pay in dollars and change them on the black market at a considerable advantage. The other embassies allowed such transactions, but they were against U.S. regulations. At least two American diplomats were caught and forced to resign. Shipments from home took four to twelve months, since cargo space was devoted to other priorities. One ship was loaded with thirteen Packards and two Studebakers presented to the Turkish government to compete with von Papen's gift to İnönü of a Mercedes-Benz.

While the war might sometimes have seemed distant from the peace of neutral Ankara, the enemy was very close at hand. Americans working in the embassy office building in downtown Ankara would look out the window to see von Papen walking by. He tipped his hat at Americans on the street, but they had been ordered to ignore him.

Shortly after arriving from the States, Huntington Damon of the OWI was driving down a street in Ankara with a U.S. air attaché. The car behind honked its horn, and Damon pulled over to let it pass. His eyes widened as he saw von Papen pass by in a big limousine flying the swastika flag. "Why did you let him pass?" the American officer shouted. "Never do that again!"

A few nights later, Damon was going to the Greek embassy. It was very dark as he drove up Cankaya Hill, trying to follow the complex directions. Finally, he reached an appropriate-looking house. He rang the bell and asked to see the ambassador. After a while, an Oriental man came to the door, sized up the visitor, and said, "Are you by any chance looking for the Greek embassy? It's next door." He pointed 50 yards up the street to an identical building. The man was too tactful to point out that Damon had mistakenly come to the embassy of America's enemy, Japan.

Everyone agreed, Archibald Walker reported, that the Germans would invade Turkey only if they concluded that the Russians were beaten. Yet an attack might still come. Those who had been in Romania,

Yugoslavia, or Bulgaria wondered whether they were seeing the pattern repeat itself. The U.S. and British military attachés drew up plans for destroying their embassies' codes and communications equipment if the Germans attacked.

Parker had commented that Turkey offered a front-row seat for viewing the war. Now the tiny band of Allied officials in Turkey understandably felt that they were down on the playing field itself.

9 | American Ignorance and Intelligence

I'm involved in a dangerous game
Every other day I change my name
The face is different but the body's the same
Boo, boo, baby, I'm a spy.
　　　　　　　　　—U.S. embassy songbook

The Park Hotel was a drab stucco building set back from Istanbul's broad Ayas Pasha Boulevard. One morning early in 1943, an old taxi swung into the hotel's circular driveway from a traffic jam of American, German, and French cars. The forlorn flower beds looked brighter than usual as the sun beamed down from the cloudless sky, but the taxi's occupant did not notice.

Since the Park Hotel was across the street from the German consulate, it had become the favorite residence for Axis agents and sympathizers. Yet if there was one man who would not hesitate to march double-time into the jaws of lions—much less enemy spies—that man was George V. Earle III. The large, handsome millionaire with wavy hair and cold blue eyes had already shown himself, as U.S. ambassador to Bulgaria, to possess great pugnacity and appalling judgment.

Earle had enjoyed highly publicized adventures since leaving Bulgaria when it declared war on the United States in December 1941. Visiting Casablanca, Morocco, just after U.S. forces liberated it in December 1942, Earle had lunched with General George Patton. Afterward, he took a walk toward the town's outskirts, absentmindedly passing beyond American lines. Suddenly, a bullet struck the muddy pavement near him, followed by another which hit a nearby wall. Earle left quickly. Although Earle swore that he told no one outside his immediate family about the incident, dramatic articles soon began appearing in American newspapers recounting his alleged heroism and narrow escape from a sniper. The White House staff was frustrated with Earle's penchant for publicity and trouble, but the president thought him a splendidly entertaining fellow.

On returning to Washington, Earle went to see President Roosevelt at the White House and asked to be sent to Istanbul. There, Earle promised Roosevelt, he would gather intelligence using his great knowledge of the Balkans and his excellent connections in Europe. Of course, Earle continued, he would always act with the approval of Ambassador Steinhardt ("a personal friend of mine"). Roosevelt agreed. It seemed a small enough request from a man who might have asked for a lot more.

Now Earle arrived at his new post. As he registered in the Park's ornate lobby, loiterers and bellboys paid by various governments to report on such comings and goings took note. Earle was not disappointed with the large, luxurious, high-ceilinged suite. The view was magnificent. His balcony looked out over a web of winding, narrow streets to the Bosporus and the Asian shore beyond. On bright days he could see the sun sparkling on the Sea of Marmara to the south. The Park's management took Earle's eccentricities in stride. Few other hotels would have let Earle keep a parrot and Great Dane in his room. Earle did not even wear out his welcome when he demonstrated the virtues of his new gun by firing it out the window.

This was an impressive arrangement for a man whose official rank was only assistant naval attaché. Although Earle saw himself as America's master spy and the president's personal representative, he was too flamboyant even by Istanbul standards and too credulous to be successful. Nevertheless, his style had certain advantages: the Germans, convinced that Earle was up to some extraordinary caper, expended much of their resources in watching him. They believed that such an important American political figure—President Roosevelt's personal friend and a former ambassador—must be on a very secret mission. German intelligence was intensely frustrated at the mystery until it finally concluded that Earle was, indeed, head of all U.S. intelligence operations in the Balkans.

A woman confessed to an American diplomat that she had been working for the Germans but wished to change sides. The Abwehr had hired her to seduce a Polish underground courier based in Istanbul, she explained, to discover his travel plans to occupied Warsaw. The next time he crossed the border into Bulgaria, the Gestapo arrested, tortured, and shot him. Qualms of conscience, she continued, made her refuse the next assignment: to seduce Earle and pry secrets from him.

Earle was not worth all this trouble. The OSS had wisely decided he was too unreliable to be given access to its codes, safes, and intelligence. This in no way stopped him from having a wonderful time spreading rumors, drinking and flirting in Taksim's cafés, and tirelessly sending Roosevelt gifts picked up in the bazaar and flattering letters hinting at his availability for a Senate seat. "Undisturbed by American political maneuvering and a press willing to sacrifice everything for sensationalism, I am able to have a clearer outlook on things," he wrote the president.

In fact, Earle was a sucker for phony intelligence merchants, passed on German disinformation, and distorted whatever useful information he came across. Hearing rumors about the V-1 pilotless bomb-plane and the V-2 rocket being developed in Germany, for example, Earle reported in September 1943 that Hitler was developing "stratospheric bombers [that] can reach America in 7½ hours. . . . Those to be used against England [will be] largely operated by wireless robots [and be] completely devastating." The OSS described Earle's source as a Turk who was considered completely unreliable and was fired by the British for having suspicious contacts with a female German agent. The OSS and the British gave no credence to any such German projects. Although there were kernels of truth in Earle's story, he typically so inflated it that he destroyed his credibility.

Some of his stories were even wilder: vast reservoirs of "the most virulent cholera bacteria" were stored "underground in the forests near Berlin." "Chances strongly favor above being pure propaganda," he added, "but because of Germany's desperation making anything possible I cannot conscientiously refrain from sending it."

Yet Earle sometimes had real insight, as when he wrote the president: The "most important and most difficult problem you will have to face in post-war Europe will be Russia. This country, today probably the most popular in America and England, thirty days after the cessation of hostilities will be the most unpopular, due not to [Communism] but to Russian imperialism."

If most of the operatives of the newly formed OSS were more reliable than Earle, most of them were also amateurs. British help was indispensable in learning the intelligence business. A June 1942 Anglo-American agreement reached in Cairo gave the OSS direct access to British intelligence on the Middle East and Balkans. The British side insisted this accord be kept secret from other U.S. agencies lest it provoke bureaucratic jealousies. Since the OSS had only four agents in this whole area, these reports were its main source of information and, as an OSS officer put it, "represented an extreme venture in faith that OSS would eventually produce something of value in turn."

In exchange for all this help, London received a major U.S. concession. The Cairo accord provided that all "special operations [in the region] operate under the direction and control of the British." This British supervision over the OSS was hard to achieve in practice. "The one inviolable principle which [we] fought, bled and stood firmly for was that of independent American operations," concluded a postwar OSS study. To achieve this, the OSS men sometimes pretended "apparent frankness" toward their British allies while circumventing them in practice.

The OSS tried the same technique of outward obedience and actual autonomy on the U.S. Army, to which it was supposedly subordinate. The OSS wanted to establish a regional headquarters in Cairo to avoid the time-consuming, inevitably confusing procedure of having Washington clear all reports and decisions. It took almost four months to convince the Joint Chiefs of Staff to approve an office in Cairo with jurisdiction over activities in the Balkans and Middle East. OSS-Cairo opened with two rooms in December 1942 and soon expanded into a villa at 8 Rustum Pasha Street near the British SOE offices. There was a standing joke that taxi drivers who were asked to go to Rustum Street would respond, "Oh, you want the secret intelligence headquarters!"

Working on intelligence in Cairo was a surrealistic experience. Far from the battlefields, officers spent their time handling papers and engaging in endless bureaucratic skirmishes. Christopher Sykes, a British intelligence officer in Cairo, wrote: "Here was the civilized world rent by the most terrible of all its conflicts, and here were we close to great events, in daily communication with men whose names will be remembered in history for a thousand years at least, and yet we never seemed to discuss anything but questions of precedence, procedure, and trifling matters of organization. The center of the storm of war [seemed] composed of Committees." Hugh Seton-Watson of SOE-Istanbul designed an SOE coat of arms: an arrangement of tennis equipment entitled "Rackets and Balls."

A British officer, assigned to parachute into occupied Greece, reported to the SOE headquarters' fifth floor only to be told, "We don't work here between 12:30 and 5." While awaiting his coming ordeal, he played squash at the Gezira Club, which also offered tennis, golf, thrice-weekly polo matches, and abundant dinner parties. "The lotus-eating existence of Cairo would have sapped anyone's morale if allowed to go on for too long," he wrote.

The combination of the Cairo intelligence lifestyle and the attendant bureaucratic knife fighting set off psychological conflicts for conscientious officers. Sykes wrote: "One lived in a kaleidoscope of emotions. . . . Hope would rise, sink, rise and sink again. . . . How I hated being well informed. How I envied people who only read the papers. The Intelligence Officer's life is an extremely depressing one. He knows much more about the enemy's preparations than about our own. . . . He inevitably becomes a pessimist. . . . He feels guilty that he is not in the battle line. He can't go there. He is suspected of cowardice; he suspects himself. He has a double share in the anxiety, none in the danger and heroism."

Yet much vital work was also done. In its charter, "A Plan for Special Operations in the Middle East," OSS-Cairo was authorized to gather information and conduct counterintelligence in the whole area and to begin clandestine operations in Albania, Bulgaria, Yugoslavia, Hungary, Romania, and the Greek islands. The OSS would now expand its small nucleus of American volunteers in Istanbul into a secret base of operations. Given the Balkans' complexities, the problems of coordination with the British and the U.S. State Department, and the Germans' proximity, a very able man was needed to run the OSS station in Turkey. The unanimous choice was a Chicago banker, Lanning "Packy" Macfarland. He was a Harvard graduate and a volunteer ambulance driver in the Balkans during World War I. When the United States entered the fighting in 1917, he became an army captain and stayed on after the armistice to run U.S. relief operations in the new state of Yugoslavia. He learned a bit of the language, received two medals from the government, and made many friends.

After World War I, he joined a Chicago bank and rose to be its vice president. But his old wartime adventures exercised a powerful pull. In early 1941, as the Germans were closing in on Yugoslavia, Macfarland visited Washington at his own expense to tell the State Department he was firmly convinced that the Yugoslavs would resist and that the United States should support them. Macfarland offered to participate in such a mission "because of my many close contacts there (even though dusty with age now)."

No action was taken at the time, but someone remembered the exchange and Macfarland's experience in the area. He was asked to join the OSS in October 1942. A few days later, while Ambassador Steinhardt was visiting Washington, the OSS director, Bill Donovan, introduced the two men and told Macfarland that the OSS must always respect the ambassador's authority and keep him informed of operations. This was music to Steinhardt's ears. Donovan approved establishing an OSS station in Istanbul and asked Secretary of State Cordell Hull to give Macfarland cover and cooperation. Hull wrote Steinhardt on December 21, "The Office of Strategic Services is anxious to send Mr. Lanning MacFarland to Turkey for a period of perhaps three or four months, for the purpose of obtaining information concerning the Balkans." Steinhardt quickly agreed, and Macfarland was made a nominal member of the U.S. Lend-Lease aid mission, a natural cover job for a banker.

Macfarland arrived in Cairo in March 1943 to meet with the OSS and British intelligence offices. Then he went on to Turkey and worked out arrangements with Steinhardt and the British. On May 4, 1943, he sent out his first cable. OSS-Istanbul was in business.

During these months of preparation, the State Department continued to take prime responsibility for information gathering and secret contacts with the Balkans. The State Department's Balkan Reporting Unit in Istanbul, under Consul General Burton Berry, was a talented group. One of its stalwarts was Floyd Black. Born on a midwest farm in 1888, Black graduated from a local college in 1911 and, shortly thereafter, answered an ad seeking English teachers for Robert College, the American missionary-run school in Istanbul. He left Illinois for the first time in his life; in Istanbul, the insular young American learned about a whole range of countries and cultures of which he previously knew nothing.

In 1926, Black became head of the new American College in Bulgaria. Over the next fifteen years he built it into the country's most respected educational institution; its graduates played important roles in Bulgaria's political and cultural life. Breaking with that country's traditional style of education, which stressed memorization, Black introduced American methods that sought to encourage independent thought.

As Bulgaria moved into the German orbit, the student body was riven with debate. Some opposed fascism; others demanded discrimination against Jewish students. Black maintained academic freedom. Even after Bulgaria declared war on the United States, the school continued until the government took it over in mid-1942. Shortly thereafter, Black and his American colleagues were expelled and left Sofia on the Istanbul train. It was a bitter moment for those who had devoted so much of their lives to the country. Amidst such reflections, the train made a brief stop at a suburban Sofia station. Suddenly, the Americans heard a chorus singing in English from the platform, and the surprised passengers looked out the windows. Through a crowd of German troops marched a delegation of graduates who had come to serenade their departing teachers and bid them an emotional farewell.

Black wanted to return to the United States, but he was persuaded that he could better serve the war effort in Istanbul as the State Department's intelligence specialist on Bulgaria. He worked long hours in the U.S. consulate building, reading the Bulgarian press, interviewing travelers and Jewish refugees, and briefing journalists. Later, when Bulgaria sought to negotiate a secret surrender to the Allies, Black was an intermediary. Many of the political leaders involved were parents of his pupils.

The Balkan Reporting Unit obtained lists of military objectives in Bulgaria, maps of Romania's Ploesti oil fields, and detailed charts of the railroad system in Hungary. A constant stream of reports poured out of Istanbul on the location and use of ports, roads, and factories in all these countries as potential bombing targets. Although hard work and research produced much of this material, good luck was also a factor. One day a short, chubby man in his forties came to the office of Walter Birge of the Balkan Reporting Unit. He inquired in a thick Viennese accent, "Are you the American consul?"

Birge nodded and asked, "What can I do for you?"

"I am here to do something for you," the visitor replied. He was an Austrian refugee now teaching in Istanbul. Was there some mission he could perform?

Well, Birge replied, he would certainly like a nice railroad map of Austria. He expected nothing would happen, but a few days later, the man returned with a huge, accurate map showing every track and bridge around Vienna.

Among the unit's most valuable finds were similar maps and detailed information on Romania's Ploesti oil fields obtained from refugees and business executives. Britain's failure to sabotage the oil fields in 1941 had meant 3 million tons of petroleum yearly for the German war machine. The refineries, pipelines, storage tanks, pumping stations, railroad lines, and bridges around the fields were high-priority targets for American bombers.

U.S. air raids on Ploesti provided American diplomats in Turkey with a unique problem and an amusing solution. After the first attack, on the morning of June 12, 1942, three off-course B-24 Liberator bombers, including *Little Eva* and the *Blue Goose*, landed at neutral Ankara airport. The Turkish ground crew received the Americans hospitably and gave them breakfast. Steinhardt rushed to the scene. Turkish officials politely turned their backs so that he could speak privately with the officers. A fourth bomber from the fourteen-plane raid landed elsewhere in Turkey. Two more B-24s, though losing altitude rapidly, made it across the border to British-occupied Syria.

As neutrals, the Turks were obliged to intern soldiers who strayed onto their soil, but the Turkish government promised that the fliers would be treated like guests if they gave their word not to escape. The aircrews were housed in barracks near Ankara. Suddenly released from daily military discipline and the strain of flying combat missions, they had a wild time. Occasional bar brawls caused headaches for the embassy, and the airmen's fraternization with Hungarian "artistes" at nightclubs forced Steinhardt to call a meeting and issue a warning: No more sleeping with enemy citizens.

Steinhardt negotiated a secret agreement with the Turkish government to allow the men to "get away" gradually in exchange for giving the interned warplanes to Turkey. Some of the aircrews were moved to a training field to teach the Turks how to fly the B-24s.

On December 19, unaware of Steinhardt's agreement and thinking they would be heroes for escaping, eight of the twenty-eight men took off in a B-24 with just enough gas to make Syria. *New York Times* correspondent Ray Brock exulted in his dispatch, "I say more power to them and strength to their good right arms on bomb releases." But the Turkish government was angry about the publicity and the broken promise that the fliers would escape only with its permission. Steinhardt cabled Washington, "It will henceforth be difficult to arrange the escape of any more American internees . . . until the B-24 has been returned or replaced." Interned German fliers, he noted, had not been allowed to escape and those caught in the attempt were confined. Fortunately, the Turks were satisfied when twelve more damaged or off-course planes arrived in the following months. These bombers were duly interned and then quietly handed over to the Turkish air force.

On August 1, 1943, the Americans staged an all-out, 177-plane raid on Ploesti from bases in Libya. A German air force unit in Greece detected them en route and alerted the defenses. As scores of bombers roared in at low altitude, they were met by heavy antiaircraft fire. Almost one-third of them were shot down. The oil installations were not seriously damaged.

Over Ploesti, the plane piloted by First Lieutenant Willard Hines dived to treetop level to escape German fighters and engaged in a desperate fight for survival. The plane lost one engine, and the fuselage was like a sieve from German shells and bullets. Dodging its pursuers, the plane was soon alone in peaceful skies. As it crossed the Black Sea to Turkey, however, a second engine conked out. That evening, Hines's bomber and three other B-24s approached Izmir, Turkey, flying low and unmolested over the offshore German-held Greek islands. A Turkish fighter plane was quickly sent up to guide them to the airport. One of the planes, its pilot dead at the controls from a shrapnel burst three hours earlier, was brought to a perfect landing by the copilot. Hines's plane and another B-24 came in smoothly at a nearby field. The fourth tried to reach British-ruled Cyprus but crashed into the sea; the Turkish coast guard rescued the survivors.

Hines and two comrades decided to escape internment and return to active duty as soon as possible. One night several weeks later, they came back to their quarters from a nightclub. In order to fulfill their promise not to escape while out on official permission, they signed the registry in their barracks and then left without signing out. Telling guards they were returning to the club, the three Americans instead took a taxi to the train station. They entered the U.S. diplomatic courier's compartment just as the *Taurus Express* was pulling out for Syria. Their host bribed the conductor to look the other way. When they reached the border, Turkish frontier guards boarded the train. One of the Americans successfully hid behind an overcoat in the corner and went unnoticed. Hines and the other pilot were caught hiding under a bunk; they were pulled off the train, charged for the fare, and put in jail.

The rules of the game were simple: the Turks would let the Americans get away if the escape could be made to look genuine. So the next morning the guards left the cell door open, and the two airmen sneaked away, hiking four and a half hours into the hills toward the border. But not all the Turkish military knew of the secret escape agreement. Just as the Americans, weak from lack of sleep and food, came to within sight of the frontier, they were again caught by a mounted Turkish police patrol. The prisoners were forced to walk back alongside the horses, and one soldier hit Hines with his rifle butt. When the Americans were too exhausted to continue, however, their captors let them ride double. The two pilots were again jailed and were put on the next train to Ankara.

The guards in the capital were under orders to give them a third opportunity. The two Americans walked to the car of Major Robert Brown, the U.S. air attaché, who hid them in his apartment until he put them on a train moments before departure. This time, no chances were taken. Brown stayed with the men until they safely boarded a British boat to Cyprus. By such methods, Brown and other embassy officials returned dozens of badly needed fliers to duty.

The arrival of American planes in Balkan skies was a signal to Germany's allies of how badly the war was going. There was no shortage of other signs. In November 1942, Rommel's North Africa army was trapped between the U.S. forces landing in Morocco and Algeria and the British army in Egypt. By the time the last Axis forces there surrendered in May 1943, Hitler had sacrificed 150,000 fresh troops in the losing battle. The Russians surrounded the German Sixth Army at Stalingrad in November 1942 and destroyed it. Romanian and Hungarian armies suffered devastating losses on the Russian front. In July 1943, Anglo-American forces crossed into Sicily and then onto the Italian mainland.

The attempt to convince Germany's allies Bulgaria, Romania, and particularly Hungary to desert the Axis and cooperate with the Allies was one of the most important OSS assignments in Istanbul. Donovan, the agency's director, noted in a memo: "The anticipated collapse of Italy intensifies the fears of the Balkan ruling classes that the Axis will be defeated and that Soviet Russia will dominate Eastern Europe. We propose to capitalize on these fears, and in agreement with Great Britain and the USSR to bring to bear upon Bulgaria, Rumania and Hungary certain subversive pressures which may induce those countries to withdraw from the war, or at least to cause difficulties for the Axis."

Hungary was an ally but not a puppet of Germany. In contrast to the situation in Romania and Bulgaria, there were few German troops in the country. Many Hungarians had mixed feelings about their country's alignment with the Germans, and a number of government officials were against it. The British were already working to take advantage of this situation. George Paloczi-Horvath, the journalist who escaped the Germans on the last train out of Hungary in March 1941 and then on the last plane out of Yugoslavia, now did anti-fascist radio broadcasts from Haifa. "I imagined that most of Hungary was listening and being infected with my enthusiasm, convinced by my convictions, fired by my emotions."

The handsome Paloczi-Horvath, now known by the more prosaic cover name of "George Howard," had flourished in the sparkling atmosphere of prewar Budapest with its rich artistic life and the brilliant conversation of the late-night cafés. He was both a bohemian, cosmopolitan advocate of cultural modernism and a liberal shocked at the near-feudal treatment of the peasants and urban poor. As with many others of his generation, these attitudes pushed him toward the political left and the conviction that the anti-Nazi battle must be followed by building a new society when the homeland was liberated.

British intelligence reassigned him from Haifa to Istanbul as a contact with Hungarians who sought to extricate their country from the Axis. "You know, of course," he was told in Cairo, "that British officials cannot talk directly to enemy representatives. They can get in touch . . . only in case the enemy offers unconditional surrender. Our task is to bring negotiations to that stage. Until that stage is reached . . . nothing you say or do can mean any commitment on our part."

With the new year of 1943, Hungarian emissaries, like migratory birds, began to arrive in Istanbul. Each of them and those they represented back in Budapest hoped to circumvent the Allies' demand for unconditional surrender. If the British took a tougher line, perhaps the Americans would prove more flexible; if Paloczi-Horvath, because of his leftist views, seemed unsympathetic, someone else might be more understanding. "If a bookkeeper at the American Embassy in Lisbon met a Hungarian courier in some night-club and listened with kind interest to a fervent description of Hungary's difficulties," wrote Paloczi-Horvath, "the courier promptly reported home that 'the American attitude is far less stiff than that of the British.' . . . Any American represented for them 'the Americans,' any Englishman 'the British'. . . . They believed everything they wanted to believe instead of seeing the simple and plain truth: Hitler was going to lose the war, and if they didn't do something instantly they would lead Hungary into a catastrophic situation."

The main movers behind the secret Hungarian peace effort—men like Count István Bethlen, the former prime minister; Miklós Kállay, the foreign minister; and Antal Ullein-Reviczky, the Press Bureau director—knew they were playing for their lives, people's future, and country's independence. These men were trying to avoid both the immediate danger of Nazi domination and the future likelihood of Soviet occupation when Germany lost the war. As the Russian army approached from the east, the moderate Hungarian leaders hoped to expel the Germans, hold off the Russians, and permit an Anglo-American occupation.

Yet these courageous Hungarians faced great difficulties in implementing any deal with the Allies. Their country was still independent, but the Gestapo's spies were everywhere. There were pro-German Hungarians in the government and army who had to be kept in the dark. And the Allies were still far away in 1943, when, as SOE operative

Basil Davidson noted, Hungary was "locked and barred behind five hundred miles of Nazi-occupied territory."

Washington and London knew that Hungary wanted to cooperate with the United States and Britain but not with the U.S.S.R. They also understood that Budapest wanted a deal guaranteeing that no Soviet troops would enter Hungary. Roosevelt and Churchill were unwilling, however, to jeopardize their alliance with Moscow for Hungary's sake. At the same time, however, if Hungary left the Axis, it would undermine Hitler's empire and divert German forces away from the Allied landings in Italy in 1943 and the invasion of France planned for 1944.

Realizing that Germany was doomed, Hungarian leaders began exploring the idea of a separate peace with the Allies as early as December 1942. A Hungarian diplomat returned to Istanbul from Budapest and met with a trusted Greek colleague. Influential Hungarians were eager to get in touch with the United States and Britain, he said, and if a meeting was arranged, they would send a responsible official to discuss the details.

In response to Allied encouragement, no fewer than four Hungarian emissaries reached Istanbul in February 1944, including Albert Szent-Györgyi, who won the Nobel Prize in medicine for his work with vitamin C, and Ferenc Vali, who was a respected legal scholar. None of them knew of the others' existence, but each carried a similar message: the Hungarian government and military would not fight British or American troops and, as soon as they approached, would join them in battling the Germans.

Vali's cover story was that he was going to give a lecture at Istanbul University. As his train jolted to a stop at the Croatian republic's border, Vali awoke to see three executed anti-German guerrillas hanging from a tree beside the tracks. The train rolled on through Belgrade, still largely wrecked from the German bombing two years earlier. On February 15, he arrived in Istanbul and, not expecting to stay long, went sightseeing. Having asked in Budapest about a good Istanbul hotel, Vali was told that the Park was frequented by the Axis and the Pera Palace was the Allies' favorite. Vali cautiously chose the Tokatliyan, which had enough pro-Axis guests to make him seem loyal to Germany but not so many as to subject him to excessive scrutiny.

The next morning, Vali went to see one of the German anti-Nazi refugee professors. Vali shook off the Abwehr man following him by leaving the hotel on foot and hopping on a streetcar. At the professor's house he was invited to meet the "Canadian-Hungarian" George Howard, whom he immediately recognized as Paloczi-Horvath. Paloczi-Horvath passed on Vali's message to British and American intelligence.

The most urgent question the OSS and SOE asked Szent-Györgyi and Vali was whether the peace forces controlled the military and whether the army would fight the Germans. "Perhaps," Vali replied honestly, but he added that many officers were mesmerized by German victories and might not cooperate.

The British insisted Budapest must prove its good faith through concrete actions. Hungary, SOE agent Basil Davidson wrote Vali, "can't behave like Germany's closest ally for three years . . . and expect to be treated any different from the way we are going to treat Germany."

On March 18, the whole secret operation was endangered by a major leak. The Czech government-in-exile in London broadcast a statement that Hungarian professors were contacting the Allies in a neutral country. Budapest issued a public denial and privately urged Vali to return home. Fearing arrest, he stayed in Istanbul.

The Germans were paying close attention to these activities. Hitler invited Hungary's ruler, Admiral Horthy, to Germany and asked him about these stories. "Malicious gossip," Horthy replied, declaring that Hungary was Germany's oldest and most faithful friend. At any rate, the German embassy in Hungary thought the Budapest regime was loyal. Still, to be on the safe side, Germany instructed its ambassador in Budapest not to trust either Kállay or Ullein-Reviczky. The latter was soon sent to Stockholm as a sop to the Germans, but Kállay stayed at his post.

German intelligence also laid some traps to discover the truth. One of its Hungarian agents, a Colonel Almassy, called the American diplomat Walter Birge one day and asked for a meeting. They met in busy Taksim Square. The Hungarian followed twenty paces behind Birge. When they arrived at Birge's apartment, Almassy said: "I've got an idea for you. Why don't you come to Budapest with me? I can arrange it for you. I think there's a chance we can get Hungary out of the war."

Birge laughed. "Do you think I'd get on a train, cross the border, and be arrested? Good try."

"Oh, it wouldn't be so difficult," Almassy answered. He had been Hungarian liaison officer with Rommel in North Africa, he explained in flawless English. "One day he wanted me to go to Cairo and find out about British plans. I asked, 'Do you think I want to be shot as a spy?' 'Wear your uniform,' Rommel replied. 'We'll drop you outside the city and you can take a train and stay at a safe house. With so many uniforms and armies in the city, no one will recognize a Hungarian one.'" And that was precisely what happened, Almassy claimed. Birge still rejected the man's offer, rightfully suspecting that he was a German agent.

The Hungarian government, realizing it was making no progress on negotiations with the Allies with unofficial envoys, sent a junior Foreign Ministry official, Laszlo Veress, to Istanbul in August 1943, ostensibly to supervise the Hungarian exhibit at the Izmir trade fair. Veress understood that there was no way to get around the Allies' requirement that the Axis powers surrender unconditionally. Over black coffee in Paloczi-Horvath's apartment, Veress broached the idea of a secret unconditional surrender. Allied leaders—the Soviets were informed as well—agreed.

On the evening of September 9, Veress was taken by motorboat to Knatchbull-Hugessen's yacht in a suitably empty corner of the Sea of Marmara. The British ambassador read an agreement for Hungary's unconditional surrender to the Allies, which would be kept secret until it could be implemented. Budapest would reduce military and economic cooperation with Germany while withdrawing its troops from the U.S.S.R. The Hungarian high command would be reorganized to eliminate pro-German officers.

As the meeting was taking place, there was a coup in Italy. A group of officers overthrew Benito Mussolini and surrendered to the Allies. The event thrilled the Hungarians. If the Allies quickly took over northern Italy, they might be in Hungary sooner than anyone expected. In addition, Italy's rapid transformation—from a member of the Axis in August, to a surrendering nation in September, to a full partner of the Allies at war with Germany in October—seemed a promising precedent for Hungary. Veress returned to Budapest with high hopes and a British-supplied wireless transmitter. Using two trusted detectives from the political police as operators, the Hungarian Foreign Office kept in daily touch with the British in Istanbul.

But the SOE and OSS were still uncertain of their interlocutors' power and the all-important question of the Hungarian army's loyalty. Moreover, the Budapest transmitter was supplying no useful military intelligence. Rectification of this situation would require a direct link to the Hungarian general staff. In August 1943, the OSS suggested that Lieutenant Colonel Otto Hatz, Hungarian military attaché in Sofia, would be the best man for this purpose. No one then knew that this obscure officer would prove to be a quadruple agent who would play a central role in determining the war's course, Hungary's fate, and the downfall of OSS-Istanbul.

During the autumn of 1943, Romanian and Bulgarian emissaries also arrived in Istanbul with word that their governments wanted to explore the possibility of changing sides in the war. When Bulgaria's King Boris died under mysterious circumstances in August, there were rumors—encouraged by British intelligence—that the Germans had murdered him because he planned to break with Berlin.

While the Hungarians desperately tried to escape the war, the Turks strove to keep from being dragged into it. The Turkish government suspended the newspaper Vatan for ninety days for publishing a front-page picture of Charlie Chaplin imitating Hitler. "Don't you know," an official asked the editor, "that Hitler is mad? Is it right to provoke a madman when he has large armed forces close to our frontier?" Equally, when the Germans tried to sneak some destroyers and submarines through the Bosporus to deploy against the Soviets on the Black Sea, the Turks refused them passage and informed the British and Russians.

Turkey's neutrality was on display at the state's twentieth anniversary celebration on October 29, 1943. Burton Berry, the U.S. consul general in Istanbul, went to Ankara for the occasion. The clothes he had bought in New York a year earlier had still not arrived. He had to scramble to find even an aged, out-of-fashion collar. Berry borrowed a vest from one acquaintance, a hat from another, and an overcoat from a third; he fit into his own old pants only "by a good deal of tugging and pulling and taking a firm resolution never to sit down." His colleagues were in even worse sartorial shape.

The rest of the diplomatic corps gathered at the reception in their best ceremonial clothes, with Allies, Axis, and neutrals in one large room. Berry wrote his mother: "Some of the new arrivals didn't know who could be spoken to and who should be ignored. I fear that some shook hands with people that they shouldn't and others failed to shake hands with those they should."

Each ambassador was to enter a room to congratulate the foreign minister as the previous visitor was ushered out another door. Knatchbull-Hugessen arrived a little late, almost colliding with von Papen. During the buffet brunch afterward, the British naval attaché's wife found herself anchored by a dress hook back-to-back with another lady. She soon discovered her Siamese twin was Mrs. von Papen. A blushing Turkish official spent ten minutes disentangling them.

Despite such meticulous neutrality, the Turks were willing to help the Allies quietly, as they had done in the case of the interned pilots. Italy's surrender and the beginning of the Balkans' collapse opened opportunities for guerrilla warfare, espionage, and the rescue of Jewish refugees that could be carried out only through Istanbul. From Turkey's shores, the British and Americans were already launching a new, secret war front on the Greek coast and the Aegean Sea.

10 | The Archaeologist's Navy:

The OSS in the Aegean, 1943–1944

Every warrior has his own way of eating yoghurt.
—Turkish proverb

John Caskey of the OSS had to get on the Ankara-to-Istanbul *Anatolia Express*. It was almost 6 p.m. on Friday, April 30, 1943. "There are no more tickets, sir," said the station's cashier.

"How about third class? I'll take anything you've got."

"I'm sorry. We can't sell more tickets than we have seats."

Caskey pleaded to no avail. He ran out onto the platform where the train stood, steam spurting from the connections between the cars, ready to leave in only ten minutes. Leaping up the steps, Caskey bustled down the corridor looking left and right into the crowded compartments. Finally, he saw a man all alone in a first-class sleeper compartment. Fortunately, it was an American diplomatic courier guarding a pile of State Department mailbags. Caskey identified himself and was allowed to use the upper bunk.

The next morning the train pulled into Istanbul's Haydarpasha Station. Caskey grabbed his bag and went to the Tokatliyan Hotel, whose clientele was less Nazi than it had been during Vali's stay there three months earlier. After checking in, he called on Consul General Burton Berry. Caskey showed his OSS credentials and asked for help in changing $5000 in U.S. currency into gold needed for a secret mission.

Obviously, Berry told Caskey, the man for this job was Earle Taylor, the wheeler-dealer commercial attaché who was making a fortune on black market currency exchanges. Since it was both a Saturday and a national holiday, shops were closed and money changers were off duty, but Taylor sent out a man who returned at 4 p.m. with a large bag full of British, Swiss, and Turkish gold coins. Taylor, Caskey noted, charged him the official embassy rate though the money had been changed at the black market rate. He estimated that Taylor made about $1000 on the deal. "Under the circumstances," Caskey wrote, "I didn't feel I could openly object. Taylor is an influential man who can be a useful ally or a difficult opponent in our work."

On Sunday, Caskey took an excursion boat to Prinkipo, a pretty island below Istanbul, for a holiday. But he took the opportunity to note the presence of fifteen German barges lying at anchor to the southeast. The next day, he took the morning boat down the Asian coast and then transferred to a train for Izmir, a trip of almost fifteen hours.

Two OSS people, Lansing Williams and Dorothy Cox, met him at the station and took him to the Izmir Palace Hotel. Their job was to use the gold for buying OSS's first caïque—a small wooden fishing and cargo boat—for intelligence work on the Aegean Sea. Special precautions had to be taken, since German reconnaissance planes flew over Turkey as far as 60 miles inland from the coast. The OSS also had to avoid subverting Turkish neutrality or stirring up the British, who wanted a monopoly on covert operations.

Williams had made a good impression, having bustled around a great deal since he arrived the previous September. He was fluent in Turkish and in touch with everyone in Izmir, gathering intelligence from the British, the Turkish police and Chamber of Commerce, and the local French, Italian, and Greek communities. Cox worked for a relief agency helping refugees from the nearby Greek islands.

The British were already well established. Their first caïque runs in the Aegean brought hundreds of Greek and British soldiers to the Turkish coast after Greece's collapse in 1941. As many as 4000 Greek escapees were housed at a camp near Izmir. While the Germans gradually tightened control in the islands, over 10,000 Greeks escaped to Turkey during the war. The SOE established a small group in Izmir to interrogate them. Some males of military age were sent to join the Greek exile army in Syria; others were persuaded to return to Greece as agents.

Covert British naval operations were supervised by the Levant

Schooner Flotilla (also known as the Levant Fishing Patrol) in Beirut. A secret base was established near Izmir under the supervision of the British consul, Noel Rees, a retired navy officer who knew the islands well and sometimes paid expenses out of his own pocket. The British had four large schooners anchored in Turkish waters as movable command posts.

Although prodded by Italian and German protests, the Turkish government usually overlooked these activities. The Royal Navy commander in the east Mediterranean wrote, "The assistance given by Turkey was entirely in keeping with a position as an ally, and its behavior throughout [was] satisfyingly un-neutral." Axis counterparts were treated differently: an Italian arrested photographing Turkish installations in Izmir was executed.

To conceal their operations, the caïques' Greek civilian crews pretended to fish, sponge-dive, or engage in interisland trading. The wooden ships had one or two masts and ranged from 5 to 250 tons. They were slow under sail and had old, sputtering engines. The British kept the boats' seedy appearance as camouflage but installed powerful new motors, one or two heavy machine guns, sometimes a light artillery piece, and a radio.

The caïques' first task was to facilitate the escape of British aircrews downed in Greece. They were so successful that a Cairo joke suggested that those who did not return quickly enough should be considered absent without leave. One captured fighter pilot who had been hospitalized evaded German guards by climbing over a wall despite his injured arms. He was rescued by a caïque which also took a group of Greek soldiers. The monks of the monastery of Mount Athos hid six British officers until a boat could be sent for them. The caïque landed in a village north of Izmir, and Rees came with two Rolls-Royces to pick them up.

The caïques also sneaked up to the Greek and Yugoslav coasts to land advisers and supplies for the local guerrillas, both royalist and Communist, organizing to fight the German occupation. By heightening resistance, the Allies convinced the Germans that Greece and the Balkans, rather than Sicily or Italy, were the next Allied objectives in 1943 and thus succeeded in tying down large numbers of enemy troops. Although the British ran these operations, they also brought in their American partners. By September 1943, there were 257 British and 17 Americans working with the partisans. Between July and September, the U.S. airlift alone brought in 570 tons of matériel, supplemented by an OSS "shipping line" that began carrying 300 tons a week between Italy and the Yugoslav coast.

While these struggles against German occupation were at their height, Istanbul was still a land of plenty. The Greek consulate there held a luncheon whose menu included a luxurious spread of poached eggs in jelly, pâté de foie gras, fillet of fish with rice pilaf and a fine sauce of mussels and mushrooms, breast of wild duck with french fried potatoes, green salad, fruit mold with whipped cream, fresh fruit, and candies. All this was accompanied by wine and followed by coffee and liqueurs. "Everything was wonderful but I didn't like it," U.S. Consul-General Burton Berry wrote his mother. "I thought of the poor people of Greece. . . . In wartime all that luxury was out of place. . . . How magnificent it would be if the representatives of governments were as fine as the spirit of the people they supposedly represent!"

Life was considerably more spartan at the OSS's secret bases set up and supervised by Caskey, whose command center was an office at the U.S. consulate in Izmir. His caïques transported, supplied, and collected the intelligence gathered from seventy-five agents in occupied Greece. The main base, code-named "Boston," was in the little town of Rasadia, 50 miles northwest of Izmir. The wind blew endlessly and sometimes reached hurricane strength, but it was a good location for the boats to anchor between missions. The barracks was an old concrete-floored stone warehouse that formerly housed an olive-oil press. It was now inhabited by ten Americans, fifty Greeks, and long-tailed rats the size of cats. An olive-oil distillery next door emitted an overwhelming smell. The OSS radio antennae, strung inside the building to keep them hidden, kept in touch with OSS-Cairo and agents behind German lines. The equipment was also used for a clandestine radio station for broadcasts to Greece; the commentators included a "reformed Greek collaborationist" (really a Greek-American sergeant), news in Greek for the underground, and news in German that was broadcast just after Berlin's own program to rebut its claims.

The other base, "Key West," was in the beautiful fishing town of Kusadasi. Its radio was kept in a four-room stone house overlooking the sea and the German-occupied island of Samos 3 miles away. The operator sat in an upstairs room facing the Aegean; the first floor office belonged to Turkish Emniyet and Customs officers, providing a perfect "cover."

Events in Italy set off the largest Allied military operation in the Aegean. A coup overthrew Mussolini, and the new regime surrendered to the Allies and then declared war on Germany. If the Italian troops who garrisoned many of the Greek islands could be persuaded to turn them over to British forces, the eastern Aegean would be liberated before the Germans reacted.

The day the Italian government proclaimed an armistice, September 8, 1943, two British officers parachuted into Rhodes, the main base in the area, to seek the Italian army's cooperation. But the Germans were already there, and 36,000 Italians allowed themselves to be disarmed by 6000 Germans.

British forces were still able to occupy three smaller islands in sight of the Turkish coast: Samos; Leros, with its Italian naval base; and Cos, where there was an airfield. The Italian garrisons gave up or changed sides; the 100,000 Greek residents welcomed the liberators. At Kusadasi, facing Samos, the British set up a secret supply dump with Turkish connivance. Labeled as food for the islands' civilians, military equipment poured in by railroad from Syria and by caïques, planes, and destroyers from Alexandria; submarines operating out of Beirut or Haifa took supplies, troops, and artillery directly to the islands.

The Germans struck back with dive-bombers from Rhodes and the Greek mainland. British soldiers watched in frustration as the German bombers stayed out of range of their underpowered anti-aircraft guns, while the captured Italian ones were too rusty to be effective. Two British destroyers were sunk near Leros. Turkey allowed British wounded to be evacuated to the resort town of Bodrum; doctors at Izmir's French hospital performed emergency operations. During the last week of September, the Germans bombed the Cos airfield daily. Engineers desperately filled in the craters. As soon as they were repaired, a new raid knocked the runways out of action again. Working at night, however, the engineers rebuilt the dirt airstrips.

On the night of October 2, cargo planes were able to land with supplies for the first time in five days. Nine Spitfire fighter planes were parked nearby, their pilots sleeping beside the office trailer. At 5 a.m. the next morning, German commandos sneaked up the beach to the airfield and began knifing the sentries. Hearing their cries, other guards started firing before being wiped out. The pilots scrambled from their sleeping bags and ran into town raising the alarm. As the sun rose a few minutes later, the drone of planes could be heard. German Junker-88s flew placidly in over the sea with navigation lights on, knowing they would face no defending fighters. They first bombed the British telephone exchange located in a small stone cottage, knocking out communications on the island.

Captain M. W. Hollum of the Second Light Anti-Aircraft Battery was already awake nearby, trying to call the shattered switchboard. Around 6:30 a.m., one of the escaped pilots told him the Germans were landing. Hollum prepared his six guns dug in next to a resort hotel while the battery commander went to headquarters to find out what was happening. He roared off on his motorcycle and did not return. The Germans had already cut the road.

Now in charge, Hollum inspected the guns and found them short of ammunition. But the road to the supply dump was unpassable, pockmarked with bomb craters and blocked by uprooted trees. German planes attacked the town, the transport ships in the harbor, and the infantry positions. Hollum's men shot down a Stuka dive-bomber, which trailed smoke as it fell into the sparkling blue Aegean.

At 10:30, fifteen Stukas appeared and circled for a half hour, pinning down the defenders. German troops arrived on the western end of Cos and advanced eastward. When stopped momentarily by a British strongpoint, they fired a white flare signaling the Stukas to blast it. As the Germans approached, the British commander ordered Hollum to sabotage his guns by throwing their breeches into the sea and to deploy his men as infantry. The British hoped to hold the town and harbor until dark so that reinforcements could be landed.

As night fell and the firing died down, the British were stretched thin across the width of the island. The Durham Light Infantry still maintained its line from the north coast to the main road, with the Royal Air Force regiment in the center and the Italians on the south. The British commander checked the Italian troops and found that only 100 out of the 4000 soldiers were willing to fight. It was clear that the

Germans would quickly break through in the morning. Reluctantly, he ordered everyone to take to the hills and try to escape.

At 1 a.m. the British, already exhausted from a day of fighting with nothing to eat and little to drink, split into small parties and moved off. Half of Hollum's soldiers became lost and he had only about thirty-seven men left. By dawn, his group found a deep ravine with a freshwater spring where they hid all day Monday and Tuesday watching German seaplanes bringing more enemy troops.

The next afternoon, Hollum went off looking for the British commander. He saw lines of Italian prisoners being marched off by the Germans, was fed by Greek peasants, became lost, wandered into an enemy camp, and arrived back just in time to see his men being rounded up by a German patrol. The Germans ordered him to halt and opened fire as he ran away. Hollum then joined a group of British soldiers marching west to the coast. They hid in a wadi near the beach while, 50 yards away, Germans swam off the deck of a patrol boat.

By October 10, Hollum was left with three men. He and a Greek Cypriot private climbed to the top of a mountain to get food and news from the peasants there. One farmer gave them cigarettes and said there was someone who wished to meet them. He led them to a Greek squatting among the rocks who produced a message addressed "To all British personnel still at large on Cos." It stated that the bearer was risking his life to evacuate as many soldiers as possible and that his instructions should be obeyed to the letter. At the bottom was a smudged rubber stamp. The last sentence said, "If this is shown to you after 11 October 1943 you must treat it with the utmost suspicion and reserve." This last statement convinced Hollum that the message was genuine, although by that point he was so desperate that he would have seized any opportunity.

The Greek introduced himself as Georges Samarkos, a civilian radio operator in Bodrum who had volunteered to carry out this dangerous rescue mission for the British knowing the Germans would shoot him without hesitation if he was captured. Samarkos told Hollum to light a small fire on the shore at midnight to signal in a rescue boat. Meanwhile, Samarkos would visit shepherds to ask their help in rounding up more soldiers. He gave Hollum a note for the ship captain, "Milton." If Samarkos was not at the rendezvous, the British were to tell Milton to return there the following night.

Hollum and his companions moved down to the beach and lit the fire. There was a full moon. After an hour, he looked through his binoculars and saw the white wake of a ship coming from the Turkish coast. "It almost seemed like a miracle—almost too good to be true. We doused the fire and ran down to the beach. The caïque came in as near as it could, and then one man put off in the dinghy and rowed toward us."

The nervous sailor in the dinghy called out, "Georges!" The private replied in Greek, "He isn't here but he told us to meet Milton." Satisfied, the man picked them up and rowed them to his boat. Three Greek crewmen wearing steel helmets pointed submachine guns at Hollum and the others until persuaded they were British. Then they were taken below to meet Captain Milton as the ship sped toward Turkey.

Milton was one of the most daring and successful Greek caïque captains. He undertook many missions through German-controlled waters and harbors without mishap. The British awarded him two medals, but he told a friend that he would have preferred more money. Captain Milton asked for the soldiers' revolvers, which otherwise the Turks would take, and gave the men a letter signed by the British consul at Bodrum. On reaching Turkey, the letter explained, they would be put ashore outside town and must walk in, claiming to have come in their own rowboat, which they abandoned on the beach. There must be no connection between them and Milton's caïque. During the stormy four-hour trip back to Turkey, however, the caïque's dinghy—tied to its stern—sank and had to be cut adrift, necessitating a change in plans.

At 5 a.m. the caïque came upon a small uninhabited island in Bodrum Bay. Despite the choppy waves, Milton maneuvered his boat right up against the rocks to allow his passengers to step off. They waited on the isle all day and were beginning to feel abandoned when they heard someone whistling from the sea. A Greek lad was rowing toward them in a dinghy from Bodrum. He came ashore and gave them water, bread, and olives. The young man started a bonfire on the cliff facing the town, explaining that the soldiers should say they built it themselves. Then he jumped back into his boat and vanished into the night.

Soon a Turkish patrol boat chugged over to investigate the fire. The four men introduced themselves as British soldiers. The Turks gave them warm handshakes and took them aboard for the trip to Bodrum. As the ship crossed the bay, Hollum looked back at Cos and saw a

British air attack in progress there. One of the Turks nudged him and, with much winking, signaled that the guests should go down into the cabin and remain hidden.

As soon as the boat tied up, the Turkish captain sent for the British consul, Whittall, who quickly arrived accompanied by a Turkish officer. The two men asked what had happened. As the Turks looked on, Hollum recounted a dramatic and false tale of how they had rowed from Cos, landed on the small island, and fell asleep from exhaustion. They awoke to find their boat had drifted away in the storm. Did they have any guns? Hollum glibly replied that they were taken prisoner and disarmed by the Germans before escaping.

The Turkish officer broke in, "Do you want to be interned or 'Go South,' " a euphemism for returning to British territory.

"We want to 'Go South,' " Hollum answered.

Whittall turned to the Turk. "We can easily fix it. You haven't seen them. I haven't seen them." The Turkish officer shrugged his shoulders, laughed, and agreed.

Whittall and the Turk then took the men a few yards down the waterfront to where two British military cargo ships were tied up in the nominally neutral port. The crew gave them a terrific meal, with toasts to the Turkish guest. Later, when they were alone, Whittall brought the men new uniforms and gear and heard the true story. Nine other British soldiers rescued by Samarkos soon joined them.

The British troops were put on a caïque which sailed all night. At dawn the next morning it put in at a small bay where caïques and over twenty dinghies were drawn up to appear like innocent local fishing vessels. There was a shack with a radio and a stock of English books and magazines. Two German planes flew low over the bay. If they knew what was going on, there was no way they could intervene in those neutral waters.

Hollum and his party were transferred to a larger caïque carrying a very mixed party of passengers including an Italian colonel, his orderly, an Italian navy officer just escaped from Athens, two Nazi agents captured in Turkey, a man who had been a British agent but who had double-crossed them and was now under arrest, and a young German Communist deserter. They set off that evening for Cyprus. The caïque passed four unidentified warships, scrambled back to hug the coast for safety, and then headed straight for Cyprus, where Hollum rejoined his unit.

Although Britain's Aegean offensive was a military failure it did have the benefit of making the Germans expect a full-scale invasion of Greece. To counter such a move, Berlin sent there dozens of planes, ships, and regiments from the Russian front, Italy, and France. British planes and warships, guided by code breakers, inflicted heavy losses on German convoys. So efficient was this surveillance system that the British were able to attack German cargo ships in the few minutes before their armed convoys arrived. In November 1943 alone, Allied forces sank 23 percent of the German ships in the Aegean.

But having lost Cos and its airfield, British forces on the other captured islands could not hold out long. A caïque armada left Turkey on the evening of November 19 and brought back the British and Greek garrisons from Samos, about 1500 Greek civilians, and over 3000 Italian troops. Two thousand more Greeks crossed in their own boats. Rescue parties continued landing on the islands even after the Germans occupied them. In the following weeks, they saved 714 British soldiers, Greek civilians, and Jewish refugees from Leros and elsewhere.

During the evacuation, one of their first missions, the OSS's caïques provided extensive help. The British commander commended Captain Caskey and his thirty-six caïque fleet for having "rendered most excellent service" in the Samos evacuation. The achievement was all the more impressive given the fact that few of the caïques were faster than the ships of Odysseus. They had to make 300-mile runs on converted tank motors whose top speed was only six knots. Missions that might have been performed in a single night took up to ten days. Supplies from Cairo came late. An order for sail-cloth made in October 1943 took ten months to arrive. Nonetheless, the caïques kept sailing between the Rema Bay and Kusadasi bases, Cyprus, Alexandria, and occupied Greece.

The Greek crews were loyal, daring, and, as an OSS report affectionately described them, "masters of smuggling, thievery and gold-bricking." No American boat was lost through enemy action, though one was accidentally sunk by a British torpedo boat, another ran aground after being abandoned by its crew during a wild Christmas party, and a third disappeared under circumstances giving rise to rumors of desertion. Although an American officer generally accompanied each mission, the OSS Maritime Unit was quick to explain that it had no one aboard on those three occasions.

The Allied operations also benefited by knowing, from broken German coded messages, that Hitler repeatedly vetoed any proposed attacks on Allied warships in Turkish waters. The Germans did, however, escalate protests to the Turkish government. In turn, Ankara complained that the British and Americans were going too far. One British caïque, for example, captured a German military boat carrying supplies and reinforcements to Cos and towed it to Bodrum. Thus, the British and the OSS issued a new order: ships could not dart from Turkish waters to attack the Germans and run back again within twenty-four hours. Boats must be moved more frequently and dispersed into smaller, better-camouflaged groups. Only anchorages approved by the Turkish government would be used. The British also took out insurance. In Kusadasi, they paid the local Emniyet chief more money than did his own government.

The attempt of the Axis and Allied powers to exploit Turkey's neutrality in the Aegean produced some bizarre situations. When the open sea became too dangerous for the Germans during the day, they began sailing in Turkey's territorial waters. It was not unusual for a British and a German ship, both flying false Turkish colors, to pass a few yards from each other. British SOE men sailing down from Izmir on the Turkish ferry could see the faces of German soldiers on the islands they passed. One of them asked that the ship's radio be switched to the BBC news, which was reporting heavy British air raids and German losses. German and Hungarian passengers objected that this was an unneutral act. The exasperated captain ordered the wireless turned back to safely uncontroversial Turkish music.

In addition to hitting German shipping, rescuing Allied fliers, and delivering agents, the caïques out of Bodrum and Kusadasi also began raiding German installations. On a moonless night in June 1944, a fast motorboat left the Turkish coast with six British marines on board. Their mission was to attack German ships shown by aerial reconnaissance to be anchored by Leros. Each man carried a rubber-encased hacksaw blade hidden in his beret, a silk handkerchief map, gold coins, and rations. A mile and a half off Leros, the marines blackened their faces and hands, made a final check of their magnetic limpet mines, and pushed their three canoes overboard.

The sea was gentle as the marines paddled into Leros' bay. A German sentry called out and a searchlight skimmed across the water, but the guard decided he had only imagined hearing something. The two-man crew brought the first canoe alongside three escort ships and attached two delayed-action mines to each. After an hour's maneuvering, the men put two more mines on a destroyer and then rowed out to a nearby island. The sun was peeking over the horizon, and the two marines hid their canoe in the rocks and laid low all day.

Meanwhile, one of the other crews, quickly sighted by sentries, had to race away. The third team put all its mines on another destroyer. Slowed by a leak, the canoe was still on the open sea at dawn. A Greek fishing boat pulled alongside and provided food and water; the Greeks offered to take the marines back to Bodrum but were scared off by a distant machine-gun volley. The next night, all three canoes met their mother ship and safely reached Turkey at dawn to a great reception: the three escort boats had blown up and sunk; the two destroyers had been knocked out of action.

The OSS, however, was unwilling to use the caïques for saving Jewish refugees. Although Kurt Waldheim, a German army intelligence officer in Greece and Yugoslavia, claimed to be ignorant of nearby atrocities committed during this era, plenty of details about them were reaching Istanbul. In March 1943, the Jewish population of Salonika was deported. Two men, allowed to leave because they had Turkish passports, told the Balkan Reporting Unit's Greek expert, Homer Davis, of the crowded cattle cars, the deliberate starvation, and the victims' probable fate. In April 1944, mass deportations began from Athens. SS officers refused to let the Jews take food. A workman at the railroad station commented, "I am a German but I can't stand this."

Davis asked if the OSS could help Jews who escaped or were in hiding. Caskey said it could do so only if the Turkish government agreed to accept the refugees. Davis sent the State Department in Washington a strong cable requesting action. Nothing happened due to bureaucratic inertia.

The caïques coming back to Turkey empty were going out to Greece and Yugoslavia loaded with military supplies. Throughout 1943 and

1944, partisans in those two countries, helped with aid and advisers from the SOE and OSS, became stronger. Refugee and intelligence reports recorded their successes in destroying bridges, sabotaging railroads, and ambushing German troops. More somber news also filtered out about German reprisals against civilian hostages. Communist and non-Communist partisans competed in seeking Allied support and sometimes fought each other. While suspicious of the Communists' postwar intentions, the British and Americans chose, as Donovan ordered, to "show preference among resistance groups or prospective successor governments only on a basis of their willingness to cooperate [in fighting the Germans] and without regard to their ideological differences or political programs."

OSS conducted many missions into occupied Europe to aid partisans, gather intelligence, and evacuate downed U.S. airmen. Operation Featherbed provides examples of their problems and achievements. British agents notified the OSS that American airmen from three B-24s shot down over Greece were being moved by partisans to a British secret airfield, code-named "Featherbed," behind the German lines. Meanwhile, Captain Ehrgott, one of the OSS military advisers who was working with a Greek guerrilla cavalry unit nearby, made an urgent appeal for vital supplies. The OSS decided to conduct a combined supply-and-rescue mission and borrowed from the air force a DC-3 transport plane which was loaded with 4800 pounds of equipment. The OSS was withholding weapons for the time being, however, because the Greek guerrilla factions were fighting among themselves.

When the OSS found that a British rescue flight was about to be sent, it was determined to arrive first. Lieutenant Colonel Paul West, chief operations officer for OSS-Middle East, reported, "I had no intention of allowing the British to land first and pick up our American airmen." The DC-3 took off just after midnight on October 21, 1943, for the four-hour flight. After landing on a makeshift runway marked with flares, the plane taxied immediately to a takeoff position at the end of the field in case of German attack. Guerrillas ran up and unloaded the plane within ten minutes, but the DC-3 was bogged down in the heavy mud. There were only enough camouflage nets to cover one wing, and the rest of the plane had to be hidden with branches. The work was finished just as the sun was rising.

West, met by Captain Ehrgott, went to a deserted summer resort about 8 miles away where he found the American airmen underclothed and hungry, shivering in the damp, forty-degree coolness, sleeping on straw scattered about the stone floor. After reassuring the Americans, West and Ehrgott inspected the cavalry regiment Ehrgott was advising and met with the Greek Communist guerrilla leader, General Serafis. Even the Communists were eager to convince their people that they had American support. "I am certain," West reported, "the General will endeavor to construe [my visit] to indicate . . . backing of his cause by the United States." He told Serafis that Ehrgott could not take command of a unit: he was there only as an adviser. West noticed that the cavalry standards consisted of the emblem of ELAS (the Communist front) together with an American flag. West explained that this was out of the question. "We cannot . . . be affiliated in any way with any political organization."

The general then gave the Americans a list of equipment he wanted: uniforms and boots, antitank weapons, automatic rifles with armor-piercing ammunition, mortars, and machine guns. West explained that the British had banned sending arms and ammunition until political differences between warring factions were settled. The Allies were not going to fly arms and ammunition to Greece for use in an internal civil war while the country was occupied by the Germans.

In addition to separating politics from warfare, the OSS had to separate rumor from fact. Shortly after meeting with the Greek general, West was told by an OSS captain that 2000 Italian troops recently disarmed by ELAS had been robbed of their clothing and were hungry. West reported: "An hour later, however, they began arriving, seemed quite cheerful, and were in reasonably good shape. . . . It is true that they had not eaten that day but neither had we. And it is equally true that they had but one meal a day before, which also applied to us Americans." West continued: "I talked with some of the Italian officers, who . . . expressed some fears of possible rough treatment at the hands of the Greek guerrillas. I asked the Italian Colonel if his fears could possibly be based on the fact that the Italian troops had completely destroyed by fire some 20 Greek villages in the vicinity, and he agreed that this might have something to do with it. That night the rumor came through the camp that four Italians had been killed by Greeks and were being placed on poles outside the camp. . . . Another check, however, indicated that they hadn't been killed outside the camp. . . . A third check indicated that they weren't killed at all . . . but had died of malaria. Peace reigned again in our camp."

On October 23, the guerrillas and British engineer officers anchored two chain pulleys which pulled the plane's wheels out of the mud and up a makeshift track to firm ground. West held a meeting of the local partisan leaders to thank them. "They replied, and I think quite genuinely, that they could never do enough to aid Americans who were fighting for their cause in Greece." The plane took off a few hours later with its ten rescued airmen and safely returned them to Cairo.

West reviewed the mission's accomplishments: "The plane had been flown into an [airfield] 10 miles from the local German headquarters . . . unarmed and unescorted over at least four large German airdromes. . . . German reconnaissance planes must have finally pierced our makeshift camouflage for, three hours after our take-off . . . a flight of Ju-88s and Me-109s bombed and machine-gunned Featherbed."

As valuable as the caïque and partisan operations were, the OSS's main job in Istanbul was to gather intelligence. Shortly after arriving, Lanning Macfarland, the head of OSS in Turkey, linked up with a remarkable network of agents that extended throughout the Balkans. In addition to supplying much valuable intelligence, this spy chain seemed able to help secure the surrender of Hungary. This operation, whose agents were all named after flowers, would be, at first, Macfarland's greatest success and then his ruinous debacle.

11 | Dogwood's Bark:

OSS Successes in Istanbul

A rich man's daughter is always beautiful.
—Turkish proverb

The value of the OSS in Istanbul, Macfarland well knew, would rest chiefly on its ability to gather intelligence on Germany and Nazi-occupied Europe. "Most important of all," Macfarland wrote OSS-Cairo in May 1943, "is action! We are now on the spot with all of them, British, Greeks, and Turks. They have done everything we have asked of them (much to my surprise) and now we must produce. Our whole future here depends now on whether we can deliver the goods."

Macfarland's job was to obtain accurate information on Nazi politics, strategy, and troop movements; the products, location, and output of factories in Hitler's empire; and the willingness of Germany's satellites to cooperate with the Allies or to surrender. Consequently, Macfarland was delighted to find a ready-made network of agents that only had to be financed and coordinated to start producing the most valuable intelligence. This group, called the "Dogwood" chain after its leader's code name, would be the most important U.S. spy ring in Europe.

Macfarland himself had no intelligence experience or training apart from a few weeks at OSS headquarters in Washington. The trench-coat and slouch hat garb Macfarland adopted, though a popular fashion, seemed to mark his trade as effectively as a calling card. One colleague said, "If he had not been a spy, dressed like that, he would have had to become one." Another commented that Macfarland "must have been a great cover for those really doing the work." Macfarland later claimed that this was indeed his purpose.

The State Department was loathe to supply cover for the OSS, arguing, "The discovery by the Turkish government that the Foreign Service was being used as a shield for undercover intelligence work could not but have the most unfortunate results." Such people were not even needed, State argued, since its own staff could easily "report on any matters in which the OSS may have a particular interest." Given this attitude, OSS people were instead made nominal employees of wartime agencies. Other OSS men went under cover as journalists or as instructors at Robert College. The latter group included Joseph Curtiss, who gathered research materials for OSS analysts back in Washington.

But Macfarland won Ambassador Steinhardt's confidence by pledging to act cautiously and to keep him well informed. In exchange, Steinhardt gave the OSS use of the diplomatic pouch and contacts with the host government. Macfarland promised the Emniyet's chief that he would exchange information, ensure that his men behaved properly, and conduct no espionage against Turkey.

Intelligence agents, precisely because of the latitude they enjoy, must possess caution and good sense. The veteran free-lancer Saffet Tozan explained that some spies were adventurers, whose loyalties or judgment were uncertain, while others were naive "missionary types." People in the first category could cause trouble, but those in the latter set might be victimized by more devious folk.

American intelligence men in Istanbul were inexperienced and more often of the latter type. They found it hard at first to maintain proper security. Macfarland's putative boss at Lend-Lease was visibly surprised when foreign diplomats asked about his new assistant, because he had not been informed about the OSS chief's cover arrangements. In July 1943, Macfarland wrote Cairo: "PLEASE, PLEASE, PLEASE! Instruct everyone to leave out any reference whatsoever to Office of Strategic Services in addressing envelopes. Today there are two more that bear this inscription on the outside." Far worse was the habit of one of Macfarland's key subordinates, a heavy drinker, who would enter a bar and greet colleagues by shouting, "Hello, spies!" British security arrangements were also sometimes imperfect. Following a leak that the designation for Germany in a British code was "1200," German officials in cafés began singing, "Twelve-hundred land, twelve-hundred land, *über alles.*" On entering the Park Hotel's lounge, intelligence agents of any nationality might be met with the pianist's rendition of a satirical song, "Boo, Boo, Baby, I'm a Spy."

The Emniyet was never fooled either. It picked up one OSS-Istanbul man as a suspicious character because he was running to keep an appointment. "We know you work for OSS," an officer told him, "but from now on walk, don't run." Sometimes the police sold photographs of Axis agents to the Allies and vice versa. Others were more confused. British Ambassador Knatchbull-Hugessen invited a low-ranking U.S. official to an elaborate, intimate dinner for two. Convinced his guest was an important intelligence agent, Knatchbull-Hugessen tried to draw information from the bewildered American throughout the evening. Finally, the exasperated British diplomat pleaded, "Won't you trust me with the truth?"

Istanbul was no place for the innocent or unwary. Over 200 people made a living by wholesaling information to both sides and retailing it to journalists. They were happy to relieve the OSS of money for false or, worse, German-planted information. Would-be spies for rent strolled up and down Istiklal Boulevard and around Taksim Square with its neobaroque monument to the republic. They lounged in Istanbul's bars, dining places, nightclubs, and dance halls and patrolled the Park Hotel, Abdullah's Restaurant, and particularly the Taksim Casino.

The music wafting from the cafés and the bells of the crowded trolleys played accompaniment as men weaved through the streets trying to follow or evade each other. Some pastry shops were fronts for espionage operations; the belligerents' propaganda experts tried to influence what the movie theaters screened. Lemonade sellers were lookouts for the Emniyet; newspaper vendors shouted out the latest war events on every corner. Agents competed to interview newly arrived refugees.

Archibald Walker (code-named "Rose"), who had been gathering information for the OSS since April 1942, was joined by a half-dozen full-time OSS officers. They leased a building a few miles up the Bosporus as a safe house, training center, and photo laboratory. Dean

Woodruff directed the Bulgaria desk and talked to the many travelers and refugees crossing the frontier into Turkey. Frank Stevens was in charge of operations concerning Romania, where he had lived for twenty years as a journalist. His many friendships with Romanian officials helped him arrange regular meetings with their country's intelligence chief in Istanbul and obtain information even from cabinet ministers. One of the most productive agents was Lieutenant Alekko Georgiades, who covered the parts of northern Greece near the Turkish border.

They all worked very hard. In addition to his own job, Macfarland had to type his own letters and encode and decode messages given the shortage of secretaries and cipher clerks. During its sixteen months of operation, OSS-Istanbul worked twelve-hour days and six-day weeks to produce over 1500 intelligence reports.

Macfarland put the most promising Istanbul contacts under the direction of Archibald Coleman (code-named "Cereus"), who, Macfarland wrote, was "one of the most experienced technicians in under-cover operations." Compared with his colleagues, Coleman was indeed relatively experienced, but his two previous missions had been failures. Sent by the OSS to Mexico, where he had been a Treasury agent in the 1930s, Coleman was quickly uncovered by the Mexicans and they demanded his withdrawal. A few months later, Coleman was moved to Spain. The U.S. ambassador to Spain was afraid, however, that OSS operations might push the Fascist but neutral Franco regime into open support for the Axis. He complained about the OSS's security, intelligence, and choice of local agents. Although the OSS denied the charges, Coleman was hustled out of Madrid in June 1942. When he arrived in Istanbul almost a year later, under cover as a *Saturday Evening Post* correspondent, Macfarland put him in charge of the Dogwood project.

"Dogwood" himself was Alfred Schwarz, a Czech businessman of Jewish background and cosmopolitan tastes who had lived in Istanbul since 1928. Schwarz had studied philosophy and psychology in Prague and Vienna. Entering a contest for writing advertising copy, he won first prize and was hired by the sponsoring company to open a branch office in Istanbul. He was so successful that he went into business for himself. The Vatican envoy, Roncalli, became one of Schwarz's friends, and the two men discussed theology over many a glass of Roncalli's favorite Italian wine. Schwarz also befriended several of the German refugee professors.

After the war began, Schwarz became the intermediary between some of the German exiles who were asked to write anti-Nazi broadcasts to Germany, and the British. He also performed tasks for MI-6. Another acquaintance, a Hungarian aristocrat named Luther Kovess, extended Schwarz's contacts with Hungary.

British intelligence chief Harold Gibson asked Schwarz to work with the newly arrived OSS officers as an adviser on European affairs. Schwarz agreed and signed a contract with Macfarland in April 1943. While Macfarland was deeply impressed with this polished, self-confident European intellectual, Schwarz was shocked by what he saw as American naïveté and ignorance about the continent's society and politics.

Schwarz chose a friend, Walter Arndt, son of an Istanbul University professor, as his assistant. The young man, though born in Istanbul, had volunteered for the Polish army early in 1939. After its defeat, he spent the next year forging documents for the Warsaw underground under the guise of running a translation bureau. Arndt's birthplace entitled him to a Turkish passport, but there was no longer any Turkish embassy in Warsaw. Having repudiated his German citizenship and fought against Hitler, Arndt could hardly visit the Turkish embassy in Berlin. He finally got word out through a friendly Turkish student who was returning home, and Arndt's father obtained the precious document. On reaching Istanbul, Arndt reported to the bureaucratic Polish military attaché. Noting that Arndt was still formally in the Polish army, the officer asked him in an annoyed tone, "Where have you been?"

"This was the earliest I could come," Arndt replied. "We had a war in Poland and I got into it." Schwarz asked Arndt to work for his intelligence operation, and the Polish army found this an acceptable duty.

Macfarland decided that Coleman should develop an independent operation apart from the OSS office at the U.S. consulate in Istanbul. It was obviously unwise to ask contacts or agents coming from occupied countries to visit the U.S. consulate to convey information. For those returning home, however, any open contact with Americans could prove fatal. Creating a cover business solved this problem. Schwarz set up a subsidiary of the U.S. Western Electric Company at his office, where he could meet subagents under commercial camouflage. Balkan businessmen and salesmen were invited to Istanbul to make transactions and then were asked to gather intelligence. Many agreed and were quickly trained; others refused out of fear or because they felt such activity would damage their reputations after the war. As one of them put it, "So many disreputable individuals are engaged in espionage operations." Working for the Americans, some reasoned, might also make one seem a foreign agent rather than a patriot.

Nonetheless, Schwarz managed to find people who, traveling in occupied countries on their own affairs, would collect intelligence as well. Each one had to be trained hurriedly and, for security reasons, individually in a bewildering variety of disciplines that included coding, concealing messages in seemingly innocent letters, transmitting by radio, selecting and recruiting subagents, organizing networks, thwarting searches, understanding Gestapo methods, enemy order of battle, security, cover, finances, and intelligence objectives.

The Dogwood network used the mail, telephone, and telegraph systems. In addition to Dogwood's own post office boxes, as many as forty Turkish businesses served as mail drops. An OSS transmitter in Algiers sent Dogwood's coded instructions to agents in the field. Bulgarian, Romanian, Hungarian, and Swiss diplomatic couriers—for bribes or out of sympathy with the Allies—sometimes carried messages in their official pouches.

In addition, two German refugee doctors became part-time OSS photographers and developed a way of copying documents onto extremely thin, transparent paper similar to cellophane. Since many agents had trouble memorizing complex codes, their ciphers were microfilmed to fit inside hollowed-out keys, pencils, razor blade wrappers, shoes, and clothing.

Enemy infiltration was an important concern. Macfarland wanted trained German-speaking American intelligence officers, but they were not available. Instead, Schwarz and other local agents, without experience, had to use their own judgment in choosing agents. But "even following the most careful security check," Macfarland later wrote, "the complete integrity of agents thus selected can never be assured."

Indeed, he admitted, the operation consciously took great risks: "It was obviously necessary to recruit agents having the possibilities of travel between central Europe and Turkey, which of necessity required that the individuals were persona grata [*sic*] with the German authorities. Furthermore, in order for them to be particularly useful, they had to have access to German officials or industries on a sufficiently high level to obtain useful intelligence. The fact that an agent had frequent contact with high German officials could be interpreted, however, in two entirely different ways." A man might equally be "considered a more suspicious character [or] an extremely valuable agent."

OSS-Istanbul sent its first intelligence reports on August 21, 1943, knowing little about how to write and evaluate them. The Cairo office conducted an on-the-job correspondence school in analyzing the work. "We must develop a critical sense," said one of its letters. "We have so much information—what we need is [good] information. In every case ask yourself, 'How did source get this information? Was he in a position to get the facts or is this just imagination or rumor? Can this be either careless exaggeration or deliberate falsehood?' "

It was of course important to keep agents' identities secret, OSS-Cairo continued, but something about the individual's background and reliability must always be included in reports. "Information is of no use unless it produces or prevents action. And nobody is going to act on a bald statement of fact without knowing where it comes from." Cairo also needed to have some knowledge of the sources so that it would not use two reports from the same agent to verify each other.

The Dogwood operation tried to avoid providing details about its sources, but it quickly grew into a structure said to control sixty-seven subagents either directly or through one of thirteen chains. In December 1943, 31 of 117 OSS-Istanbul reports came from this network; it produced 83 in January and 43 in February. Dogwood "looms large in the Istanbul picture," OSS-Istanbul commented, "having provided for some time both the bulk and what appears to be the best of the secret intelligence from Germany and [Czechoslovakia]." Since Dogwood produced such impressive results, its reports were sent directly to Washington rather than being held in Cairo for evaluation. Schwarz's team produced dozens of items on the top priorities of the war effort: bombing targets, antiaircraft defenses, troop movements, political developments, and other enemy activities.

Although Allied troops had not penetrated the Reich, British and American planes flew over it daily to bomb strategic factories. The air forces desperately needed all available information on these plants' locations, outputs, shipping routes, and defenses. Planning new raids required knowing whether earlier attacks had damaged factories or forced the Germans to shift production elsewhere. Allied planners decided to focus on several items whose production was highly concentrated and could not easily be replaced. Rubber, oil and synthetic gasoline, aircraft, and ball-bearing production were at the top of this list. In January 1944 Dogwood's agents provided important information on them all.

Cut off from natural rubber supplies in South America and Asia, Germany had to make its own rubber to keep the Luftwaffe and ground forces rolling. Dogwood's agents provided details on the location of artificial rubber factories. Their reports also claimed that production of Messerschmitt fighter planes had been moved from Viennese plants damaged by Allied bombers to three former textile spinning mills about 15 miles from the city.

Allied experts identified ball bearings as a weak point in the German arms and transport industry because two-thirds of them were made at a single complex in Schweinfurt, Germany. A Dogwood source claimed that Allied bombing had so damaged these installations as to force production to be moved elsewhere.

If the information coming from Dogwood's sources was accurate, the Allies could inflict devastating damage on the German war effort. But if Dogwood's information came from men under German control, the truly vital factories would be protected and Allied planes might even be lured into traps resulting in heavy losses.

Neither OSS-Istanbul nor the Washington office, however, knew the identity of Dogwood's subagents. Dogwood insisted on concealing them, fearing leaks from careless OSS personnel or intercepted transmissions. Some OSS officials in Istanbul, kept in the dark about its activities, criticized the operation's independence and expenditures. One OSS officer wrote a friend in Cairo: "Actually, the stuff is gathered, written and processed by [Schwarz]. . . . [Coleman] almost never sees the reports." When the British asked for the names of American agents so that they could evaluate individual reports, Macfarland and Coleman refused, arguing this would give too many clues as to the agents' true identities. The British might even try to steal or control OSS agents.

This attitude, understandable as it was, made it impossible for Allied intelligence analysts to evaluate the reliability of individuals hidden behind code names like "Cassia," "Stock," "Jacaranda," and "Iris." Special Anglo-American boards in London compared reports with each other and with aerial photographs in order to judge their importance and accuracy. The names of proposed agents were supposed to be checked against British intelligence's list of German spies compiled through communications intercepts and other means. But this precaution had not been taken for Dogwood's subagents because the operation did not reveal their identities. Given the OSS's inexperience, mistrust of the British, lack of a counterintelligence unit in Istanbul, and pride in maintaining an independent operation, the Dogwood ring was insufficiently protected against German penetration.

Some of Dogwood's intelligence was deemed too vague or disproved by other sources. Most of it, though, was enthusiastically received and used for planning bombing missions. The intelligence chief of the U.S. Fifteenth Air Force, responsible for most Balkan missions, wrote: "The Istanbul reports have been of great value, and the greater the flow from this source the better. . . . OSS-Istanbul has recently been obtaining . . . valuable data on strategic targets, on enemy aircraft factories and plane dispositions in the Balkans. Time is obviously of the essence in supplying air intelligence to operational units. Accurate intelligence on the number and disposition of enemy aircraft [or] the number and calibre of anti-aircraft guns might represent the difference between a successful mission with light losses and a partially successful mission attended by heavy losses." Another officer gave Dogwood a rave review, saying the reports were "extremely valuable . . . fresh, reliable, and relevant," particularly the ones on the dispersion of Messerschmitt production.

A graphic example of the need for timely intelligence occurred when Dogwood reported a heavy concentration of antiaircraft guns around a Messerschmitt factory in late 1943. The information went to OSS-Cairo and was immediately sent to U.S. Air Corps Intelligence. Unfortunately, a bombing mission had taken off a few minutes earlier to attack that target, having been briefed to expect no serious defenses there. Five planes were lost that otherwise might have safely returned. In retrospect, the earlier information appears to have been enemy disinformation, supplied by a double agent.

By the end of 1943, Macfarland could be proud of his achievements and particularly of the Dogwood network. Starting from scratch, he had within a few months made numerous contacts in Czechoslovakia, Bulgaria, Romania, Hungary, Greece, and Austria. The results, including the securing of an address book listing all major German industrial concerns, had been praised by superiors. Interviews with refugees were producing a great deal of useful information, couriers connected Istanbul with the Reich and occupied countries, and OSS caïques sailed the Aegean. Good working relations existed with the British, Turkish, Zionist, Polish, Czech, and Yugoslav intelligence agencies.

But even this was not all that OSS-Istanbul and Dogwood had achieved. They were now working on nothing less than fomenting a coup in Germany, a revolt in Austria, and the shift of Hungary from the Axis to the Allied side.

Following devastating defeats in Stalingrad and North Africa, the hitherto expanding German empire had begun to shrink. It was beset on too many fronts by enemies with superior resources and manpower. Those not blinded by fanaticism could see by early 1943 that Berlin's fate was sealed. The only questions were how long it would take: How many lives would be needlessly sacrificed; and how much of Germany would be wrecked before the end came?

Helmuth von Moltke, a staff officer and member of Germany's most famous military family, knew that his country's defeat was inevitable. As head of a small group of idealists with links to some higher-ranking officers and anti-Nazi politicians, von Moltke came to Istanbul in April 1943 to meet the British and Americans. He was helped by two men there: Paul Leverkuehn, the local Abwehr commander, who had close personal links with members of the anti-Hitler opposition, and Professor Alexander Rustow (code-named "Magnolia"), a German refugee who was liaison between the OSS and the German underground.

Rustow himself had ample evidence of Germany's changing fortunes. When his own father died, a high-ranking German officer had written Rustow a condolence letter—opened and passed by German censorship—commenting that it was fortunate the old general had not lived to see the army's current catastrophes. Rustow was struck by the decline of Hitler's prestige, the poor state of German morale, and the openness with which criticism was now expressed by military commanders.

Nevertheless, Rustow warned his American friends not to expect the Nazi regime's quick collapse. A good many more Allied victories were needed to destroy the idea of Germany's invincibility. Bombings might damage the country physically or psychologically, but only an Anglo-American invasion of western Europe would force Hitler to fall from power. And there was another factor to consider: fear of Soviet imperialism united most Germans, whether Nazis or anti-Nazis. They worried that Moscow would wreak a terrible revenge on Germany and impose Stalin's system on it. The best hope for a quick end to the war was that the Allies could persuade Germans an occupation was inevitable but Soviet rule was avoidable. This was the assessment behind von Moltke's mission. To save Germany from complete annihilation, his group sought to overthrow Hitler and create a democratic anti-Nazi government when the British and Americans landed. It would welcome their occupation but resist a Soviet one.

While the German opposition's attitude toward Stalin's regime was understandable, it posed a tremendous problem for the United States and Britain. As in the case of Hungary, any Anglo-American initiative which could be interpreted as making a deal against their Soviet ally might split the Allies and severely undermine the war effort.

Nevertheless, Schwarz was excited by this opportunity to work with the German opposition toward overthrowing Hitler. "The magnitude of the promise held out by the proposed collaboration can hardly be overstated," he wrote. "No limited intelligence effort . . . can offer even a remotely comparable chance of ending the war in the West at one stroke and save perhaps many hundred thousand lives of Allied soldiers and civilians. . . . We are positive that [von Moltke] and his associates . . . are absolutely reliable and sincere German patriots and that their combined resources . . . are such that their assistance would make the success of an Allied invasion of western Europe a foregone conclusion."

Von Moltke asked for a secret meeting with an important American official to discuss these ideas. Macfarland endorsed the initiative, cabling OSS headquarters: "Our Nazi penetration group is getting in touch with top-notch Axis economic and military officials and former diplomats; some are renowned. Proceding very well under the close surveillance of my assistant [Coleman]." Rustow's assessment was shrewder. The British and Americans were not going to bargain with German officials or risk a split with the Soviets. "Roosevelt, Churchill, and Stalin have decided to demand Germany's unconditional surrender," he told von Moltke. "Do you think you are going to change their minds?"

The resistance also contacted von Papen himself. It was widely rumored in Istanbul that he was in despair and considered the war lost. In an interview, he told the pro-Ally Jewish editor of an Egyptian newspaper: "The war in its present stage can go on for years and can bring nothing but a total ruin of the world and civilization. This is neither in German nor Allied interests. Only the Bolsheviks would derive some profit from it. It is therefore essential to finish the war by a reasonable peace. The occupied territories ought to be returned to the countries they belonged to." Talking to Turkey's foreign minister, von Papen claimed that Germany could hold back an Allied invasion in the west and the Soviets in the east long enough for him to replace Hitler and make peace.

But when Leverkuehn asked von Papen to allow a resistance man to be stationed as a diplomat in Istanbul with the secret task of negotiating with the Allies, the ambassador refused lest Berlin discover the plot. While others were risking their lives in Germany to overthrow Hitler's regime, von Papen would make no commitment to the resistance despite—or because of—his personal ambition to rule Germany.

When von Moltke returned to Istanbul in November, he was disappointed to discover that the U.S. government would only let him explain his plan to its military attaché in Turkey. Even then, Washington and London did not respond. They were unsure what forces von Moltke actually represented. Moreover, if the German army was encouraged to topple the regime, hold the Russian front, and surrender its country and arms to the British and Americans, Moscow would feel betrayed and continue to advance even against its former allies. As Rustow predicted, Roosevelt and Churchill were unwilling to dilute their unconditional-surrender demand. The heroic resisters were caught in a trap.

Trying to break the logjam, Leverkuehn himself wrote Donovan a personal appeal on German embassy stationery. If the Allies were willing to negotiate with a new government formed after an anti-Hitler coup, Leverkuehn suggested, officers would sabotage German counterattacks on an Allied landing in France. Donovan forwarded this note to Roosevelt with his endorsement.

To strengthen his contention that a broad spectrum of Germans were ready to overthrow Hitler and surrender to the Allies, Donovan had taken the highly unusual step of launching his own diplomatic initiative without White House approval. He used Theodore Morde, one of his former staffers who was now a *Reader's Digest* correspondent. Under Donovan's sponsorship, OSS stations in Cairo and Turkey were ordered to help Morde, though his affiliation was deliberately kept vague.

OSS-Istanbul put Morde in touch with Rustow, who, in turn, contacted von Papen through a mutual friend. Rustow, the exiled democratic scholar, must have found it most unpleasant to chat with the man he hated for delivering Germany to fascism. But he was nonetheless persuasive. Von Papen agreed to meet the mysterious American who carried a Portuguese passport and claimed to be Roosevelt's representative.

In the midst of making these arrangements, Rustow had a family problem that threatened the project. His son, Dankwart, had just received a draft notice for the German army. It was a ridiculous situation: the son of a leading anti-Nazi being told to join Hitler's forces. Dankwart tore up the letter. A few days later, the director of the Istanbul German hospital called him to ask why he had not come for a medical exam. "It is up to the doctor to say whether you are fit and I am the doctor. I will make a deal. If you report to me, I will reject you."

Dankwart asked his father what to do. "I don't want to elaborate," said Professor Rustow, "but it is a good idea." While meeting with von Moltke and von Papen, Rustow did not need any attention focused on his family; he worried that his son's loss of citizenship would damage his own credibility in trying to save the country. Dankwart went for the physical examination, and the doctor kept his promise.

On October 5, 1943, Rustow accompanied Morde to the German embassy and left him with von Papen. The ambassador had two armed guards ready should the appointment prove to be another assassination attempt. Morde opened the meeting by promising secrecy and pledging that he was neither an intelligence agent nor a trickster. The United States, he continued, wanted the war to end quickly and its peace terms were contained on a single sheet of paper that had been microfilmed.

He dramatically handed von Papen a small piece of film and a magnifying glass. The document's main point was that the United States would make peace if the Germans turned over Hitler and other leading

Nazis to the Allies for trial. Morde never quite said he represented Roosevelt but certainly strove to leave this impression. Von Papen should think over this proposal, Morde said, and his response would be given to the White House.

Appealing to von Papen's boundless egoism, Morde said: "You are the one man who can form a new Germany. You are respected, not only in your own country but throughout the world, as one who has Germany's interests foremost in your heart." This was, Morde later dryly noted, what the ambassador wanted to hear. Von Papen accepted the compliment, commenting that if he had stayed in power as chancellor there never would have been any war. Von Papen accompanied Morde to the anteroom to rejoin Rustow. The two Germans stiffly bowed to each other; Morde and Rustow left.

A second meeting was held the next day at an intermediary's house on the resort island of Prinkipo. Von Papen went on a family outing on his yacht; then he left his wife and children for a ninety-minute discussion of "business matters" at a friend's house. Inside, Morde was waiting.

The moment had come, von Papen had decided, to take his rightful place as Germany's leader. He asked Morde to convey his ideas only to the president. The ambassador then presented his personal peace terms. Germany should be economic leader of a federated Europe after the war, and Austria must remain part of Germany. Von Papen's pompous self-image had been reinforced; he thought Roosevelt was endorsing him as Germany's new leader.

Most of the German people were not really behind the Nazis, von Papen continued, and would welcome a new government as long as they believed it possible to avoid harsh terms, Communism, and the partition of Germany. Overthrowing Hitler would be difficult but possible if the Americans gave him an attractive enough incentive to offer his friends. Von Papen added that he would be honored to be in charge of the new government and that Germans admired and trusted him as their leader. He looked forward to hearing Roosevelt's response. The whole idea, of course, was ridiculous. Von Papen represented no one but himself and was deeply distrusted by anti-Nazis.

Three weeks later, Morde arrived in Washington and came to see presidential adviser Robert Sherwood. Sherwood, who already thought

Morde rather unreliable, was horrified. The White House, he ascertained, knew nothing of this whole harebrained project—although Morde did not mention his OSS connection—and should certainly have nothing to do with it. Morde had acted in an incredibly irresponsible manner, Sherwood concluded, and should be denied a passport so that he could not leave the country again.

Having been rejected at the White House, Morde turned to Donovan, who forwarded his report to Roosevelt with an enthusiastic letter of support. "It contains an idea that your skill and imagination could develop. I don't pretend to suggest what price should be paid by our government for the hoped-for result. *If* the plan went through, and *if* the culprits were delivered and fittingly tried and executed, and *if* unconditional surrender resulted, it would strengthen your position morally at the peace table."

These were quite a few "ifs." Since Roosevelt would not even permit secret negotiations with the resistance through von Moltke, he certainly was not going to countenance them with a man like von Papen. Indeed, the very contact with someone seen as a slippery, pro-Nazi character hurt rather than strengthened Donovan's overall case. Washington never replied to von Papen at all. Von Moltke was arrested by the Gestapo in February 1944, as he was preparing a return trip to Istanbul, and was later executed. If the von Moltke episode was a tragedy, the contacts with von Papen were something of a farce.

The Nazis had at least some notion about these activities and, as Roosevelt feared, tried to exploit them. Using a captured Soviet spy's transmitter, Berlin fed Stalin false reports that the British and Americans were pursuing anti-Soviet negotiations with the Nazis. The Soviet media ran stories on von Papen's peace feelers and a fabricated one on a secret meeting in Spain between the British and von Ribbentrop. It was precisely fear about this kind of German disinformation and Soviet mistrust that had inhibited London and Washington from more serious contacts with the German underground. The United States and Britain did live up to their bargain with Moscow, but Stalin never got over his suspicion that they planned to betray him.

The Dogwood operation had followed Donovan's orders to build bridges to the German opposition. As Allied armies moved north through Italy and Soviet forces advanced westward, the OSS also worked behind the scenes to subvert Germany's empire. Now was the time for an all-out campaign to persuade Berlin's allies and satellites to leave the Axis. OSS-Istanbul first turned to anti-Nazi Austrians and Hungarians, who would become the source for much of its intelligence.

Despite some later attempts to revise history, many Austrians were as enthusiastic as most Germans toward the Nazi regime. Hitler himself was an Austrian and his compatriots accounted for many of the German agents in the Balkans and some of the most fanatical SS troops. Still, other Austrians did not approve of either their country's absorption in the Reich or Hitler's policies. A contemporary Istanbul joke told of three German soldiers ordering coffee in a Greek café. The waiter sarcastically told the chef, "Three cups of poison!" One of the soldiers, who understood Greek, shouted, "Only two, please! I'm Austrian." As defeat appeared inevitable, Austrians who had previously identified themselves as Germans—and even some Germans who were born in Germany—began to claim they were Austrian citizens unwillingly forced into Hitler's Reich. One anti-Nazi Austrian in Istanbul joked, "It's amazing how big our country is becoming!"

Beginning in the fall of 1943, OSS-Istanbul began working with a group of brave but naive resisters calling itself the Austrian Committee of Liberation and known at the OSS as the Cassia ring. "Cassia" was Franz Josef Messner, managing director of the Semperit Company's Vienna operations. Messner's job made him ideally situated to supply industrial and bombing intelligence. Semperit was one of the Reich's biggest corporations, with tens of thousands of workers and factories in a half-dozen countries. The Vienna complex specialized in processing rubber, one of the Allies' main targets.

Ironically, Messner's first clandestine activity had been on Germany's behalf. At the war's outset, he set up a contraband rubber trade between Brazil and Germany. Returning from South America in 1940, Messner was captured by the French and sentenced to death. Before execution could be carried out, however, France surrendered to the Germans and Messner was freed.

Messner's partners in his new, pro-Allied endeavor included Semperit's Istanbul representative, along with a priest and several Viennese businessmen. Although the OSS thought the group much larger, it apparently included only about twenty people. Its activities up to then had been largely limited to distributing leaflets, but its members, despite the constant threat of torture and death, wanted to do more.

As Macfarland and Coleman—with frequent advice from Donovan—developed links with his group, Messner himself came to Istanbul. Worried about being followed by the Germans, he took a clever but simple precaution. Messner visited a seemingly apolitical German teacher at Istanbul's technical school who was actually one of Schwarz's chief subagents. Schwarz came to the building well before Messner arrived, and the two men met in their mutual friend's office.

On February 3, 1944, Messner signed an agreement to cooperate with the OSS "toward the defeat of Nazi Germany and the liberation of Austria." The Austrians would supply intelligence, prepare for military action, and distribute propaganda. The OSS supplied ciphers, broadcasting instructions, and $6000 in German currency. A Dogwood courier would smuggle a radio set to Budapest for Messner to pick up and take back to Vienna.

American advisers would be parachuted into Austria to help launch armed resistance. The OSS even planned the details of their arrival with the Austrian underground. On a previously designated moonless night, agents and arms would be dropped into a remote area of the country. On hearing a plane's motors, the resistance reception team would mark the landing site by arranging four white signal beams in a square with a fifth in the center and a red light outside to indicate wind direction. Two kilometers to the east, a flashlight would be switched on at two-second intervals to guide the plane. Macfarland asked Washington to recruit a team of OSS men to go into Austria to work with the resistance.

Parallel plans were under way in Hungary, where Donovan and Macfarland hoped to stage their most successful operation. The Budapest government had already secretly surrendered to the Allies at a clandestine meeting in Istanbul and pronounced itself ready to oppose the Germans. The prime minister was in secret contact with the OSS, intelligence chief General Istvan Ujszaszy was a British agent, and the interior minister was protecting trade union and democratic opposition leaders from arrest. The Hungarians did not fire at overflying Allied planes, and Chief of Staff General Sombathay was lobbying Hitler to permit Hungary's troops to withdraw from the Russian front for home defense.

If the OSS was able to split Hungary away from the Axis, the Germans would have to divert their attention and troops away from the coming Normandy landing. But the OSS's activities had gone beyond the scope of merely misinforming the enemy. Its ambition was to make the covert actions in Hungary and Austria the first step in the internal collapse of Hitler's Reich. Dogwood and OSS-Istanbul now turned their attention to this high-stakes, dangerous endeavor.

12 | Dogwood's Bite:

The Fall of OSS-Istanbul

He who loves roses must learn to deal with thorns.
—Turkish proverb

One evening in September 1943, a slim, baby-faced man with wavy hair strolled across Istanbul's Pera Bridge, enjoying the view. A large car pulled up alongside and stopped. The man in the backseat rolled down the window and leaned out, inviting the pedestrian to join him. Lieutenant Colonel Otto Hatz of the Hungarian army, whose military bearing was apparent despite his civilian clothes, entered the car and sat next to Andre Gyorgy.

The auto took them to the elegant neighborhood where the OSS owned a safe house. There, Schwarz and Coleman met Hatz to discuss how Hungary might quit the Axis and join the Allied side in the war.

The turning of Hungary was OSS-Istanbul's most ambitious operation and Schwarz and Coleman sought to monopolize it. Since early 1943, the State Department and the OSS had been meeting secretly with Hungarian envoys. The British had reached an agreement with a Foreign Ministry representative of the civilian government. A Hungarian diplomat later wrote, "We were all full of optimism that step by step we would be able to remove all the pro-Nazis in the government" and make peace with the Allies. The OSS sought to deal directly with the Hungarian high command because it knew that any arrangement which did not include the Hungarian army would be militarily worthless.

Both Budapest and OSS-Istanbul thought Lieutenant Colonel Otto Hatz the ideal intermediary. A professional officer, he had served as Hungarian military attaché to Turkey and Bulgaria. Hatz was handsome, well-mannered, and had an excellent sense of humor. His satirical imitation of Hitler was particularly successful at parties. He had been a member of Hungary's medal-winning Olympic fencing team and enjoyed good connections throughout the Hungarian military and intelligence hierarchy. Hatz avoided politics and got along well with pro-German officers as well as those more inclined to the Allied cause.

On the Allies' behalf, Andre Gyorgy—who himself combined lucrative smuggling with work for the Hungarians, British, OSS, Zionists, and, unknown to these four groups, the Germans as well—got in touch with Hatz and urged him to visit Istanbul in September 1943. Hatz asked his superior, Colonel Gyula Kadar, to let him attend Turkey's famous international trade fair in Izmir. Along the way, he visited Istanbul for separate clandestine meetings with the British and Americans. A British officer and Teddy Kollek of the Zionist service asked Hatz to gather intelligence for them in Hungary. Coleman and Schwarz told him to give the Hungarian high command an OSS offer to cooperate against the Germans.

Hatz returned to Budapest carrying a special suitcase given to him by Coleman. "I don't care even if you arrest me," he told Kadar. "But I must tell you that I reached an agreement with these Americans." He opened the bag to show Kadar a radio transmitter which, Hatz said with some overstatement, could be used to get in touch with President Roosevelt. If the Hungarians wanted to talk further with the Americans, he added, the 8 o'clock radio news should broadcast for three nights an item referring to the Izmir fair. The American radio would also carry a special phrase to confirm the deal, appropriately enough, "Sincerity above all!"

Kadar and Hatz then went to see Hungary's chief of staff, General Sombathay. The general's reaction was positive: "Thank God! Finally an opportunity to start a contact. I have always wondered how we could find a way out of this terrible darkness." After consulting the Foreign Ministry, Sombathay instructed Kadar and Hatz to continue discussions but to avoid using the radio. Thus Hatz began his career as the Hungarian military's secret envoy to the Americans, telling his superiors everything that had happened in Istanbul.

But Hatz also discussed his experiences with someone else. On the way back to Budapest, he had made a brief stopover in Sofia and eaten dinner at the home of an old friend, Otto Wagner, the Abwehr chief there. Hatz told Wagner all about the Istanbul meetings. He claimed to have virtuously resisted British and American offers to become a spy but admitted he would continue talks with the OSS on ways to end the war. Above all, Hatz wanted Wagner to keep his betrayal secret from the Hungarian government.

"It's good for us to be able to learn through him whether his government is really informing us about . . . his contacts with the Americans," Wagner told Berlin. "In this way, nothing can happen against the interests of the Reich." If the Hungarian regime kept Hatz's activities secret from the Germans, Wagner warned, this meant Hungary planned to defect from the Axis.

The Germans did not completely trust Hatz, and he was not totally honest with them either. He claimed Hungary's leaders were merely drawing information out of the Americans in the Axis's interest rather than pursuing a serious peace initiative. The Abwehr reported that Hatz chased women and spent money too freely; there were rumors that he shared in Gyorgy's smuggling profits. But the Abwehr also felt that Hatz was personally pro-German and had already rendered valuable services to Berlin.

The Americans were confident of Hatz's loyalty. Unaware of Hatz's double-dealings, Coleman told Macfarland on November 8, "Our original choice for Hungarian plan has been appointed." The U.S. Joint Chiefs of Staff approved Macfarland's proposal to try to obtain Hungary's withdrawal from the war.

Hatz continued to shuttle back and forth between the OSS and the Hungarian leaders, stopping each time in Sofia for a chat with the Abwehr. On December 18, Hatz was picked up by an OSS car in Istanbul, driven in circles, and transferred to another car that delivered him to the OSS's Bebek apartment, where Coleman and Schwarz were waiting.

Time was passing quickly, Coleman warned, and Hungary must

decide where it stood. The Axis had lost the war. Hungary's treatment at the peace table would depend on whether it now took active measures against Berlin. Hungary must accept a secret OSS advisory mission and prepare to rise against the Germans as soon as possible.

Hatz promised to convey the message faithfully. And he did so twice. On his way back to Budapest, Hatz stopped in Sofia and again went to Wagner's house for dinner. He accurately reported on what the two OSS men had said, but falsely and cheerfully maintained to Wagner that he had rejected the OSS's offer. His government would make no deals and provide no intelligence; it was only feigning an interest in U.S. proposals for Hungary to switch sides. He promised to inform the Germans of any anti-German actions by his country.

At their next meeting, Coleman and Schwarz made an incredible security blunder by telling Hatz they had been warned he was a double agent. If Hatz had told the Germans about this statement, they might have realized that the Allies had obtained this information by decoding Abwehr cables about meetings with Hatz. The Allies' most valuable asset in the war might have been jeopardized because of a single slip-up in Istanbul.

Hatz, however, merely shrugged off the American accusation with an unconvincing rebuttal. He replied that a former Hungarian diplomat had congratulated him in the lobby of Budapest's Ritz Hotel for saving Hungary by winning the Allies' goodwill in Istanbul. If the secret talks were so well known in Hungary, the Germans must be aware of them without his saying a word. Hatz later repeated the same story, justifying his contacts with the Abwehr as attempts to convince the Germans that the Istanbul contacts were harmless.

Hatz's apparent objective was to cover himself so well with each side that his position would be protected no matter who ultimately won. The damage done by him would be grave indeed. When the Hungarian government said nothing about its feelers to Istanbul, the Germans assumed that the regime was planning to desert the Axis. Hitler began planning to take over his wayward ally.

The Hungarian embassy in Berlin found the city abuzz with talk about the secret Hungarian-Allied dialogue. Budapest was panic-stricken, knowing that time was running out. "We have to find a way out of this war," Sombathay dramatically told his intelligence chief,

Kadar, and Hatz. "We must continue these contacts to get some help. . . . If I fail in this I will go to my hanging with pride because the nation will justify what I have done later."

The more down-to-earth Kadar later recounted: "This sounded very good. . . . But what could we do in this situation? It was necessary to keep talking and we somehow had to get the suspicion away from us." After long discussion, the Hungarians decided that Kadar and Hatz would tell the Abwehr's chief, Canaris, that the Americans had approached them and suggest that these contacts might be used to obtain useful information about Allied military plans.

The meeting took place in Munich on January 9, 1944. Hatz told his new story in a very convincing manner while the poker-faced Canaris listened without saying a word. Finally, Canaris responded: "It's out of the question to give permission for something like that. You are naive. The Americans are cunning and would give away nothing. The only thing that would happen is that you would be suspected as spies and this would have immeasurable consequences." Kadar could only feign agreement and tell Hatz to have no further contact with the Americans.

Of course, as a German officer, Canaris opposed Hungary's defection. But his statement's wording also suggested a friendly warning that Berlin knew a great deal about Budapest's plots and would destroy Hungary before letting them succeed. Certainly, many Abwehr officers doubted that Germany could win the war and some openly criticized Hitler. After dinner, a German infantry officer argued that the Soviets would be exhausted, the Atlantic defenses were too strong, and the Reich would soon produce miracle weapons. A member of Canaris's staff pulled Kadar aside and asked mockingly, "Do you believe all that you have just heard?"

Unsure whether this was a provocation, Kadar replied, "Obviously, that's the way we judge the situation, too."

"Please, colonel, don't pretend," said the German. "You absolutely cannot believe this stupidity. We already have lost this war. We might be able to drag it out for a while but if we get attacks from the west as well we will not be able to hold back the Russians. Within days we will collapse." Kadar preferred to be thought stupid rather than to fall into a trap, so he repeated the optimistic talk he had heard earlier. The man gave him a disgusted look and walked away.

But despite feigning pro-German sentiments, the Hungarians could not convince Canaris to endorse their feelers to the Allies. "So," Kadar recounted, "our trip was useless. Even worse, we were definitely forbidden to continue the contacts." Nevertheless, the Hungarians decided to go on with only a slight change: instead of Hatz meeting the Americans directly, most of the talks would go through his friend Luther Kovess.

Hatz continued to play a central role in the affair while tipping off the Germans. The Allies had enough evidence of Hatz's betrayal, but it came from the highly secret breaking of German codes and thus few people could be told how definitive was this proof. Macfarland neither knew of the reliable source of the information against Hatz nor properly heeded Donovan's warnings.

On January 9, 1944, Donovan again cabled Macfarland that an extremely reliable source indicated that Hatz (given the Dogwood code name "Jasmine") was working "under double-cross orders" and giving information to the Germans. Eight days later, OSS-Cairo radioed Macfarland that Dogwood's courier, Gyorgy, was involved in currency smuggling "approved by Hungarian intelligence. He is a Hungarian agent and has assured Germans he would keep them informed of his contacts." The fact that Gyorgy was a Hungarian agent was not so bad, but his German connections were another matter.

"As you know," Macfarland wrote OSS-Cairo on January 19, "I have never been very enthusiastic about this whole project and probably would not have gone as far as [Coleman] did with Donovan and the Joint Chiefs of Staff." Macfarland was fatally wrong in underestimating the disastrous effect of Hatz's behavior. "We assumed," Macfarland wrote, that Hatz's contact with the Germans "was his method of keeping his cover. It may of course be a perfect double cross and we are very much on our guard. The same message has come to us from the British here. It is perfectly possible of course that the story of his wishing to double cross us is a German plant in order to scare us away from dealing with him. . . . We shall do everything we can to be cautious about our dealings or the making of any plans based upon his statements. If our good friends of [OSS counterintelligence] would loosen up on a few of their trained agents, we would have a little better chance of following up matters of this kind."

Yet OSS-Istanbul was hardly cautious in its dealings with Luther

Kovess, the man now charged with the responsibility of maintaining its secret links with the Hungarians. Kovess, a personal friend of both Hatz and Schwarz, was enlisted as Dogwood's agent "Jacaranda." The son of an Austro-Hungarian aristocrat and himself a naval officer of that vanished empire, Kovess had come down in the post-1918 world. After the war, Hungary had no seacoast and thus no navy. Kovess became a Socony-Vacuum tanker captain and then worked for Archibald Walker in Istanbul as superintendent of the company's ships. He applied for British citizenship in the 1930s, a fact he later hid with shame when his outspoken pro-Nazi views brought him the nickname "Hitler's first lieutenant" in Istanbul.

British intelligence put him under close surveillance but found no hint that Kovess had sabotaged ships under his care. The U.S. company fired him only after America entered the war and Hungary became an enemy state. Kovess stayed in Istanbul to represent the Danube Shipping Company, an Abwehr front.

It is hard to understand how a man who was so suspected of pro-German sympathies could have become Dogwood's supervisor of Hungarian operations. But the OSS's Walker, Kovess's boss for years at Socony-Vacuum, vouched for him, as did Schwarz himself. Kovess, Schwarz wrote, "is a devoted sympathizer with the Allied cause and an inveterate enemy of Nazi Germany." Kovess admitted having friends in German intelligence but insisted that he was very careful. He traveled to Budapest twice at great apparent risk to gather information. To survive, however, he trafficked with both Hungarian intelligence and the Abwehr. His loyalties did not lay exclusively with the Allies.

On January 22 a special meeting was held between Hatz, Coleman, Schwarz, and Colonel Vala Mocarski, who had come from Cairo as Donovan's personal representative. Walter Arndt interpreted. Another member of the small group at this top-secret gathering was Baron Luther Kovess. Unaware that two triple agents were sitting across the table, Colonel Mocarski explained the situation: "The leaders of Hitler's satellites will be considered guilty of war crimes and punished after the war. If Hungary's generals would escape that fate, they must seize the present opportunity of leading a revolt against Germany." The Hungarian general staff, he continued, must provide the Allies with military intelligence and its plans for sabotaging the German war effort.

Hatz replied that the high command might not consider it advisable or ethical to divulge military secrets. Mocarski was annoyed. Questions of ethics had not stopped the generals from betraying Yugoslavia and cooperating fully with Hitler, he complained. Tactfully but firmly, Mocarski explained that nothing less than complete and genuine collaboration would count. Otherwise, there was no sense in continuing talks.

The word "collaboration" was disturbing, Hatz said, as it implied unpatriotic submissiveness. If Coleman and Mocarski had known of Hatz's betrayal in Sofia, they would have been outraged about his delicacy on this point. More fundamentally, Hatz continued, Hungary was inhibited from acting because it feared German or Soviet occupation.

If the Nazis tried to take over Hungary, explained Mocarski, the United States expected it to resist and destroy strategic facilities. As for Hungary's worries about the Soviets, Mocarski continued, all the Allies had pledged to let people choose their government democratically rather than imposing any particular system on them. The Soviets posed no more threat to Hungary than did Britain or America. To central Europeans, such ideas seemed an example of the Americans' hopeless naïveté.

After the patient explanation came the hard sell. Time was critical, Mocarski warned, and any indecision or further delay would be interpreted as a rejection of the U.S. offer. Hatz promised to return to Hungary and provide a definite answer.

One reason for Macfarland's carelessness in dealing with Hatz and Kovess was Donovan's demand for quick results. "Our work calls for action and not speech," the OSS chief radioed Macfarland the day after the meeting. Macfarland was focusing on Budapest's response, not on the reliability of his intermediaries. His main concern was to reassure superiors that he would make no binding political commitments. "We are seeking military cooperation with Hungary . . . not political negotiations," he told Washington.

Even so, the question of Hatz's betrayal was seriously mishandled. Donovan radioed Macfarland on February 5: "My warning regarding Hatz has been followed by you I trust. Inform me fully concerning this matter."

The next day, Macfarland replied: "We received your cable on Hatz. . . . He [only] still serves the function of courier . . . he possesses no information concerning our organization or plans the disclosure of which might prove embarrassing. [The] memo which he carries to Sombathay for suggested collaboration is a simple outline of how this group can proceed if they want to collaborate and in German hands could do no harm." Macfarland could not have been more wrong.

At least, however, Hatz obtained a quick and positive response to the American ultimatum from Hungary's military command, which agreed to receive an OSS mission to help manage the preparations for its switch from Axis to Allies. Kadar moved his radio to the apartment of his beautiful mistress, Hungary's most famous stage actress, so he would have it ready for contacting Istanbul.

The plan was code-named "Operation Sparrow." God might note even a sparrow's fall, but the parachuting of three OSS men into Hungary would hopefully pass unnoticed by the Germans. In command was Colonel Florimond Duke. A college-football star player and an officer in World War I, Duke became advertising director of *Fortune*, *Time*, and *Life* magazines. He joined military intelligence in 1940, served as an army attaché in Cairo, transferred to the OSS, and directed its Balkan desk from Washington. The 49-year-old Duke, who had never parachuted before, insisted on coming from Washington to lead the dangerous mission.

While all these plans were coalescing, some OSS men in Istanbul were growing increasingly doubtful about the Dogwood operation. If they had known about Hatz and Kovess, they would have been even more alarmed. The British, also suspicious, demanded more information on the network's sources. One OSS officer noted that a Dogwood report from Budapest about German troop movements was almost identical to a statement made by a known German agent.

A second OSS man complained on February 6 that Coleman "has fought any attempts on our part to trace down [German] 'plants,' get information on reliability of sub-sources, etc. . . . Eventually our pressure seems to have had some effect. [Coleman] has been separated from the Dogwood show. . . . We are not holding our breath until it happens, but things should eventually work out. Then we will be able to give [Cairo] and Washington the necessary check-up on sources, additional information desired, etc. Dogwood has possibilities but must be watched closely as he evaluated his [German] plants as high as his reliable stuff."

The chief of the OSS's regular Istanbul operations, John Wickham, argued that Coleman's organization was overrated, too costly, and out of control. Another matter worried Wickham even more. "The subject of 'double agents' is with us constantly," he wrote in his February 1944 report. "Many here believe [double agents] to be the best sources of information on our enemies," arguing that such men knew a great deal and that American agents could outsmart them "to get more than they give." This idea was misguided, Wickham warned. The double agents knew only what was necessary to do their job, "namely, to feed out enemy propaganda."

Since the OSS men had little training, Wickham added, it was not clear who was fooling whom. "We are trying to steer clear of these characters," he concluded, unhappy with being nominally responsible for Dogwood while having no say in its direction. Donovan angrily wrote that Wickham's report "ought to be put through the wringer." But Wickham's concerns would turn out to be correct. The network was riddled with double agents, and its mistakes were about to prove disastrous.

The Germans knew a great deal about the Allies' operations from Istanbul. The reports of Hatz and other Abwehr-Hungarian-OSS triple spies working with Dogwood tipped them off that some very big operations were under way. These agents, driven by venality and fear, were playing a complex, dangerous game. Hatz, Gyorgy, Kovess, and the others had the most privileged view of the war, since their duties constantly took them across the lines.

They had to tell the Germans just enough to protect their skins but not so much as to put their own behavior in question. At the same time, they had to make themselves useful enough to the Allies in order to continue enjoying the OSS's confidence and financing. By traveling across the battle lines, these men saw enough to know that the Allies were likely to win the war. In this situation, they were clever—or foolish—enough to believe they could play both sides, avoiding German punishment in the short run while reaping the victorious Allies' gratitude.

Those working also for Hungary had to convince each side of Budapest's loyalty as well. German intelligence officials worried that the triple agents might really be working with OSS to manipulate them. Berlin knew, for example, that Hatz had ignored Canaris's order to stop seeing the Americans and understood that all these shadowy figures were also working for Hungary and their own personal interests.

Being a triple agent was no easy profession; there were many moments when discovery and execution seemed imminent. But there was also plenty of money to be made by those willing to offer their services to more than one intelligence agency. Gyorgy was a common criminal, Budapest's smuggler king for gold, diamonds, and oriental carpets. He inhabited a world where espionage and gangsterism met. Gestapo and Abwehr officers wanted to use Gyorgy's proven abilities to make money for them. The Abwehr saved him from a Hungarian prison sentence in 1942 so that he could set up dummy companies to circumvent the Allied embargo on Germany. A few months later Hungarian intelligence demanded that Gyorgy keep it informed of German activities. Under orders from Budapest, Hatz helped Gyorgy carry out his missions while probably taking a share in his smuggling profits.

Hungarian Jewish groups turned to Gyorgy in the spring of 1943 to carry money and travel documents from Istanbul to Budapest. It was a calculated risk, but they had no alternative: Who else but a smuggler having good relations with the enemy could cross the border? Thus, Gyorgy came into contact with the Zionist and British intelligence services in Istanbul. His connection with Hungarian intelligence did not deter them, since they wanted to use Gyorgy to establish regular contact with the men he worked for in Budapest. The Hungarians were quite willing to employ Gyorgy to carry messages to the Allies. If pressed by the Germans, Hungary could always deny responsibility for Gyorgy's activities by branding him a common criminal.

Gyorgy's efforts to gather intelligence were laughable. His own "reports" might have been copied from British radio broadcasts. On one occasion, he was sitting in an Istanbul apartment with Allied officials. Trying to figure out their plans, Gyorgy wagered a large sum that the Americans would be in Budapest by Christmas 1943. Knowing there was no chance of this happening, the others accepted the bet. Gyorgy paid promptly when he lost. But Gyorgy was being employed as a man who could get across borders, not as a man of integrity.

Known as "Trillium," Gyorgy became the main OSS courier between Budapest and Istanbul. British decoding of German communications told the OSS that Gyorgy was a "double agent who works for the Germans, Hungarian Counterintelligence, the British and OSS." Nonetheless, Dogwood blandly and naively described him as an "uncompromising Allied partisan."

Berlin also had other means for discovering the secrets of Dogwood and the Hungarians. The Abwehr in Budapest had a budget of $3000 a month for suborning Hungarian officers and officials. It also ran covert counterintelligence operations. In one case, a German agent was disguised as an envoy from Tito, the Yugoslav Communist partisan leader, to contact Hungarian officials and ascertain their true sentiments. Those who helped him were later arrested.

The Abwehr's best single source on Dogwood may have been a Prague native named Frantisek Laufer. Tall, slim, and blond, he looked more Aryan than did most of the Nazis. Since he was half-Jewish, however, he was marked for deportation when the Germans seized Czechoslovakia. Instead, he made a deal: the Abwehr gave him papers as an Aryan in exchange for collaboration.

As early as April 1941, Czech anti-Nazis observed Laufer riding in a car with German officers, though he tried to avoid being recognized. When later asked about it, he responded lamely that he had paid the Germans to give him a ride. Laufer moved to Budapest, where Czech intelligence had its main base of operations. He traveled to Istanbul "on business" in June 1941 and picked up $5000 to finance Czech underground work. But resistance members working with him tended to be arrested. Laufer bought his wife expensive jewelry, though he had previously complained of being penniless. Despite his warning to keep the gifts secret, she could not resist showing them to friends. A Czech informant tipped off an American diplomat about Laufer in November 1941, but the report was lost in the files.

Laufer rose in the Abwehr hierarchy to the rank of chief subagent. At the same time, he infiltrated the Dogwood ring. The OSS's tight-lipped policy kept Allied counterintelligence from discovering that Laufer was the network agent code-named "Iris." While Gyorgy handled the Istanbul-Budapest run, Laufer was courier for the Budapest-Vienna leg and visited Czechoslovakia, Switzerland, and Istanbul itself.

Unaware of these penetrations in his espionage ring, Macfarland held a meeting to launch the Hungarian operation in Istanbul on February 27. For the first time, he met directly with Hatz, with Schwarz and Kovess also present. Hatz would go to Budapest. Through him, the Hungarian military command could send high-grade intelligence over the OSS radio set already there. The Hungarian generals would also secretly receive OSS advisers and draw up plans to fight the Germans.

As Russian armies closed in from the east and the Germans threatened from the west, Budapest's people engaged in giddy wishful thinking in the face of impending doom. "Never," a diplomat there said, "was the season as filled with dinners, luncheons, teas and cocktail parties. . . . The streets were still crowded with well-dressed flaneurs, the shops with luxury goods at immense prices which yet found buyers." Historian C. A. Macartney wrote: "Three-quarters of Budapest society openly feted the coming victory of the Western Powers. . . . Those Socialist politicians who a month later would be either prisoners in [a concentration camp] or lurking in the attics of friends addressed the largest audiences of their lives, which they tickled with promises of a democratic world just around the corner—a world which neither speakers nor audiences would ever see."

At 11 p.m. on March 15, 1944—Hungary's independence day— the OSS's Colonel Florimond Duke and two fellow officers climbed into a British plane at a base in Brindisi, Italy. The flight first detoured over Austria to drop two Austrian underground men dressed in German army uniforms. Their radio was pushed out the door after them; its parachute had been set to open automatically. But as Duke watched in horror, the wireless came loose from its parachute and smashed into the ground, leaving the two men isolated far behind German lines, unable to transmit any intelligence they gathered.

The plane flew onward. Just across the Yugoslav-Hungarian border, Duke's team jumped and landed safely near a Hungarian village. The uniformed Americans were quickly surrounded by peasants who called a nearby army outpost. The men stuck to their cover story: they were headed for Yugoslavia to advise the partisans, but they had become lost and ended up in Hungary by mistake.

Now, as planned, the chief of Hungarian counterintelligence arrived at the backwater border town and took control of the prisoners. He drove the "captured" Americans to Budapest in a closed ambulance, arriving there at sunset on March 18. When the "prisoners" emerged at intelligence headquarters near the city's center, Hungarian soldiers politely showed them to a large, comfortable cell and closed, but did not lock, the door.

A few minutes later, waiters entered with wine and a huge silver tray of food from one of Budapest's best restaurants. They bowed and set the table. "Royal treatment!" exclaimed one of Duke's men. Dessert was followed by the entrance of General Ujszaszy himself. The intelligence chief bowed crisply and asked, "Well, gentlemen, what is your proposition?"

"You know the proposition, sir . . . unconditional surrender," answered Duke. It was an absurd situation. Unarmed, alone, and hundreds of miles from Allied forces, three Americans were demanding the capitulation of an entire country and army. "Meanwhile," Duke continued, "we are here to see what can be done, and how we can help Hungary do it."

"Precisely," agreed Ujszaszy. "We shall be working together." Unfortunately, he continued, there was one complication. Duke would have to wait a few days before meeting Horthy and other high officials because they were out of town. Duke was surprised and angry. He wondered how the country's leaders could be so irresponsible as to go on a trip at this crucial moment. In fact, they had been summoned to Germany for a critical meeting with Hitler.

In preparation for Duke's mission, Hatz had smuggled two radios into Budapest and delivered them to Kovess, who was in town to help receive the Americans. Kovess was supposed to give one radio set to Laufer and the other to Messner's Austrian underground group. Once direct wireless communication was established with Messner, another OSS team was to parachute into Austria in mid-April.

To coordinate this plan, Messner went to Switzerland to meet Allen Dulles. Dulles approved of the operation. "I wish to offer my congratulations to Packy [Macfarland] for his accomplishments in developing this line," he cabled Donovan. Messner "impressed us very favorably. We are convinced that he is worthy of all our support and we will make arrangements to give him some modest financial assistance from here if he requests it."

But the Germans had not been fooled. They knew of all these plans through the triple agents. To forestall Hungary's desertion, Hitler had decided to take over that country and smash the Austrian resistance simultaneously, a decision justified on the basis of Hatz's reports to the Abwehr. Hitler proceeded with his usual diabolical cleverness. He made Horthy and General Sombathay visit him in Germany. Then, after delivering a harangue about Hungarian perfidy, Hitler ordered them held as hostages. The Germans told Budapest that the delegation's return was delayed by an Allied air raid that disrupted rail service.

On the night of Saturday, March 18, as Duke and his men were meeting their Hungarian hosts, a half-dozen German divisions entered Hungary. Troop trains bound for the eastern front stopped in Hungarian stations and, as onlookers watched in amazement, disgorged their armed passengers. Without orders from Horthy or Sombathay, the Hungarian army refused to fight. Telephones rang all over Budapest summoning the peace conspirators to flee for their lives or burn papers at their offices. By morning, the sky over the government ministries on Buda Hill was gray with smoke.

The unsuspecting Colonel Duke was awakened at 5 a.m. on Sunday and called into General Ujszaszy's presence. The intelligence chief had been up all night trying to deal with the crisis. His eyes were bloodshot and his hands trembled as he announced that the Germans would arrive within an hour. The Americans demanded to be evacuated, but they were told the Germans had seized all the airfields and sealed the borders. Two days later, the Hungarians turned the OSS men over to the Germans, claiming—so that the Americans would not be shot as spies—that they were ordinary prisoners of war. Although the Germans knew this was a lie, Duke and the other two officers refused to admit anything; they were sent to a high-security prison for the rest of the war.

Prime Minister Kállay, leader of the efforts to make peace with the Allies, eluded the Gestapo and took refuge in the Turkish embassy. When the Germans threatened to kill others unless he gave himself up, Kállay surrendered and was sent to the Dachau death camp. He survived. Under pressure from the Germans, General Ujszaszy and Colonel Kadar were court-martialed by the Hungarian army, but their fellow officers only put them under house arrest. Veress, the diplomat who had secretly negotiated Hungary's agreement with the Allies, took a train to Romania using his still-uncanceled diplomatic passport and crossed the border just before a Gestapo order to arrest him arrived there. He made his way to Yugoslavia and was safely conveyed to Italy by the partisans.

The Germans had also laid their trap for the Austrian resistance. When Messner and his secretary went to Budapest to pick up the radio, the Gestapo arrested them, acting on leads supplied by Hatz, Laufer, or Kovess. Under torture, the Austrians gave the names of others. Twenty people, including Messner, were killed; only two of the most active members survived. In April 1944, Laufer brought a German-inspired message to Istanbul, trying to lure Franz Josef Ridiger, who ran the Austrian underground's operations there, to Budapest. Ridiger wisely refused. "If Cassia['s group was] ever a possibility," Macfarland cabled Washington, it was "now unreliable and should be dropped."

The Germans were unsure about how to treat Hatz, Kovess, and Gyorgy. They faced the classic problem in dealing with double agents: deciding for whom they were really working. If Macfarland felt Hatz was only pretending to help the Abwehr, the agent's captors wondered the same thing. For their part, the imprisoned triple agents were miserable, not knowing whether they would be shot or tortured and having to conceal their double-dealings from anti-Nazi fellow prisoners.

Part of their problem was that their Abwehr bosses were now disgraced in Hitler's eyes. Having finally discovered the Abwehr's connections with resistance elements, the führer had dismissed Canaris and put the fanatically Nazi SD in charge of intelligence. The SD suspected that anyone connected with the Abwehr was a probable traitor and only decided to release the triple agents after three weeks of tough questioning.

With the collapse of all its operations in Hungary and Austria, the OSS now had even more reason to distrust Hatz. When Laufer sent word that he had managed Hatz's release, OSS headquarters in Washington ordered Macfarland to have no further dealings with the two men. If the Germans let Hatz return to Istanbul, Donovan warned, it would prove that he was working for them. Ironically, it was Hatz's release from prison that finally persuaded the OSS that he was untrustworthy, yet he had been arrested in the first place only because the Germans also mistrusted him.

Despite Washington's orders, both the OSS and the State Department met Hatz when he came back to Istanbul on June 8. Hatz had an explanation for everything. He claimed Gyorgy had betrayed him to the Gestapo, but he said the Germans had no proof of his involvement in the Sparrow mission. Hatz credited his release to an appeal from the Hungarian high command and to his promise to report for duty on the eastern front. As he left Istanbul for the last time, Hatz's parting words were, "After all, I wouldn't worry very much. The whole business [the war] will certainly be over in a very few months."

For Hatz, it was finished even sooner. He was already engaged with Kadar in a new conspiracy. Kadar's mistress introduced him to the Communist underground's leader in Budapest, and the two men met secretly. Hatz urged his government to make a separate deal with Moscow.

On November 7, 1944, as the Soviet army advanced into Hungary, Hatz defected to the Russians in a reconnaissance plane. In retaliation, the Gestapo sent his parents, brother, and fiancée to a concentration camp in Germany, where his mother and fiancée died. When the Red Army occupied Budapest some weeks later, it made Hatz the mayor's security adviser. Having worked almost simultaneously with Hungarian, U.S., two German, and Soviet intelligence agencies, Hatz was one of history's most remarkable spies.

But the events in Austria and Hungary also destroyed the reputation of the Dogwood ring and almost everyone connected with it. The treachery of Hatz, Gyorgy, and Laufer was inescapably clear. When Laufer asked Istanbul in May 1944 to set up secret meetings for him in Switzerland, the OSS concluded he wanted to penetrate Allen Dulles's operation. OSS-Washington radioed Macfarland on May 31, "Dogwood himself as well as the entire Dogwood chain is dangerous." The OSS ended all contacts with Laufer. He was last seen fleeing with German forces to Vienna at the end of the war.

All Dogwood's reports were reassessed in light of the debacle in Hungary. The very analysts who had so highly praised that work a few months ago now rushed to ridicule it. The OSS's London office told the Istanbul station: "Your questioned reports were probably [German] plants, the idea having been to play down target importance of [a] factory complex until it was better defended and then to play it up. Source and subsources all part of one chain composed mostly of double agents. . . . By definition our reliance on same source for clarifying data would be futile. Currently have no other sources [providing] original intelligence [on] this subject."

A similarly skeptical report from London comparing examples of Dogwood's dispatches with aerial photoreconnaissance noted: "According to the best available information here there is no [aircraft] engine plant at Ruzyno. . . . The production figures are fantastically high, in fact well informed sources here believe that very little production is going on there. . . . The drawing is so wildly inaccurate that it is of no use."

The Austrian spinning mills which Dogwood's agents reported to have been making fighter planes were still making cloth for uniforms. Fifteenth Air Force intelligence commented that the Messerschmitt works outside Vienna, reported to have been under repair, had been knocked "deader than hell. . . . The main plant was knocked out in November [1943] and never recovered." Another airplane factory, which the Dogwood network had reported destroyed, made only parts. "It was hit but not put out of action. Vital buildings escaped." One of Dogwood's most important scoops—the shifting of ball-bearing production—was now viewed as quite doubtful. "The series of little wooden shops alleged to be location of ball-bearing plant is absurd on the face of it; ball bearings could not be manufactured except in big buildings." Reports on the Heinkel plane works at Haidfeld-Schwechat, said London, "are usually highly exaggerated."

Messner's Cassia ring was also accused of feeding distorted production figures and distracting the Allies from more important targets. The U.S. Fifteenth Air Force reviewed the entire file of its reports and now concluded they were "inaccurate, vague, and exaggerated. Maps [were] out of scale, erroneous and useless." The OSS concluded, "In view of his presumable access to the true production picture in Germany, [Messner's] apparent efforts to 'load' us with such exaggerated figures are clear-cut indications that all material from him should be treated with great reserve."

The British concluded that many of Messner's reports were exaggerated or formulated to divert Allied bombers from more important bombing targets. There was, postwar research would show, some truth to this view. Sometimes, Cassia's businessmen wanted to protect their own factories and tried to divert Allied raids from plants even in the immediate vicinity. But the main problem was that the Austrians' lack of training or experience in spying made them overrate data from low-ranking German soldiers and draw maps inaccurately. Still, if the Austrians were amateurish, they were also courageous patriots who were rightfully judged heroes after the war.

If some of Cassia's reports were considered questionable, the very worst ones came from agent "Dahlia," Dogwood's source inside the German embassy in Turkey. This man was revealed to be one Fritz Fiala. Although his name means "daisy" in his native Slovakia, Fiala's character was closer to the exotic flower of his code name. Of the five double agents known to have penetrated the Dogwood ring, Fiala was the only one who was a dedicated Nazi.

A journalist by profession, Fiala was an early Nazi party member. Once, at the behest of Gestapo official Adolf Eichmann, he wrote a series of articles for the newspaper he edited—*Der Grinzbote* in Bratislava, Czechoslovakia—claiming that the Auschwitz concentration camp was humanely run. In Istanbul, Fiala was editor at Europapress-Transkontinent, a German propaganda news agency. A State Department report called Fiala "the Gestapo's man of confidence," so trusted by the SD that it made him one of the three men who took the gold from the German courier plane to pay its staff in Turkey.

Fiala's OSS employers argued that these credentials only enhanced his value as a spy, but using such an individual further undermined Dogwood's credibility as Fiala's game became increasingly clear to the OSS. The last straw was a "ridiculous, exaggerated" April report overestimating German forces in the Balkans. Schwarz was ordered to stop meeting Fiala, who was considered too clever for him.

After all these disasters, one battered OSS-Istanbul officer wrote a colleague in Cairo: "We are pretty well reduced to the white-flowering tree [Dogwood]. And events have imposed a pretty severe blight on that. Most of the blossoms fall to pieces in your hands before you can put them in water."

Macfarland defended Dogwood. "I am convinced that the major contacts established through this chain are extremely valuable ones," he wrote Washington. While Dogwood's information had, he agreed on June 10, "deteriorated considerably during the past 3–4 months . . . it has some valuable contacts which should be retained. Please bear in mind that, in the early stages, we used the Dogwood office as a [middleman] for many unrelated agents. . . . There seems to be a tendency . . . to make it appear that every Dogwood sub-source is known to the other" and thus German infiltrators could expose loyal OSS agents. "This is far from the truth although security has not been too good." He also pointed out that OSS headquarters had not fulfilled his requests for men knowledgeable about Germany, Hungary, and counterintelligence.

Macfarland's defense was partly accurate. Dogwood's Western Electric office was a clearinghouse for many agents, some of whom had provided good intelligence and important contacts with German, Austrian, and Hungarian anti-Nazi groups. And OSS-Istanbul's task had been inherently difficult. As a British intelligence report noted: "However reliable, well-briefed and trained, agents cannot be sufficiently aware of the general enemy situation in Europe accurately to assess all information which comes their way. They therefore naturally pass on a proportion of information, particularly that obtained at second-hand, which is distorted or false." Those who had been too willing to accept Dogwood's reports at the beginning quickly reversed their views when the network came under fire. An OSS-Istanbul intelligence analyst wrote years later, "Dogwood, fashionable at one time, became a villain at another."

Nevertheless, Dogwood was taken in too often. Any good work done by an enemy-penetrated ring only underwrites the credentials of those using it for deception. Agents like Laufer, Fiala, Hatz, Gyorgy, and Kovess made the network's balance sheet quite negative. The final report on Dogwood himself by OSS-Istanbul's regular analysts—always his severest critics—complained, "The man is a consummate egotist who apparently believes himself omniscient and . . . crafty, and it [seems] that through his vanity and desire for power he has . . . been made the tool of any number of German agents." Macfarland and Coleman had shown poor judgment in handling Hatz and Kovess. Other men paid with their lives for these mistakes.

Macfarland's direct superior, the chief of OSS-Cairo, wrote the commander of the OSS base in Bari, Italy, on July 25, "I have recommended to General Donovan that [Macfarland] be replaced by [Frank] Wisner and the staff be cut approximately in half." Everyone liked Macfarland, he continued, but "my own observations of the work he left behind him in Turkey have given me the strong opinion that he did considerable damage to OSS's work and reputation there." The other officer replied, "Your information about Macfarland sent cold chills up and down our backs . . . all of us have the highest respect and appreciation for Macfarland personally but do not under any consideration wish to have him attached to Bari in any capacity."

The OSS terminated the Dogwood network on July 31, 1944. Macfarland was removed from his position as OSS chief in Turkey on August 9 and assigned to evacuate downed Allied fliers from Yugoslavia. Coleman was sent home to resign. Schwarz was fired; he stayed in Istanbul, where he prospered in business before retiring to Switzerland.

Schwarz's aide, Arndt, had been told little by his boss and was judged blameless for everything that had gone wrong. He worked as an OSS radio broadcaster and then emigrated to the United States. There he became a respected scholar and produced a popular translation of a book quite relevant to life in Istanbul at a time when so many men sold their souls: Goethe's *Faust*.

13 | Rescue from Hell

The things that are happening to the poor people who live in this part
of the world make one wonder what God's intentions are.
—letter home from U.S. officer in Ankara, 1942

Throughout the war, horrible news drifted down to Istanbul from Poland
and the Balkans about the genocide that was an integral, high-priority
part of German strategy. Those who escaped tried desperately to reach
the city. Many people during the war came to Istanbul in rickety refugee
boats that sometimes fell apart or were sunk by submarines. Those more
fortunate rode the train from occupied Europe through Bulgaria or
even—for diplomats and businessmen or spies posing as either—on the
twice-weekly plane from Vienna via Sofia.

All was not well, however, even in that safe haven where economics
and xenophobia made local minority groups into scapegoats. Compared
with costs in 1939, prices in Turkey doubled in 1942, tripled by 1943,
and were five times higher in 1944. There were shortages of many
foods as well as cigarettes, matches, and beer. Bread rations were repeatedly cut. Store-bought loaves were dark and often soggy or gluelike
inside; the ingredients sometimes included ground straw or even saw-
dust. Better-quality black-market goods were expensive. Sugar cost
$1.35 and coffee $9 a pound. Hardships provoked bitter criticism of
the government.

There were several reasons for these problems. Faced with inflation and an uncertain future, peasants hoarded food. Military call-ups reduced the number of farm workers, and shipping was delayed or diverted. The poorly maintained road and rail systems were overwhelmed. U.S.-supplied trucks stood at dockside with their tires rotting. Expensive machinery rusted, shipping cases were crushed by poor packing, and bottlenecks delayed everything.

The government, however, adopted the simple expedient of blaming merchants as "profiteers" responsible for these difficulties. To punish them and to finance military preparedness, the government ordered a new tax in December 1942—the *Varlik Vergisi*—to raise $360 million ($265 million of it from Istanbul). The authorities organized commissions which consisted of Finance Ministry employees and Moslem businessmen, from which there was no appeal, to determine each individual's obligation. Those unable to pay—or whose property and household goods could not be sold for enough money—would be sentenced to hard labor. When the assessments were posted in tax offices and published in the press, they hit Istanbul like a bombshell. Due to prejudice and the opportunism of their Moslem competitors, virtually the entire burden was put on the non-Moslem minorities.

Moslem Turks traditionally preferred farming, the army, or government bureaucracy, leaving much of Istanbul's commerce in the hands of Greeks, Armenians, and Jews. Each of these groups retained its own religion and language and fearfully avoided politics. Istanbul's rich, distinctive culture was a blend of their traditions. Personal friendships often formed among members of the different communities. Still, many Turks were jealous of the minorities' wealth and suspicious of the Jews and Greeks as pro-Ally and of the Armenians as friendly to the Axis or Soviets.

The new tax paralyzed business as merchants spent all their time trying to arrange payment and often went bankrupt after the government froze their bank accounts and property to prevent them from concealing or selling assets. American and British residents—and not a few Turks—were disgusted by the discrimination against the Christians and Jews. "Many of my friends here have been all but crushed," wrote Burton Berry. "In some cases the tax demanded is considerably more than the total wealth of the tax payer." Poor clerks and shoemakers were ordered to pay as much as they made in a year.

An American doctor wrote his son in Philadelphia that all the victims' goods were confiscated to pay the tax. "And when I say all I mean all. They go into the homes and take their rugs, furniture, valuables of every sort. . . . In all my years here I have never been so discouraged. . . . I can't see how [anyone can] say that a doorkeeper who gets $32 a month and has to support a family on that can be profiteering. Yet those poor devils were assessed at $450 apiece." Nine policemen entered the home of a Greek woman and locked everything but her bed, dining room set, curtains, and lamps into one room to await collection. She saved her clothes only by paying baksheesh. Another woman, pleading to keep her gas range, was told she could cook with charcoal instead.

Businesses and furnishings were sold at auction to Moslems at ridiculously low prices. Store signs on Taksim Square and Istiklal Boulevard changed overnight. Walking through Istanbul, one came upon furniture being dragged from homes and loaded onto carts or trucks as the owners stood weeping.

Those who could not pay were imprisoned and then sentenced to work camps. The jails were packed with tax prisoners. In one group, noted an American visitor, "were two old men lying on the boards who were very ill, one with a bad heart and the other with a fever. It is doubtful if they ever reached their destinations alive." Among those deported were Greek fruit dealers, a Jewish hardware man whose shop measured only 6 feet by 4 feet but whose assessment was $32,000, and an Armenian insurance broker who collapsed physically after selling all his possessions and was taken to jail from a hospital bed. Istanbul's most prominent lawyers—fifteen Jews, nine Armenians, and eight Greeks— were taken away one freezing midnight in an open garbage truck for a trip of hundreds of miles. Thousands of people were thrown out of work as their employers were exiled or bankrupted.

Since tens of thousands of the minorities' young men were already drafted into road-building crews, most of the families were left with no means of support. The arrests continued into the summer. Finally, groups of prisoners were assembled in the jailyard and made to stand five hours in the hot sun without food or water. The gates facing the Bosporus opened, and the men filed through. Women and children, carrying blankets and baskets of food for relatives, sobbed and shouted.

The prisoners marched to the little boats that carried them across the Bosporus to the Haydarpasha railroad station. Three hours later, the train began its long trip east to the work camp.

After a day's journey without food or water, the tired men reached the last station at 6 p.m. Finding dry branches and twigs, they built fires by the tracks. Although carts and carriages waited, the guard captain ordered them to march 20 miles to the camp. The hot sun and dust added to their thirst as they passed through eastern Anatolia's bleak, treeless landscape. One man found a spring and the prisoners were allowed to drink. After climbing steep hills, they came into camp after sunset. "All the taxpayers lined up on the edge of the road for the evening roll call gave us a triumphal reception," wrote an Istanbul Jewish businessman in his diary, "but I soon saw that all of them were crying and it was up to us, exhausted and miserable as we were, to comfort the others."

A dozen men were forced to share leaky tents made to sleep only four. "You are all bad citizens and traitors," warned the camp commandant. "If anyone gives me the slightest trouble I will cut all your throats." About 1400 deportees, mostly middle-aged and unused to manual labor, were forced to build roads in the summer and clean snow off railroad tracks in the dead of winter.

Greek and Jewish groups in the United States complained, but the State Department would act only for victims who were U.S. citizens lest the Turks resent or Germans exploit any intervention. Hitler praised the Turkish policy. A group of disgusted Americans from the Istanbul consulate took matters into their own hands. They detailed and documented injustices for Sulzberger, the *New York Times* correspondent. Knowing that Turkish censorship would not let his stories out, Sulzberger showed the press-office director, Selim Sarper, that he had a Soviet visa in his passport. If Sarper blocked his articles, Sulzberger explained, he could file them from Moscow. "I doubt very much if the Russians would care whether I wrote the truth—or greatly magnify it —on this subject. In fact, they don't care very much for Turkey these days."

"Let's be reasonable," Sarper said. He promised to talk to the prime minister.

Sulzberger wrote a series of articles on the tax's effects. He avoided censorship for his tougher pieces by sending them out of the country with travelers. U.S. public opinion was outraged, and Steinhardt hinted that aid might be cut off. Worried about American pressure, Ankara canceled the remaining unpaid taxes in September 1943.

Three months later, the prisoners faced another rainy night as the south wind blew in great gusts. Tents shook so hard they snapped loudly like laundry drying on a line. The prisoners took turns using newspapers to cover holes in the canvas. Around 10 p.m., a man was heard yelling outside, "Nichan! Nichan! We're going to Istanbul!"

"What's bitten you? Do you want to play a joke like that on me?"

"A messenger just arrived and brought the news to Agopian."

"You're making fun of me," cried Nichan. But the man kept shouting, "Istanbul! Istanbul!"

One Jewish prisoner threw on his overcoat and went out into the rain. He crossed the camp, navigating by faint lights coming from the tents and stumbling in sticky mud that came up to his ankles. He finally found Agopian's tent, lit by two candles tied halfway up the center pole.

He went inside. "What's happened, comrades?" he asked.

"A messenger has brought us word from a radio broadcast. Parliament ratified a law allowing us to go home right away. A farmer heard the first evening broadcast. Everyone was skeptical, but the second program repeated it."

"Don't worry," another man told him. "We're going to Istanbul. I'll meet you next Sunday at the Park Hotel!"

Nobody slept that evening. In the morning, the rain stopped. A young prisoner, Frangi, who served as camp secretary, promised to call from the office outside the gate to confirm the story. If it was true, he would signal with his hat. A man was posted by the wall to watch.

Suddenly, the lookout cheered: "To Istanbul! To Istanbul! Frangi threw his hat into the air!" Everyone ran to see. Frangi waved his hat up and down, back and forth. Men embraced each other and even the guards, some of whom also began to cry. An indescribable din arose as prisoners struck empty cans against the tent poles.

"Assembly! Assembly!" shouted a guard. Usually it took a half hour for the men to line up and then only after being bullied by swearing guards. This time, within five minutes all the inmates stood along the road facing the commander's tent. The colonel's car drove up to the gate. Hundreds of men shouted greetings. The startled officer, used to threatening prisoners, was speechless for a moment. Then he pulled himself together.

"Comrades! You've heard the news. In its magnanimity the government has given the order to free you. You are no longer prisoners!" Even he choked up. "From now on you are free citizens. You will now return to your homes. Be good citizens. Love this country. And may God continue to keep war away from us!"

But the suffering of Istanbul's minorities was nothing compared to events in lands plagued by war and the Germans. The tax deportees in Turkey went to labor camps. Some kind of similar treatment—confinement, forced labor, and only mild mistreatment—was what Jews in Poland, Czechoslovakia, Romania, and Greece expected at first. But in contrast to the situation in Turkey, there was no happy ending in those other countries.

News of the Nazi concentration and death camps leaked out from a variety of sources. One of the first reports was made by an escapee from Auschwitz—he had hidden under a pile of murdered prisoners' shoes taken out for sale—who made a long, perilous journey through the Balkans in early 1943. Arriving in Istanbul, he told his story to the Zionist delegates there from Palestine and to U.S. diplomats. The small, red-haired man explained that the German deportations of Jews were a prelude to mass murder. Asked about his family, he burst into tears: they were all dead.

Even before direct communication of this dreadful news, David Ben-Gurion and the Jewish community in Palestine had begun to act. In 1941 they sent a team to Istanbul to investigate conditions in occupied Europe and to rescue as many people as possible. But most of these efforts were dependent on the support of the same British government whose anti-Semitic elements and appeasement of the Arabs so limited immigration to Palestine. Hundreds of thousands of Jews died because London's stance barred their escape from occupied countries and their safe transport to Palestine or elsewhere.

The British government's behavior was shameful. Early in the war, it encouraged Balkan states to block Jewish emigration and pressured the Greek, Panamanian, and Turkish governments to prohibit ships sailing under their flags from carrying Jewish refugees. A Foreign Office bureaucrat wrote, "The only hope is that all the German Jews will be stuck at the mouths of the Danube for lack of ships to take them." When one refugee ship, the *Struma*, sank with the loss of 769 people because no country would accept them, British Colonial Secretary Oliver Stanley told Parliament that his government could not "be party to any measures which could undermine the existing policy regarding illegal immigration into Palestine in view of the wider issues involved." The British even tried to prove that the Germans were behind the escape efforts. "It is a pity that we cannot find an authentic Nazi at the bottom of it," wrote the British ambassador to Greece, since that would provide a useful excuse for turning back refugees. During the war's first three years—when hundreds of thousands of Jews tried to escape from Germany, Austria, Czechoslovakia, and Poland, and the Nazis were willing to let them go—the British allowed only 10,000 into Palestine. The Zionist movement smuggled in another 9000.

When the ill-fated *Struma* arrived in Istanbul in late 1941, the Turks would not let its passengers land unless Britain guaranteed that they could proceed to Palestine. Otherwise, they would be sent back to Romania. Following London's instructions, Knatchbull-Hugessen said they were not wanted in Palestine, but he added on his own that instead of returning the ship to German-controlled territory, "let her rather go toward [the Mediterranean]. It might be that if [the refugees] reached Palestine, they might despite their illegality receive humane treatment." The ambassador's decent words outraged some of his superiors. A Colonial Office official in London wrote that the Turks were discouraging the refugee ships "and then the Ambassador goes and spoils the whole effect on absurdly misjudged humanitarian grounds." Another bemoaned the waste of "a heaven-sent opportunity" to return the refugees to Romania. Colonial Secretary Lord Moyne complained that if these people escaped it would have the "deplorable effect [of] encouraging further Jews to embark." While Prime Minister Winston Churchill was more willing to save refugees' lives, he often did not act to control what he himself characterized as "the usual anti-Zionist and anti-Semitic channel which it is customary for British [official] to follow." As late as June 1944 a senior Foreign Office official warned against "letting the Germans flood the Middle East with Jews in order to embarrass us. There is fortunately not much sign of it yet."

But Zionist leaders like Ben-Gurion and Chaim Weizmann knew they had to fight alongside Britain as this offered the only chance of defeating Hitler. Thousands of Zionists volunteered for service with the British forces, while Arab leaders were secretly or openly allying with the Nazis. In exchange for this help, the Zionists wanted British aid in rescuing Jews from Europe. Their advanced post was the Istanbul "delegation" led by Jewish Agency representative Chaim Barlas. His younger colleagues, known collectively as "the boys," had the mission of circumventing officialdom.

The murderous regulations blocking the escape of refugees were hard to cope with through either proper channels or circumlocution. States would not let Jews leave or pass through unless they had exit permits, transit visas, and guaranteed destinations. The Turks permitted few refugees to enter their country and none to remain. The prerequisite for admission was an entrance certificate for Palestine, which the strict British quota on Jewish immigration made difficult to obtain and slow to come. Thus, along with the official Aliya (immigration) movement, the delegation set up "Aliya Bet," a parallel structure for "illegal" immigration.

Beginning in late 1942, about twenty young Jews, including Yehuda Pomerantz, Menahem Bader, Akiva Levinsky, Teddy Kollek, and Ehud Avriel, came from Palestine to Turkey for rescue, immigration, and intelligence work. Istanbul's location and neutrality made it the ideal advanced base for reaching into occupied Europe. Istanbul, Kollek said, provided "a narrow crack in an otherwise impenetrable wall."

Except for Barlas, all these men lacked official standing and thus were vulnerable to harassment or expulsion by the Emniyet. As cover, Pomerantz was nominally a timber buyer, Kollek a hazelnut merchant, and Avriel a journalist. Of course, Emniyet officials knew exactly what was going on; and after the war they showed Levinsky two thick books of reports and photographs about his activities. But the delegation was protected by its alliance with British intelligence. Major Arthur Whittall, another member of that ubiquitous Anglo-Istanbul family, served as the British liaison man. Flashing a whimsical smile, he explained: "We shall help you get the sources. Do your best to get us their information."

If an "illegal" refugee ship arrived, the delegation's Greek agent would come to the man in charge of receiving the passengers and announce: "Police says arms on board. Had to stop and search." The proper response was "How much?" Using an expression in Ladino, the Hebrew-Spanish language of Turkish Jews, the agent would reply, *"Todos comen,"* meaning "Everybody eats." The Turkish official would then specify the size of his grocery bill and, in exchange, would look the other way as the refugees disembarked.

Members of the delegation also met refugees arriving on the trains from Bulgaria. The agents made valuable contacts on the station platform while waiting alongside police and customs officials. Often one of the terrified escapees would hide and make his own way to the delegation's office. But everyone had to have an entry stamp to get an exit permit. In such cases, Simon Brod was called upon to make arrangements through the magic of *"Todos comen."* Brod was a Turkish Jewish merchant who had been impoverished by the tax but who refused to be paid for his services. He would list his expenses on cigarette packs which he would then throw away while chain-smoking through the day.

Brod was a little man with a chubby, rosy face crowned with silver hair. Avriel describes his eyes as being "like the heads of steel-blue pins that darted around to take in every new situation; they could be angelic one moment and scornful the next." Always the first to find out what was going on and the last to give up, he was particularly adept at smoothing relations between the delegation and the Turkish authorities.

Levinsky recounts a typical example of harassment. He lived with a Jewish family who had to sleep on the floor, since all their beds had been confiscated. They were all asleep with the lights off, late one night, when the front doorbell rang. Two policemen stood outside. "There is light," they said. A blackout violation was a misdemeanor; three meant deportation. Levinsky called Brod, and the next day someone appeared at the family's door to accept the policemen's "tip." No offense appeared on the records.

At first, the delegation worked out of Istanbul's Continental Hotel, but there were too many prying eyes around. It soon moved into three centers: a five-room apartment called "the Palestine Office," Barlas's headquarters, and a center for unaccompanied child refugees. The Jews from Palestine and local volunteers—speaking fourteen languages among them—worked from 8 a.m. to 8 p.m. There was a huge amount of paperwork, and the corridors were always full of people. Everyone awaited travel documents or news of relatives; each day's mail call was taken for what it was: a matter of life or death.

Some of the delegation's activities centered on Turkish Jews. After the tax oppression, many of the younger people wanted to leave the country. Levinsky taught Hebrew to small classes that produced teachers for groups eventually totaling 800 students, and he gave lectures preparing those who were leaving for Palestine.

The situation in Europe, Barlas wrote Jerusalem, was truly devastating. "If I use the word 'desperate' it is not enough to express the cruelty and the torture and above all the risk of being shot as a dog to which are exposed all our poor brethren in Romania" and the other occupied countries. Nothing in history had ever equaled "the killing of Jews by ten thousands and their transportation without food and water, their exile in this part of the year without permitting them to take with them their own winter garments." Those Jews still in Bucharest were fired from their jobs, dispossessed of their businesses, and placed under humiliating restrictions. "The cries [of] S.O.S. for immediate help [are] pouring from Romania and it is heartbreaking to know that you are not able to help."

Beginning in September 1942, the Zionist delegation in Turkey launched its rescue effort by sending thousands of letters through the post and by courier into Poland, Bulgaria, Romania, and Czechoslovakia to establish contacts with the Jews there. To show these people that they were not forgotten, Kollek later commented, was almost as important as the actual work of rescue. Prewar mailing lists of Zionist and other Jewish organizations and publications were scoured for names and addresses. Letters requesting information were phrased so that, to the censor, they would seem to have been written by the recipients' relatives. Thousands of responses told heartbreaking stories of roundups and deportations to concentration camps from which no one ever returned. Using simple codes so that their letters would pass censorship, the respondents begged for food parcels and passports. Hebrew words were transliterated into the Roman alphabet to disguise their news—"escape," for example, was indicated by "*tiyul*," meaning "a trip." If fifty people in a city were said to have attended a wedding or party of some long-dead Zionist leader or Jewish cultural figure, it meant that 50,000 had been murdered there.

After contacts were made, attempts to send aid followed. Couriers smuggled funds in the form of diamonds, gold coins, or local currency into the occupied lands to sustain the impoverished Jews. Some Turkish and Latin American diplomats helped, though only for a large fee. The Polish underground's couriers and the parcels sent home by Polish engineers working in Turkey were used to reach Poland. Contact with Greece was done through the British caïque shuttles.

All the information obtained was shared with the British. The Zionists also provided them with a number of other services. For example, Kollek rang up Bucharest on the telephone every other day to get the weather report as guidance for Allied planes. He also obtained information on bombing damage and the names of captured fliers.

Because of the urgency and difficulty of reaching Hungary, the delegation had to use experienced smugglers and known double agents as couriers. These included Gyorgy, who claimed his own involvement might "whitewash part of my soul." In fact, he gave information to the Germans, but at least he also delivered the mail, money, and immigration documents which otherwise would not have gone through.

In the Zionist efforts to rescue Jews, the Germans were often not the greatest obstacle. Refugees could obtain exit permits from their own country only after they received visas from each state they had to cross. These states, in turn, required evidence that Turkey would admit them. But the Turks would not give an applicant an entrance visa unless there was proof that the British would allow the person into Palestine. All this paperwork had to be pried from unsympathetic governments and slow-moving bureaucracies, transmitted through poor wartime communications, handled on minimal funds, and delivered to people who may have been deported or driven into hiding. To secure British cooperation, moreover, the Zionists had to persuade London that the refugees would be a prime intelligence source.

The delegation was willing to try any route that offered hope for escape. When Afghanistan's ambassador to Turkey commented in 1942 about his country's difficulties in recruiting technicians, doctors, and engineers, Barlas immediately proposed that Afghanistan hire Balkan Jews for these positions. Even the ambassador was unable to get the necessary transit visas.

Neutral ships could not be found to carry refugees, so the delegation tried to find its own boats. It convinced the United States and Britain to explore whether Romania would lease two large passenger liners sitting idle in Istanbul's harbor since the war began. Bucharest refused, fearful that the ships might be lost. The Red Cross said it had no money to buy them.

Once refugees arrived in Turkey, they had to be housed and fed for weeks or months before they were put on the *Taurus Express* to Syria and thence to Palestine. Brod worked selflessly and endlessly to find them places to stay, clothing, food, and toys for the children. It was also hard to find funds, since the British forbade sending money from Palestine and the Turks closely controlled all currency transactions. The delegation was financed by smuggling diamonds into Istanbul in toothpaste tubes, shaving cream bottles, and hollowed bars of soap. Secret reports were sent home by similar methods. One secretary's moral reputation was damaged because she constantly bought condoms to keep dry the papers sent in this manner. An elderly black-suited Greek man, who looked more like a country parson than Istanbul's black-market financial wizard, was hired to turn diamonds into cash and foreign currency into Turkish pounds.

Every tiny gain was a victory. After months of pleading and pressure from the delegation, the British persuaded the Turks to grant transit visas to nine families a week beginning in April 1943. This step allowed about 1350 people to get out of Hungary, Bulgaria, and Romania between April and December. Another 312 escaped from Greece on British caïques. About 2100 people already in Turkey, including Turkish Jews, were sent on to Palestine. These estimates undercounted those rescued by "illegal" methods. Still, as Barlas commented, "The results of the immigration in numbers are in no comparison with the tragic situation of Jewry in the enemy-occupied countries, but taking into consideration the almost unsurmountable difficulties, I may say that it is a miracle that even this small number has escaped from the hell."

Roncalli was one of the Jews' sincerest allies, although he, too, made compromises. When New York's Cardinal Spellman visited Roncalli's house in 1943, he was shocked by something he saw in its courtyard. Spellman shouted, "Hey Giuseppe, what are you doing with a bust of Mussolini out here? This is terrible."

"Oh," answered Roncalli, "what we think in our heart and say with our mouth are not necessarily the same thing."

In January 1943, Barlas asked Roncalli to relay three simple requests to the Vatican. Would the Pope ask neutral states to grant temporary asylum to Jews who managed to escape? American Jewish organizations would pay for their relief. Would the Vatican inform Berlin that the British have provided 5000 Palestine immigration certificates for use if Germany would free some Jews? And might Vatican Radio declare plainly that "rendering help to persecuted Jews is considered by the Church to be a good deed?" The answer soon came from the Vatican secretary of state, Cardinal Maglione: the Vatican would do none of these things, as Jewish presence in Palestine might interfere with the Holy Places. At that time, Maglione was receiving reports from Vatican emissaries that only 100,000 of 4 million Polish Jews were still at liberty and that "it is said that hundreds of people are sometimes locked up in trucks where they die under the effects of gas."

Roncalli forwarded messages to the Vatican; sent personal appeals to colleagues in occupied countries; and asked his old friend, Bulgaria's King Boris, to let Jews emigrate. There were some—usually temporary—successes. Rabbi Isaac Hertzog, chief rabbi of Palestine, wrote Barlas in December 1943: "All Italian Jews [are] in extreme danger [and] about to be sent to concentration camps. Please contact His Eminence the Papal Nuncio in Turkey [in] view [of] his cabling urgent petition to his Holiness the Pope [to] use [his] influence [to] save our brethren." Roncalli did as requested, and the deportations of Italian Jews stopped for a while. A similar appeal had some effect in Slovakia. More often, however, the Vatican did nothing, local prelates failed to act or were openly pro-Nazi, or satellite regimes and German authorities ignored the pleas.

Even those motivated by greed had to be flattered as well as paid before they would help. Barlas wrote the venal Turkish ambassador to Romania in September 1943: "I know that it is thanks to your benevolence that many [Romanian Jews] have been saved. . . . Allow me, Excellency, to express to you, in the name of the Jewish Agency, our profound gratitude for this aid. I take this occasion to call your attention to the frightful situation of the Jewish population [of 150,000] deported. . . . It would be an act of humanity on your part to use your influence with the members of the Romanian government on behalf of these unfortunates, so that they might be authorized to return to their homes. A certain number of Jewish children . . . have received authorization to enter Palestine. . . . It would be highly desirable that the Romanian government implements the promises it made toward facilitating their emigration."

There was barely time to mourn one tragedy while trying to avoid new ones. In September 1943, Barlas wrote Sokolnicki, Poland's ambassador to Turkey, that he had finally obtained transit visas for 380 Polish Jews. "I must communicate that unhappily these immigrants cannot use these transit rights because of recent acts of terror and massacres in Poland in which the majority of the Jewish population located there has perished." There were, however, 542 refugees from Poland who had come through the U.S.S.R. and were now stranded in Tehran because they could not get transit visas to cross Iraq on the way to Palestine. The British embassy in Tehran had already confirmed their Palestine immigration certificates. Would the ambassador ask if they could instead come through Turkey? This effort succeeded.

Such bright spots were rare. Pomerantz's roommate returned to their apartment one day to find everything in disorder and Pomerantz himself collapsed on a bed, exhausted from crying. Nearby lay a letter from Poland that Pomerantz had dropped on the floor. Avriel picked it up and read the note just delivered by a courier. It was dated July 17, 1943, and began with a long list of extinguished communities and death camps. "In . . . Warsaw, Lublin, Czenstochau and Cracow," it continued, "there are no Jews left. They were gassed mostly in Treblinka. This is a notorious camp, where not only Jews from Poland but also from Belgium, Holland, and other Western countries have died.

"The most beautiful chapter in our struggle was the uprising in Warsaw. . . . There were terrible battles in the ghetto. To our sorrow only about 800 of the enemy fell. The result: all the Jews and the ghetto utterly annihilated.

"There seem to be no more Jews in the [land] once called Poland, except for about 30,000 in three forced-labor camps. In a few weeks they, too, will be gone." The same conditions prevailed throughout the Ukraine.

"In the near future the district from which we write to you will also be 'Judenrein.' When you receive this letter, none of us will be alive. . . . Our hope to reach Palestine will unfortunately never be realized. . . . We greet you warmly. Aranka, Hershl, Zvi, Koziak, Shlomo."

Again and again, the delegation's efforts were foiled not so much by the Nazis themselves but by other regimes' bureaucratic timidity or criminality. This frustration was expressed in a November 1943 letter by one of its members, Kalman Rosenblatt, who sought "to rouse, perhaps at the last moment, the conscience of the free world and to induce them to act. . . . Above all my lines are addressed to [the British] government. . . . All evidence coming from beyond the Nazi wall is proving that the foe has decided to pay the cost of his retreat and defeat with Jewish blood. In Berlin a new attack is being prepared against those few countries where Jews have still remained. . . . On the eve of those developments we are obliged to save the maximum of our brethren— the last European Jews. It is at the moment permitted to leave Hungary and Romania, and Bulgaria does allow the transit through her territory. . . . The key rests with Great Britain. It is in her power to increase the number of transit visas through Turkey a hundred-fold."

If the British would immediately make available several years' quota of Palestine immigration certificates, Rosenblatt continued, "there would be a possibility to rescue now tens of thousands of Jews who are in a terrible impending danger." If the British gave certificates, the Turks would provide transit visas. There was no time left for London's bureaucratic delays. Lives were being lost every day. Since the British claimed that some refugees might be German spies, they could organize "detention camps" in Palestine "to examine the people more thoroughly." It would be easy to move 30,000 people. "Even youths of military age are able to leave Hungary and Romania . . . two of them arrived here today from Hungary. But our heart is full of pain—for hundreds of thousands will be left behind. . . . Why should Great Britain and U.S.A. not hear our cry of agony—now at the last moment."

By refusing to admit refugees, the Allied countries "did not save from death the Jews of Holland and Belgium, France and now, Italy, Denmark and Poland." The refugees could be sent to Mauritius, Cyprus, or anywhere they would be safe. "All symptoms are showing that [the Germans] want to make an end to all Jews in Hungary, Romania and Bulgaria. . . . After the complete destruction of Polish Jewry (woe to myself and woe to all of us—that I simply put down on a sheet of paper this sentence and my hand does not wither away)—perhaps we shall still awake, for all that, the conscience of the world and shall rescue those who remain." These and other pleas had little effect on the Allied governments.

American diplomats were constantly faced with individual appeals as well. In the summer of 1943, a Jewish couple came to the U.S. consulate in Istanbul. "Could you give us a visa? We aren't interested in going to the United States," they explained, "but we must get out of Turkey." A stuffy young official who shared the office passed his colleague a note: "You can't give a visa to these people. They could become a public charge." Ignoring the advice, the consul provided a temporary visitors' visa. "We will never forget that you saved our lives," they wrote their benefactor from safety. Years later, he reminisced, "This is the kind of thing that makes one's life worth living." Many State Department officials were less helpful at a time when each visa saved a family's life. Strict U.S. immigration limits were not even temporarily bent to admit refugees.

The British were reluctant to help in rescue efforts even when they were combined with intelligence missions. The Zionists begged to be allowed to send saboteurs behind Nazi lines. "We ascertained," went one such request, "that there are still in Bulgaria, Romania, Hungary organized Zionist cells which would be able and willing to receive and give shelter to 'envoys' sent by us" to gather intelligence, organize resistance, rescue downed Allied fliers, and operate radios. But Britain rejected this plea, and the first such agents only reached Hungary in June 1944.

Meanwhile, the delegation found the ideal front man for its own shipping line. He was Yanaki Pandelis, nicknamed "the fat one," a charming Greek Oxford graduate, promoter, and confidence man living in Bucharest. His junior partner, an Italian ex-naval officer, looked like Peter Lorre and was known to the illegal immigration agents as "the gnome." They combined efficiency and reliability with the deviousness needed to get the job done.

The plan to create a Zionist rescue fleet was given a boost in August 1943 when Whittall met with Simon Brod and with delegation members Avriel and Dani Shind to read them a message from London. The dozens of pleas and pressures had at last brought results: the British government had finally decided that any Jews reaching Turkey would be admitted to Palestine. The catch, however, was that this policy must remain a secret. Ignorant of this development, the Turkish government was still reluctant to admit refugees. Avriel thought the decision just "half a message of redemption."

Pandelis bought a Bucharest travel agency, whose business had understandably declined, and moved in Zionist youth group members to organize passengers for the *Maritza* and another ship, the *Milka*. Local officials were bribed to accept the idea that these people were "tourists" taking excursions to neutral Istanbul. Pandelis telephoned Istanbul to announce the *Milka*'s departure. The delegation's members nervously followed the ship's progress on a large map, constantly worrying about an attack by German ships or submarines. Each time the phone rang, everyone froze. Barlas rushed to Ankara to ask the Turks to admit the refugees. The foreign minister relented only when the British embassy committed itself to allow the 240 passengers into Palestine.

When the ship arrived in Istanbul, Avriel, Brod, and Whittall met it at its mooring. A police officer let Whittall stamp the passenger list with an official seal transforming it magically into a collective visa. Then, whistle blowing joyously, the *Milka* headed down the Bosporus to the Haydarpasha railroad station's dock, which was only a short distance from the train waiting to take the refugees to Palestine.

Whittall smiled. His work with the Jews had made him sympathetic to their plight. These people would not be his intelligence sources, he said, "but never mind, it was a privilege to have set the seal to their deliverance." Brod ordered breakfast. Raising a glass of red wine, he proposed a toast: "To the safe arrival of all the boats to come!" Everyone—Haganah members, British intelligence men, and Turkish policemen—joined in. Then, Avriel, Brod, and Whittall raced to the railroad station to watch their wards board five special passenger cars carrying the miraculous sign "Reserved for passengers to Palestine."

Most of these refugees were women or elderly people, each carrying the one suitcase permitted. "We are saved! We are saved!" one told an OSS man. "We don't know how to thank you enough. We are now praying for all the Jews who have remained there. They are running the greatest dangers. Nobody can realize the atrocities we have suffered."

"When did you leave Hungary?"

"About a month ago. Friends who had come from Budapest told us that the number of German soldiers was rapidly increasing. The behavior of the pro-German Hungarians was becoming more and more intolerable. I had already taken the decision to leave, so my papers were ready. One cannot say they were all in order, but I managed to get through."

"What do they think about the Germans in Hungary?"

"Everyone is sure the German army will be unable to hold out. But . . . the Germans are sure that they will manage to make a compromise peace with the Anglo-Saxons against the Soviets. The Hungarian people also believe this and it incites them to continue to fight against the Russians." The Germans harassed the refugees until the last moment, when they reached the Turkish frontier. "I heard a German soldier say: 'You think you are making your escape, but we will catch you nonetheless.' "

Tragically, the remaining British and Turkish barriers and U.S. passivity were not overcome until after the Germans occupied Hungary. Only on May 19, 1944, did London at last allow Barlas a free hand in granting visas. Each of them was like a lifesaver tossed onto the sea. "I have the honor to approach you on behalf of _____," read these forms, "who has been granted permission for entry into Palestine. . . . I shall be very grateful if you will be so kind as to inform the British Embassy." One ship brought 150 Jews, including 120 orphans, from Bucharest to Istanbul. The *Milka* arrived in Turkish waters with 272 more people, mostly escapees, who were sent on to Palestine.

A concerted campaign of threats against Germany's allies was also tardy. The U.S. War Refugee Board's representative in Istanbul, Ira Hirschmann, cabled Washington in February 1944: "Hungary, Romania, and Bulgaria are most anxious to whitewash themselves in the eyes of the Allies. . . . We must exploit this anxiety at once." He warned those countries' envoys to Turkey that their leaders would be held responsible as war criminals unless they ended persecution of the Jews. But by this time, their regimes were reduced to total dependence on Berlin. Hirschmann's own trip to Istanbul had been delayed by the anti-Semitic State Department official Breckinridge Long.

Similarly, Ankara stalled on permitting privately owned Turkish ships to carry refugees from Romania or Bulgaria to Istanbul. They complained that no boats could be spared or put in danger of being sunk. Ships might be chartered only if the Germans guaranteed their safe passage, which, of course, Berlin refused. When the United States promised to replace any boats lost, the Turks objected in June 1944 that they might be held responsible if refugees died in transit. Steinhardt replied that the Jews' situation was so desperate they would prefer "to run the risk of attempting a passage without safe conduct rather than to be left to the tender mercies of the Nazis."

British opposition to the Zionists' long-standing plea to parachute Jewish agents into Hungary to organize resistance and guide people to safety ended only in March 1944, when a trio was dropped near the Yugoslav-Hungarian border. While the Zionists were preparing to cross, they heard the news about the German invasion of Hungary. One of the parachutists, 22-year-old Hannah Senesh, burst into tears. "We are too late," she sobbed, "we are too late." She was right. Nevertheless, she still continued her mission. Crossing into Hungary, she was captured by the Germans; she gave her life in trying to save Hungarian Jews.

The Horthy regime in Hungary had, for three years, resisted Berlin's demand to send Jews to the death camps. When the Germans took over in 1944, they quickly remedied this delay. Between April and July, 400,000 Jews from provincial towns were sent to extermination camps in Poland. Trains streamed toward Auschwitz unchecked, since the Allied air forces would not bomb the tracks. It was too low a priority, the U.S. War Department said, though planes were available for such a mission. About 300,000 people were murdered within the first seven weeks. New pits had to be dug in which to burn the bodies.

The lack of transport to Istanbul, reported the Red Cross, and the impossibility of getting exit visas from Hungary were "virtually insurmountable" barriers to rescue. In July the Germans began to deport the remnants of Budapest's 350,000 Jews, both Hungarians and refugees from other countries. Frantic messages came from the Jews in Budapest: "The only rescue possibility is: 1) to give warning about reprisals against Germans interned in allied countries, 2) to grant foreign citizenship to Hungarian Jews." The U.S. embassy in Turkey suggested the massive distribution of visas, since "holders of such documents may enjoy immunity from deportation or may actually succeed in leaving Hungary thereby." The collaborationist Romanian leaders, knowing their country would soon be in Allied hands, let Jewish refugees cross from Hungary and organize an underground railroad. But the Jews saved numbered in the hundreds, while those killed were in the hundreds of thousands. By August, there were few Jews left in Hungary.

Denied the use of neutral boats, the delegation had to charter dangerously dilapidated Romanian and Bulgarian vessels that might be confiscated by the Axis. In May, the *Maritza* foundered while sailing empty back to Romania; the *Milka* was detained by the German authorities in Bulgaria.

New ships had to be found to replace them as the Nazi extermination campaign reached top speed. Pandelis's assistant came to Istanbul and advertised himself as a shipping magnate interested in hiring boats at generous rates. Flooded with offers, he chose one Greek and four Turkish ships. Between January and August 1944, 2672 refugees were brought by sea and 408 by land to Istanbul. Some of those taken by train through Hungary and Romania passed cars that carried other Jews to concentration camps.

Tragedy still spoiled minor triumphs. A Soviet patrol boat sank one of Pandelis's ships just 40 miles north of Istanbul. The captain and crew immediately took the lifeboat; all but five of the passengers, including ninety-six children, drowned.

Nevertheless, the pace of rescue accelerated. During a three-week period near year's end, 1200 Romanian and Bulgarian refugees were granted visas and moved across Turkey by railroad. Eight hundred more were saved from Greece in the summer of 1944. A Jewish official meeting a group in Haifa reported: "All the people lack weight and strength. Signs of great suffering in the past are visible on their faces. . . . [Many needed] hospital treatment. All suffer from undernourishment."

If the Romanian, Bulgarian, Hungarian, British, and Turkish governments had acted differently in 1942 or 1943, over a million Jews might have been saved. It is estimated that the Haganah saved 55,000 Jews during the war, most of them directly through Istanbul. Hundreds of thousands of others, particularly in Bulgaria and Romania, survived thanks to the Zionist movement's aid and demands for Allied and Vatican pressure on the Balkan regimes. But at best this figure equaled only one-twentieth of the number of those who perished in Europe.

The Bulgarians did not permit the deportation of their "own" Jews to death camps—though they were expropriated and sent to slave labor camps—but had no such compunctions toward allowing the murder of over 11,000 Jews in Bulgarian-occupied Yugoslavia and Greece. While King Boris and other Bulgarian leaders protested against the killing of Bulgarian Jews, they also acceded to German demands to prevent Jews' emigration or free passage for Jews to safe haven in Turkey. In Romania, where local anti-Semitism was more powerful, 380,000 of 765,000 Jews were murdered. In Hungary, about 560,000 of 750,000 died. There were more victims in Slovakia, Greece, and Yugoslavia. All these countries were accessible to Istanbul even in 1944, and most of their Jews could have escaped if not for the obstruction of a half-dozen governments. Despite the efforts of Roncalli and some others, the Vatican had done little. In some areas, particularly Slovakia and Croatia, Catholic prelates supported the genocide; in other places, most notably Hungary, the church was mainly interested in helping converts. Even in Roncalli's own Istanbul parishes, two Italian Catholic priests organized Fascist meetings.

Dani Shind, one of the delegation's key organizers of rescue efforts, explained the lesson learned in Istanbul. Referring to the happy day when the *Milka* came into port, he wrote: "Our feelings were mixed: we were overjoyed by the arrival of the ship, yet fearful of what lay ahead and thoroughly disgusted with our 'well-wishers' who had left the remnant of our people to fend for themselves. We shall never forget the proud entry of the ship filled with Jews saved by the efforts of Jews after our 'sympathizers' had announced that all possible steps had been taken to advance the rescue effort. Let the *Milka* bear witness to the sin of neglect on the part of the enlightened world. We have often met with setbacks, but our work has not been in vain after all."

The Holocaust was created by the German Nazis, but it was implemented with collaboration by some states and passive acquiescence by others. These events were clear from Istanbul, as was the lesson that Jews had to act on their own through their own nationalist movement—and eventually their own state.

But Istanbul was also the scene for another drama: the downfall of German intelligence.

14 | Germany's Defective Intelligence

> An Istanbul man trained his cat so well it carried a candy tray to guests. A friend, tired of his boasts, brought a mouse in his pocket. The cat entered with the tray; the guest put the mouse on the floor. The cat dropped the tray and chased the mouse. "Ah, well," the Turkish gentleman told his abashed host, "a cat is always a cat."
> —anecdote recounted by Burton Berry, 1943

The inevitability of Berlin's defeat and a distaste for Hitler's regime led six German intelligence operatives to defect from Istanbul in early 1944. The results were explosive: the Abwehr's destruction and the ruin of Germany's most productive spy.

Paul Leverkuehn, head of Abwehr-Istanbul, had helped von Moltke and the anti-Hitler underground while conscientiously performing his own espionage work. Like many other Germans, Leverkuehn's sense of duty to the fatherland was powerful enough to overcome his distaste for the dictatorial, criminal Nazi regime that ruled it.

It was a paradoxical situation for those who simultaneously risked their lives to oppose Hitler while refusing to shirk professional responsibilities. After an all-night discussion with two of his subordinates about ways to overthrow the regime, Leverkuehn told them, "You have my support, but I cannot do anything to break my officer's oath." In that case, one of them pointed out, the oath required "that you take your pistol and shoot us as traitors."

Leverkuehn was an able intelligence officer. His men analyzed Turkish forces on the Bulgarian border, tried to pry secrets from Allied personnel, and closely monitored Turkey's intentions toward the war.

The Abwehr's minions, wrote the OSS's Cedric Seager, "have as many aliases as a rainbow has colors. . . . The city is riddled with their agents; one's movements are frequently watched and occasionally followed."

The Abwehr used a variety of techniques. A female Nazi agent seduced a Swiss diplomat; the Turks expelled both on discovering the man had become a spy for the Germans. An Abwehr officer elicited information from a Greek diplomat by keeping him supplied with liquor. Hildegard Reilly, the German wife of a former English official, worked at the Taksim Casino's bar, where she specialized in making Britons and Americans more talkative. An OSS investigation discovered that a Hungarian bar hostess, expelled by the Turks as a German agent, had successive affairs with a half-dozen Americans. Elli's Bar was financed by the Abwehr as both a rendezvous for Axis agents and a place whose Allied patrons could be systematically plied for data.

One of Leverkuehn's agents with a particularly colorful background was a Russian-born Spanish diplomat whose career had begun as a czarist officer. He took refuge in Istanbul after the Bolshevik revolution and worked as a croupier in open and clandestine gambling houses. Expelled from the country in 1933, he moved to Yugoslavia and then France to become a spy in several governments' service until the French police threw him out in 1936. As a virulent anti-Communist, he fought for the victorious Fascist side in the Spanish civil war. Taking Spanish citizenship, the man joined Madrid's diplomatic corps and became press attaché to Paris until the police dug out the old dossier and demanded his recall. After being transferred to Istanbul, he ran a ring of Russian émigré agents for the Abwehr.

Leverkuehn's Abwehr also tried to foment subversion in the Middle East, despite its earlier failures there, and in the Soviet Union. One of its most ambitious plans was to build an underground revolutionary and espionage group in Iraq called the National Liberation Column. The movement began with remnants from the pro-German revolt which the British had put down in 1941. Its leader was a Baghdad doctor whose henchmen—including high-ranking government officials—met in a pharmacy next to the physician's office to exchange information as they waited for "prescriptions." A full-time liaison man was sent to Istanbul to make contact with the Germans and obtain aid from the Abwehr.

British intelligence quickly realized that the Germans were up to something in Iraq and put the Arab group under surveillance for over eight months to uncover its plans. In fact, the Iraqis were so amateurish—losing one German-supplied wireless radio and being unable to operate its replacement—that the British wondered if the whole affair was a diversion. They were forced to take the plot more seriously, however, after capturing three German agents parachuted into Iraq in July 1943. Leverkuehn planned to send reinforcements to start a revolt among the Kurdish tribes.

The British were determined to infiltrate the Abwehr's network through an Iraqi undercover agent, code-named "Zulu," who arrived in Istanbul on August 3. He went to a café on Istiklal Boulevard, gave a secret password, and was taken to the house of the movement's Istanbul representative. Zulu was shocked to realize that he had once met this man in Baghdad in the course of his police work. Fortunately, the revolutionary did not recognize him. When Zulu again gave the secret password, the blasé agent replied, "Such formalities are unnecessary."

Thus cleared, Zulu was accepted by the Abwehr too. Posing as a delegate from the Baghdad underground, Zulu requested supplies from the Abwehr. The Germans demanded intelligence in exchange and brought models of British military vehicles to teach him how to interpret their unit markings.

On the night of September 3, a Mercedes car picked up Zulu for a talk with Leverkuehn himself. The two men drove to an isolated spot and sat in darkness. The future of the Arab cause, Leverkuehn told him, depended on German victory, which, in turn, required intelligence about British oil refineries and forces in Iraq. Unaware that his three agents had been captured, Leverkuehn asked about them. Zulu replied they were doing well. Leverkuehn gave him $2000 for expenses and an English book with a radio code skillfully sewn into its back cover.

At this moment, British intelligence heard that the Iraqi movement's treasurer was coming to Istanbul. Worried that he might uncover Zulu's true identity, the British arrested the entire pro-German ring in Baghdad. The Abwehr, not realizing that the British had outwitted it, thought the arrests were routine. "After all," one German told Zulu, "this is a dangerous game."

During 1942 and 1943, the Abwehr shifted its attention from the Middle East to the Soviet front. It recruited dozens of Soviet Moslem émigrés in Istanbul—some of whom reported everything to the NKVD—and contacted purported antigovernment groups in Soviet Georgia, Azerbaijan, and Uzbekistan. The Armenian nationalist Dashnak party worked closely with the Germans (though Soviet intelligence also penetrated Armenian communities throughout the Middle East). Leverkuehn subsidized these movements and tried to smuggle their operatives from Turkey into their home areas in the U.S.S.R.

Since the Turks feared the U.S.S.R. and its intentions more than any other country, Turkey's foreign minister and the Emniyet regularly exchanged data with the Germans about the Soviet Union. The Turks permitted a small Abwehr radio and supply base near the Turkish-Soviet frontier, but they drew the line at allowing direct sabotage from their territory. German intelligence officers who tried to sneak into the U.S.S.R. were detained, and the Emniyet arrested two Azerbaijanis caught smuggling machine guns, radio sets, and explosives across the border.

Ankara also feared that rightist Turkish nationalist groups, which the Germans aided, might make trouble at home or try to stir up Turks across the border in the U.S.S.R. When it became clear that Germany was losing the war, the Emniyet banned such clubs and arrested their leaders. There was, however, little support for these organizations. "Had German fortunes in Russia not deteriorated so rapidly," an exaggerated British intelligence report claimed in December 1943, pro-German Turkish groups in the southern U.S.S.R. "might have proved a most efficacious and possibly decisive aid to the German forces in their planned advance . . . to Persia and the Middle East." Unfortunately for the Crimean Tatars and thousands of other Soviet Turks, Stalin deported them as a precaution and most were never allowed to return home.

But German fortunes were now clearly in retreat, and the Turks were increasingly cooperating with the Americans and British. This development made it harder for the Abwehr to operate in Istanbul. The liaison man between the OSS and the Emniyet was Cedric Seager, an American who had grown up in Istanbul. The Turks kept him informed of the Abwehr's every move. He knew, for example, that four German agents equipped with radios and sabotage material were living at a house belonging to Paula Koch, one of Leverkuehn's most energetic agents. Since the Emniyet was watching them closely, however, it was better to follow them and discover their contacts than to take them into custody. "Paula Koch is more valuable to us free than under arrest," Seager concluded.

Two members of Leverkuehn's Istanbul-based sabotage group, a Persian and a Turk, offered to sell Seager even more information, one of them demanding a $700 down payment. "He thinks," quipped Seager, "he is a dollar-a-word man." Instead of paying him, the American told the man that the Emniyet would no longer tolerate German agents. He could either talk or be "entirely at their mercy." The Turks cooperated by seizing his passport for "routine inspection." As a result, reported Seager, "the names of the Azerbaijanis, Persians and Caucasians who work for [German intelligence] are now known to me, and therefore to the British. Where they congregate of an evening, where they work and what they look like."

While it was increasingly difficult for German intelligence to operate in Istanbul, German defeats were making it even more vital to do so. The new top-priority issues were the timing and location of the next Allied offensives and Turkey's intention as to entering the war.

Meanwhile, some Germans were battling with their consciences over whether to continue serving Hitler, while others were merely eager to join the winning side. Eric Vermehren and his wife, Countess Elisabeth Plettenberg, were in the former camp; some defectors were of a more opportunistic type.

Eric Vermehren had won a Rhodes Scholarship in 1938 to attend Oxford University, but German officials suspicious of his political views held up his passport. By the time they relented, the war had begun. Unfit for regular military service because of an accidental gunshot wound as a child, Vermehren worked in German prisoner-of-war camps. Needing an aide he could trust, Leverkuehn recruited this 24-year-old son of an old friend and brought him to Turkey in April 1943. Both Vermehren's mother and Plettenberg's fervently Catholic parents had links with anti-Hitler groups. An exiled German resistance leader later questioned the sincerity of Vermehren's anti-Nazi feelings. Would anyone not entirely reliable, he asked, ever have been given an intelligence job? The answer was that Canaris and his lieutenants had welcomed many anti-Nazis into their organization. From Hitler's standpoint the Abwehr had more unreliable people than any other German institution.

When Vermehren went home to see his wife, she insisted that they break with the government and defect. This step, however, was made more difficult by a new Gestapo regulation prohibiting citizens from leaving the Reich. Diplomats' relatives were virtual hostages to discourage defections. Through influential friends, the countess arranged her own Foreign Office assignment in Istanbul. She divided her bank accounts among younger brothers and sisters and set off to join her husband in Turkey. Leverkuehn worried about such an open violation of the Gestapo's rule and had her stopped at the Bulgarian border. But the strong-willed countess again used her connections to obtain a seat on the courier flight to Istanbul. When she arrived on December 24, 1943, Leverkuehn ordered Vermehren to submit a report dissociating himself from his wife's trip.

But matters were even more complex than Leverkuehn knew. A few days later, Vermehren contacted Nicholas Elliott of British intelligence. Vermehren went to dinner at Elliott's apartment at 7 p.m. and the men talked through the night. He did not want to see his beloved fatherland ruined by the Nazis, Vermehren explained, but he also feared appearing to be a traitor to Germany or a dishonorable rascal in his friends' eyes. Therefore, he did not want to defect openly or join the British war effort. Elliott agreed to these conditions.

To prepare for escape, the Vermehrens moved to a new apartment and told Leverkuehn they did not yet have a telephone. On January 27, 1944, the couple attended a neutral embassy's cocktail party. As they left, two men pushed them into a passing car to persuade any witnesses that the Vermehrens had been kidnapped. When Vermehren did not show up for work the next morning, Leverkuehn sent a search party which became lost trying to follow Vermehren's deliberately inaccurate directions to his new home.

When the Germans realized what was happening, von Papen sped back from a skiing vacation, but the Vermehrens were already en route to Cairo. They were intensively debriefed for a month. Vermehren made a radio broadcast attacking Hitler. As a new, junior officer, he knew few major secrets, but he did tell about German-Turkish intelligence exchanges regarding the U.S.S.R. The British passed this information to Moscow, and a Soviet protest led Turkey to stop this practice. When the Vermehrens went to London, a British counterintelligence officer named Kim Philby loaned them his mother's apartment. Perhaps the Soviets' gratitude explains Philby's hospitality to the couple. Philby was, after all, the NKVD's top mole in British intelligence.

The defections had an explosive effect in Berlin, where the Abwehr's old rivals—Heinrich Himmler's Security Ministry and von Ribbentrop's Foreign Ministry—pounced on a chance to discredit Admiral Canaris and his intelligence organization. Canaris's enemies, ignorant of British success in this area, claimed Vermehren might reveal the workings of German codes. Von Papen insisted Vermehren had no such information. The OSS had so many good sources in the Abwehr that it followed the process closely. On February 24, 1944, Dulles cabled Washington: "659's [Canaris's] position and his whole outfit has been seriously jeopardized by the . . . V[ermehren] affair in Turkey. Abwehr will probably be taken over by Himmler. . . . It is unlikely that 659 [Canaris] will offer a strong protest since he is somewhat of a Buddha. . . . It may be wise to encourage certain Abwehr men in important jobs to decline to go back to Germany, if as appears probable, they will lose all value for our purpose."

Himmler's men were determined to destroy the hated competitor who had dominated foreign intelligence gathering. Ernst Kaltenbrunner, Himmler's intelligence chief, wrote Hitler on February 7 that the Abwehr's Istanbul operation was a traitors' nest. Vermehren's flight "has gravely prejudiced the activities not only of Abwehr-Istanbul but of our other military agencies in Turkey. The entire work of the Abwehr station has been exposed and its continuation seems impracticable."

Five days later, Hitler abolished the Abwehr, ordering: "A unified German espionage service is to be created. I entrust the Reichsführer SS [Himmler] with the command." Canaris was fired and placed under surveillance; Leverkuehn was sent home. In addition to demanding Leverkuehn's firing, Kaltenbrunner had named as enemy spies a number of Abwehr agents, including Willi Hamburger and Karl Kleczkowski, a 43-year-old journalist who, with his wife's help, gathered political gossip and spread German propaganda around Istanbul.

The twenty-five-year-old Hamburger was the best-known Abwehr officer in Istanbul. His grandfather was founder of Austria's paper industry; his father was a prominent Viennese industrialist and Nazi party member. Hamburger had grown up amid great wealth; on coming of age, each child in the family had received a paper mill. Hamburger had attended the same school as Kurt Waldheim, and he was active in a fascist student group to which the future UN secretary-general belonged. After earning a doctorate in Middle East studies, he was recruited into the Abwehr and sent to Istanbul under cover as a buyer of hemp and flax—items about which he knew nothing. Most nights he could be seen with his entourage at the Park Hotel or an Istanbul nightclub. This group's philosophy was that if one could not have a good time with the espionage business and the lavish expense accounts, it was not worth being a spy at all. One of Hamburger's colleagues, a German officer who had won an equestrian medal at the 1936 Olympics, unharnessed a carriage horse and led it into the Park's dining room. When a local informant proposed that Hamburger meet him in a graveyard at midnight, the Abwehr officer replied, "Are you crazy? Let's have dinner on the Park Hotel's terrace."

Hamburger's main work for the Abwehr was to smuggle goods through the Allied blockade on Germany and to gather intelligence on Middle East political and military developments. It was like assembling a giant jigsaw puzzle in which the smallest piece might prove the most critical. He found American and Middle East magazines good sources of information. Reports of military sporting events, officers' marriage announcements, and other items helped the Abwehr locate Allied units.

But Hamburger was also an Austrian patriot and a stubborn individualist. The confident young man talked freely with Leverkuehn about his discontent. Hamburger and the Austrian-born Kleczkowski had contacted the Americans to offer cooperation even before Vermehren decided to defect. When Kleczkowski told Italian friends that he hoped Austria would soon regain its independence from Germany, they thought him an agent provocateur. Through a Turkish contact, however, Kleczkowski met the flamboyant George Earle in October 1943 and began giving him fairly unreliable information, including a purported plan for a German-Bulgarian attack on Istanbul should Turkey enter the war.

Hamburger's encounter with Earle was more dramatic. Earle's great love in Bulgaria had been a Hungarian singer named Adrian Molnar. She was a breathtakingly beautiful woman who resembled the young Ingrid Bergman. After Earle left Bulgaria, she returned to Hungary, having refused to go with him to Turkey. Earle insisted that he was going to bring Molnar to Istanbul even if he had to go into Axis Budapest himself to fetch her, and his behavior was erratic enough to convince some people he might be serious. Earle once tried to hire the Dogwood courier Gyorgy to bring him a prize bulldog from Hungary.

To accommodate Earle or to spy on him, Leverkuehn and Hamburger arranged for Molnar to come to Istanbul. She was hired to sing at the Taksim Casino, but she had a falling out with Earle just before her debut. Hamburger was in the audience that night, and he asked the manager why Molnar did not begin her performance. She was crying in her dressing room, the man told Hamburger. The Abwehr officer went backstage to see what was wrong. She was upset after having an argument with Earle. Hamburger and Molnar met for the first time and quickly fell in love.

Earle soon heard about this romance and decided to meet Hamburger to take the measure of his rival. Either through fickleness or through willingness to acknowledge defeat, Earle told Hamburger that he was giving Molnar up. The two men began to talk about politics. When Hamburger maintained that he was loyal to the Austrian resistance, Earle made him kneel down to swear allegiance to a free Austria. The Abwehr officer was willing to propitiate the eccentric American who, after all, seemed to offer a direct line to President Roosevelt. But Earle proved a poor conduit: he had little credibility in the White House and garbled all the information he was given.

Earle also had a poor sense of security. One of his minions, a well-known American agent, once brought Hamburger a message at his little bungalow next door to von Papen's summer house. Hamburger saw the motor launch sailing up the Bosporus with the American carrying a briefcase and standing conspicuously in the back. The boat tied up at a pier in front of his house, and the man marched blithely up to his front door. It is not surprising that pro-Berlin Germans became suspicious. From its office near the furnace in the consulate basement, the SD watched the Abwehr's activities and plotted revenge.

When Hamburger, Kleczkowski, and the other Abwehr men accused of working with the Allies were ordered back to Berlin, the Kleczkowskis resolved to bolt. Hamburger thought he could talk his way out of any charges by using his family's connections with several German generals. Unbeknownst to him, however, the Kleczkowskis had gone into hiding in Istanbul and the Abwehr panicked, ordering the arrest of the other suspects. Hamburger was awakened at dawn on February 12 by two Abwehr men pounding on his door. "You are under arrest," they proclaimed, "and will be put on the next train to Germany."

Hamburger promised to cooperate but asked to telephone his chief Turkish agent lest his disappearance provoke controversy. The security men let Hamburger do so. "I am going to Berlin for a week and will be back," he explained. "Tell our friends to 'Tell it to the Marines.' " The last phrase was the contemporary American slang for calling something nonsense. Understanding this simple code, the Turk sought help from the British.

Meanwhile, Hamburger stalled by selling the security men his radio and packing his bags slowly. Then the telephone rang. It was his Turkish agent. "Everything will be all right," he told Hamburger. "A car is waiting in front of your door." Hamburger casually put down the phone, raced outside, and jumped into the auto before the guards could stop him. The driver took him to the British consulate, where he was given breakfast and a new identity. On the way to the airport, an Abwehr officer passed within a few feet of Hamburger without noticing him. The OSS and the British successfully evacuated all three Austrians to Cairo. Despite von Papen's demands, the Turks did nothing to find them.

The Americans and British exulted. "Cairo bade fair to be swamped by an invasion of evaders and turncoats," cheered an OSS report. Hamburger did radio broadcasts and psychological warfare work in Cairo for the Americans and British. His papers identified him as an American lieutenant from Seattle. Hamburger's confessions blew the cover of twenty German agents in the Middle East who had been working for him. But interrogators found the Kleczkowskis less helpful. The couple was taken to New York under armed guard and incarcerated as "dangerous enemy aliens." They were deported in 1947 to Colombia, where they prospered in business.

Istanbul's German community was in a panic. No one knew who might next make a break; everyone was frightened of being arrested and sent back to Germany to face a firing squad. Suspicious officials paid unannounced "visits" to each other, almost surprised to still find colleagues at their desks. Von Papen sent his deputy to Berlin for a Gestapo hearing on these events. The meeting was interrupted by an air-raid alert and never reconvened. On a street in the capital, the aide picked up leaflets dropped by the Allied planes announcing the defections and claiming the German embassy in Turkey was in chaos.

Hans Fritzsche, deputy propaganda minister and a talented orator, soon arrived to shore up German morale in Istanbul. "Due to the fact that you are always exposed to the full impact of virulent propaganda, you are deserving of sympathy," he told an audience of 200 at the Teutonia Club. "You are also deserving of congratulations," he added sarcastically, "for your escape from the hardships of wartime and from bombings."

He reassured them that Germany would still win the war. "There is no need to worry about the Eastern front," he claimed. "Instead remember that the armies of Germany are still far from Germany and on foreign soil." Germany was working on secret weapons, but it did not yet have something which would "sweep Britain off the face of the earth in five minutes, after which twenty minutes will be all that is needed to blast America to hell." Nevertheless, Germany's triumph and revenge were inevitable. "We must await the day when victory is ours. It will come with a vengeance when that day arrives."

If the Germans were receiving any indication about what the future really held, however, that news was coming from a most peculiar source, the German agent code-named "Cicero." His occupation: valet of the British ambassador to Turkey.

15 | The Valet Did It

He who tells the truth is driven from nine villages.
—Turkish proverb

Cicero's real name was Elyesa Bazna. His parents had migrated from Albania to Turkey when he was a child. Bazna's knockabout youth made him amiably amoral, leading him first to small-scale criminality and then to a series of abortive get-rich-quick schemes. Bazna's lowly position made him easy to underestimate, but his drab appearance camouflaged an underlying cunning and a burning ambition to make his fortune.

In the late 1930s, Bazna began working as servant and chauffeur for a series of diplomats. Fired by a Yugoslav official whose letters he was caught reading, Bazna found a job with a businessman named Albert Jenke. Jenke was from an established German family in Istanbul that owned a florist shop. Otherwise undistinguished, he enjoyed one stroke of marvelous luck by marrying the sister of von Ribbentrop. When von Ribbentrop became the Nazi foreign minister, Jenke was made the German embassy's number-two man.

Bazna would later make good use of this connection. In a progression possible only in neutral Istanbul, however, the restless Bazna left Jenke's employ to work for a British diplomat and, in September 1943, became Ambassador Knatchbull-Hugessen's valet. Bazna was in his forties, a small, roundish man with a high forehead, thick black hair, and a large drooping moustache. One acquaintance compared Bazna to "a clown without his make-up on—the face of a man accustomed to disguising his true feelings." For the British elite of that era, servants were taken for granted. The idea that a valet might spy on his master was as shocking and frightening as the notion that a vacuum cleaner or a pet might attack its owner.

Many people liked Knatchbull-Hugessen but thought he was a dilettante. Ironically, hard work rather than gentlemanly sloth brought his downfall. After a long day at the office, he would take boxes of secret documents to study at his next-door residence before bedtime. When security men came around to lock everything in the safe for the night, Knatchbull-Hugessen retained items for further reading. Bazna saw this routine as the long-awaited opportunity to make his fortune.

On October 26, 1943, Bazna visited Jenke's home in the German embassy compound and made a proposition. Not knowing how to deal with the matter, Jenke called in Ludwig Moyzisch, the SD's Ankara chief, who was operating under diplomatic cover. An early member of Austria's secret Nazi party before the German annexation, Moyzisch had been a favorite of Hitler's governor there. Among the embassy staff, he was known as a zealot.

Moyzisch met the valet alone in Jenke's drawing room. Speaking in French, Bazna offered to sell photographs of the British ambassador's documents at the astonishingly high price of 20,000 British pounds per roll of film. Promising to telephone Moyzisch for an answer in four days, Bazna slipped away.

Naturally, Moyzisch was skeptical. But he had seen many strange things happen before in intelligence work. He told von Papen the story and cabled Berlin for instructions. October 28 was Turkey's national day when belligerents and neutrals alike gathered for President İnönü's reception. At the annual military parade, warring diplomats sat a few feet apart in the Ankara racecourse's stands. After the ceremony, Moyzisch returned to his office to find Berlin's go-ahead and the money. Bazna called as promised, using the cover name "Pierre," and scheduled a meeting.

At 10 p.m. that dark night, Moyzisch met Bazna at the end of the embassy garden where a back gate, shielded by a toolshed, could be used by those wishing to enter the grounds clandestinely. The two men walked to the embassy in silence and entered Moyzisch's office. Bazna asked for the money first. Moyzisch opened the safe and counted the bank notes so that Bazna could see them, but he refused to pay until he saw the material. The money was returned to the safe and Bazna handed over two rolls of film, which Moyzisch took to a basement where a waiting code clerk had set up a darkroom for the occasion. Within fifteen minutes, Moyzisch inspected the prints with a magnifying glass and read across the top of one: MOST SECRET, FROM FOREIGN OFFICE TO BRITISH EMBASSY, ANKARA. Obviously, he could not evaluate the negatives, but the product seemed good enough to buy. Bazna stuffed the bundle of cash under his coat, pulled his hat down and collar up, and left.

The excited Moyzisch stayed up until morning enlarging the fifty-two photos. Then, rumpled and unshaven, he took them to von Papen. The ambassador was impressed. "Fantastic," he exclaimed, looking through the pile. "Good heavens! Did you see this one?" There were reports on British pressure for Ankara to enter the war and on the infiltration of British air force personnel into Turkey, as well as details about U.S. military aid sent to the Soviets.

These documents, von Papen cabled the Foreign Ministry on November 4, were provided by a source "whose material is—for reasons of security—known only to a few persons." So valuable was this source that von Papen continued, "In future, I will refer to information provided by this source as 'Cicero.' " He named the new agent after the great Roman orator because the documents had so many exciting things to say.

The material was sent to Berlin, where Walter Schellenberg, Himmler's bright young head of foreign intelligence, was as astonished as von Papen had been. He routed the documents to Hitler via Himmler and also sent some copies to German code experts. The latter could only confirm that each of the British reports had been sent on an unbreakable "one-time pad" that was altered after each use. The documents were useless for German code breakers but appeared to contain authentic top-secret information. They were certainly no crude forgeries.

As his meetings with Bazna continued, Moyzisch was impressed by this amateur's knowledge of espionage tradecraft. They usually exchanged money for film in Moyzisch's office or at the house of one of the German's friends. Sometimes, Bazna jumped into Moyzisch's car in a dark empty street and, after a short ride, left the same way. Moyzisch personally developed and enlarged the pictures, which revealed documents providing detailed accounts of decisions made at high-level meetings in Cairo and Moscow and at the Tehran summit conference by Churchill, Roosevelt, and Stalin.

To believe that the documents were genuine, Berlin had to be confident about the man who was selling them. Through Moyzisch, the German intelligence chiefs asked the valet about his methods and motive. Bazna made up a tale about seeking revenge against Britain because an Englishman had murdered his father. His real motive, however, was purely mercenary. As for his technique, Bazna insisted that he worked alone. When Knatchbull-Hugessen gave his trousers to Bazna for pressing each evening, the valet sometimes took the ambassador's keys from the pocket. If Knatchbull-Hugessen went out to a party or diplomatic reception, Bazna could open the ambassador's red dispatch boxes and photograph the contents with a borrowed camera. The Germans gave him a better camera. But neither Moyzisch nor his superiors had direct proof that Bazna's claims were true.

Moyzisch was brought to Berlin by special plane to explain more about the mysterious spy. There he found the issue was being used as a pawn in an internal power struggle. Schellenberg of the SD thought Cicero was genuine, while von Ribbentrop of the Foreign Office—who hated von Papen and resented the ambassador's supposed intelligence triumph—told Moyzisch that Cicero was "too good to be true." Though carefully questioned, Moyzisch could provide no information that would definitively settle the issue one way or the other.

On the negative side, Bazna's photographs were suspiciously well done. Moreover, one picture showed a hand holding the page being photographed. This would have been impossible if Bazna were telling the truth about working alone, since he needed to grip the camera with both hands.

Yet the highly secret nature, and sometimes clearly accurate contents, of the British documents should have overwhelmed these doubts. When an espionage agency launches a double-agent operation, it must give the other side some true and verifiable intelligence so that the recipient will accept the false data as also being valid. The double agents working for Dogwood, for example, followed this pattern exactly by providing genuine political gossip to validate their phony industrial and military information. The higher the stakes, the greater the required value of these "giveaways." Yet Bazna's product was so valuable as to make it inconceivable as a mere cover for a double agent operation.

The most persuasive item should have been a message saying that Sofia would be bombed in mid-January 1944. The Allied raid took place as predicted. If the Germans had accepted Cicero's intelligence and prepared for the air raid, they could have turned a devastating attack into an Allied debacle. The British would not have risked losing scores of planes to validate Cicero's credentials.

Von Papen also believed Bazna because the documents' information on Anglo-Turkish relations was accurately reflected in his own meetings with Ankara's leaders. Moyzisch and von Papen were frustrated by Berlin's unwillingness to use the Cicero information and by their superiors' insatiable doubt over the spy's credibility.

Berlin's suspicion was understandable. The Germans had, after all, been fooled several times before, most notably by a 1943 British operation in which a dead soldier was dressed in an officer's uniform, handcuffed to a briefcase of documents purporting to show an impending Allied invasion of Greece, and ejected from a submarine so that the body would wash ashore on a Spanish beach. As the British expected, the Spanish government gave the material to the Germans, who swallowed the false story and diverted several divisions away from the real Allied attack: the invasion of Sicily.

But even if the documents were accepted as accurate, interpreting them on the most critical issues for Germany remained difficult and inevitably controversial. The cables showed, for example, that Churchill wanted to invade the Balkans while the Americans and Russians preferred to funnel all resources into the coming invasion of Europe's Atlantic coast—code-named "Overlord," as one Cicero document told the Germans. Yet Berlin could not rule out the possibility that Churchill might ultimately have his way. After all, another Cicero-supplied document designated a landing to capture the Greek port of Salonika as a major Allied objective for 1944. Even Schellenberg, who ridiculed the idea of such an attack, still rated it as 40 percent likely.

A second controversial issue was how seriously to take friction between the Anglo-Americans and the Soviets. As Germany's military defeat seemed increasingly likely, even the most fanatic Nazis began to think that only a civil war among the Allies could save them. The debate on military strategy between the Anglo-American and Soviet leaders, as discussed in the Cicero documents, could be interpreted as indicating that there was a widening split or as proving that the Allies would stick together until victory. Hitler concluded from these messages that Germany must fight to the end. If Berlin held out long enough, the Allies would fight among themselves; if the Allies remained united, Hitler thought national suicide better than submitting to Soviet occupation. In contrast, other German leaders were starting to think that Germany should sue for peace.

Finally, the documents prompted a debate over Turkey's policy. They revealed both Allied pressure and Turkish resistance to joining the war. The 1943 Allied foreign ministers' conference in Moscow, Bazna's information correctly told the Germans, concluded that Turkey should be pushed into belligerency by the end of 1944 so that it would furnish a base for attacking the Balkans. But ironically, if the Germans had thought Turkey was about to enter the war, they would have more eagerly swallowed Allied disinformation and kept their troops in southeast Europe at a time when the Allies were about to invade France. In short, the "good fortune" of having inside information on Allied deliberations concerning these key issues could have led Berlin to dangerously wrong conclusions.

Meanwhile, Bazna continued to deliver his film. He used some of his new income to buy fine clothes and jewelry. In December, he brought Moyzisch a wax impression of the key to Knatchbull-Hugessen's dispatch box. The Germans made Bazna a copy in order to speed up production. Bazna was in such an ebullient mood that he sang Moyzisch an aria at one meeting. At that moment, however, his survival was being threatened from unexpected directions.

The events leading to Cicero's exposure remained secret for many years after the war. The greatest asset of British intelligence was its ability to break German codes, and this played a critical but incomplete part in uncovering Cicero. A number of von Papen's messages about Cicero were sent to Berlin in the Foreign Office code that the British could read. Yet these telegrams were carefully worded. The code breakers had to clarify the meanings and unmask code names from a mass of deliberately enigmatic messages whose individual importance could be ascertained only with great difficulty. Code groups were often garbled or incompletely broken. Reading the German traffic remained a tough, time-consuming jigsaw puzzle with many missing pieces. In addition, Cicero's direct output was shielded from Britain's code breakers, since it was usually sent on the twice-weekly German courier plane to Berlin. Thus, it took some time before British intelligence was aware that there was a mysterious but dangerous leak of information in Istanbul.

Other clues also suggested danger. Beginning in November 1943, the Allies possessed a "Cicero" of their own in Berlin. Fritz Kolbe (code-named "Wood") was an anti-Nazi Foreign Office official whose job gave him access to many incoming cables and allowed him to make regular trips to Switzerland. During the course of his visits there, he began giving copies of German messages, including some of the British documents coming from Turkey, to the OSS's Allen Dulles. The Allies were more energetic and systematic in taking advantage of Kolbe than the Germans were in listening to Cicero.

By December 1943, Dulles had sent Kolbe's news about the leak on to London. British intelligence was now aware that someone in its Ankara embassy was giving the Germans its deepest secrets, but it had no idea of the spy's identity. The British could not risk sending a message to alert Knatchbull-Hugessen, since it might also reach the spy and alert the Germans.

In early January, London dispatched two security men to warn the ambassador and install improved security measures. Good investigative work turned up an additional clue. Kolbe provided the text of one document from the British embassy in Istanbul which contained a typographical error. By chance, the embassy's typist had corrected the mistake on all the copies except the one belonging to Ambassador Knatchbull-Hugessen. But a central problem was Knatchbull-Hugessen's failure to admit his habit of keeping material overnight in his home. Consequently, it had to be assumed that the leak occurred in his office, and suspicion focused on a secretary in the embassy's office rather than on the ambassador's home, where Cicero worked.

The Germans quickly became aware of the British investigation.

Angered by proof that the British were secretly moving military personnel into Turkey with that government's approval, von Papen protested with such detail that it persuaded the Turkish foreign minister there was a leak. Alarmed, he quickly contacted the British embassy. When Knatchbull-Hugessen cabled the news to London, Bazna was there to photograph this warning about himself and give the Germans a copy. Von Ribbentrop told von Papen to be more careful. The ambassador replied on February 10, "Of course, I'm always very cautious in my political talks. But there is no way to avoid using the available information." Von Papen added, however, that his spy worried about tighter British security and was already "financially satisfied." Thus, von Papen predicted, "Cicero will probably soon cease to operate."

Realizing the heightened danger, Bazna had already reduced his activity. He photographed documents less frequently and more hurriedly. As a consequence, the Cicero material was now less exciting for the Germans. By late February or early March, just as the British security men were starting to close in on Cicero, he stopped his espionage career. Bazna passed his last roll of film to Moyzisch by early March.

The British had no definitive proof against Bazna, however, and he stayed on as the ambassador's valet. The story of Cicero's final unmasking because of an Allied spy is as fascinating as the tale of Bazna himself. On visiting Berlin to discuss the Cicero case, Moyzisch had joked with his superiors, "I hope none of you has a valet." But Moyzisch himself had two secretaries, one of whom was the blonde, quite pretty 24-year-old Nele Kapp. Kapp's father was a career diplomat who had been the prewar German consul in Cleveland, Ohio, and she had gone to high school and college in the United States. Kapp still lived with her parents, who were now stationed in Sofia. Seeking to protect Nele from Allied air raids, they wangled her a job at the German embassy in Ankara.

Kapp arrived there in early January 1944 and was assigned to Moyzisch's office. About two months later, she asked an anti-Hitler Austrian friend to set up a meeting with an American diplomat. On the night of March 17, Kapp took a taxi to the Iranian embassy and then walked over the hill to her friend's basement apartment. She was very nervous. Awaiting her was Richard Gnade of the U.S. embassy. Ten minutes later they were joined by Gustav Rengers, a German pilot who had crash-landed his fighter plane in Turkey and was interned there. Rengers claimed that he had been attempting to desert and that the German air attaché, who suspected this, was trying to send him home for a court-martial.

Speaking German, Kapp asked Gnade for an American cigarette; then she switched to English. "Let's get down to business. I want to go to America where I spent the happiest years of my life. I know that there will be a price and I'm prepared to pay" by supplying information gleaned from Moyzisch's files and cables.

Gnade suggested she might remain at her job for a while to obtain more intelligence. "No," she replied. "The war will be over in two or three months. Besides, I might do that, and at the end of the time you Americans would say, '*Danke schoen*, thank you very much, finish.' And where would I be?" Kapp had another reason for being eager to get out of the country. She was in love with Rengers, and the couple hoped to begin a new life together in the United States.

Gnade reported the meeting to the U.S. embassy and received his instructions. The trio met again two days later. Gnade told Rengers that the United States would not help him. Exfiltrating German agents who possessed useful intelligence might be justified; snatching interned pilots from Turkish authority, however, could mean a political crisis with Ankara. Rengers then asked Gnade to forward a letter requesting help from his father, who lived in Brazil. "I'm coming past this house on the way to a party at the Iraqi legation on the 20th," Gnade told him, "and I'll pick up the letter to your father then."

Kapp's case was more productive. She promised to make shorthand notes of German secret documents and transcribe them at home. Kapp also casually told Gnade a detail that must have seemed obscure at the time. Every Saturday afternoon the clerks had orders to await a telephone call from a man who would say in French, "Mr. Moyzisch is expected for poker tonight at the same house." They were told to reply, "Mr. Moyzisch regrets that he cannot come." No call ever came. Neither Kapp nor the Americans realized that the expected caller was Cicero, then laying low due to the strengthened British security.

Gnade was to meet Rengers alone the next evening, but when the American arrived, the pilot told him, "I have a surprise. There's someone else here to see you." Kapp appeared. She was so serious about her new job for the Americans that she had already copied three messages from Moyzisch's desk. She gave them to Gnade. Two were about Arab propaganda and subversion; the third was from Berlin: "Decision about dispatch of pound notes will only be made when Cicero has delivered again." Cicero was obviously a code name but she did not know what it meant.

A few days later, Gnade heard startling news that might have endangered his whole operation. A German refugee told him that Rengers had mentioned the secret meetings in his conversations. At their next meeting, Gnade warned Rengers that his carelessness could endanger everyone. Then he turned to the evening's important business—the new material Kapp had brought from Moyzisch's office.

This haul showed a good cross section of German knowledge and activity. It reported on secret Bulgarian and Romanian contacts with the Allies, the flow of military aid to Turkey, and German intelligence's attempts to stem more defections. There was an intriguing item about an American spying for the Germans. Kapp looked up the file but found it sealed. She promised that she would try to take it when she defected.

Kapp also brought a little more news about the mysterious Cicero. Moyzisch had expected him on the train from Istanbul, she recounted. When he did not appear, Moyzisch was upset all day. Yet after the man finally turned up in the evening, Moyzisch was even more nervous the next morning.

Kapp did not know that the reason for her boss's distress was Bazna's announcement that he would deliver no more intelligence: British alertness made it too dangerous to continue, the valet had explained. This was Moyzisch's last meeting with Bazna. The German's greatest intelligence opportunity of the war had come to an end.

On April 6, Kapp telephoned Gnade in a state of panic. Moyzisch had ordered her to leave on that night's train for Istanbul en route to Berlin, she claimed, and the Americans must help her get away immediately. According to Moyzisch's later account, however, the trip was Kapp's idea. She had requested leave to visit her parents. If Moyzisch was telling the truth, Kapp made up this story about being under suspicion because she was impatient to reach the United States and unsure that the Americans would keep their word.

Gnade quickly made arrangements for the escape while Kapp packed her bags. He alerted Cedric Seager, the OSS man in the U.S. military attaché's office who had managed the earlier defection by the Abwehr agents. At 3 p.m., Gnade picked up Kapp in front of her apartment building and drove her to Seager's apartment.

A few hours later, Moyzisch and Rengers, who was apparently ignorant of Kapp's defection, arrived separately at the railroad station to see her off to Berlin. When Kapp did not show up, Moyzisch was annoyed, then upset, and finally quite frantic. He searched the building, grabbed and interrogated Rengers, and rushed to Kapp's empty apartment.

Realizing he would be held responsible for the defection, Moyzisch himself was distraught. At 2 a.m. the same night, he was yelling into the telephone loud enough to wake the neighbors: "Kapp must be found dead or alive!" He offered a large reward for a clue to her whereabouts. "You have no idea what I have been through," he told a friend. Moyzisch eventually lost over 15 pounds from this ordeal.

The OSS had to sneak Kapp past the alerted German agents and Turkish police who were watching all the train stations and border crossings. She was moved three times that first night. One stop was the apartment of a U.S. embassy secretary who shampooed Kapp's hair with henna to change her appearance. Suddenly, there was a knock on the door. Kapp, Seager, and the American woman froze. When the secretary answered the door, however, it was an American journalist with whom she had a date to go to the opera. She told him that she was not feeling well and had decided to wash her hair. He found out years later that he had missed not only a date but a great scoop as well.

The next night, Seager took Kapp to Izmir, where she was hidden in the home of an American couple. The OSS's John Caskey, an archaeologist turned secret warrior, stood as an armed guard all night outside her door. A most mild-mannered man, he later confessed he was unsure what to do if someone showed up to kidnap her. On April 13, Seager took her to Cairo by ship. She was interrogated there for two months.

The defection set off a heated argument in Berlin. The SD insisted that Kapp's parents must have known about her plans and should be arrested. Defending its own people, the Foreign Ministry replied that Kapp had been in such a state of nervous tension that she must have acted on her own and without premeditation. To reinforce this claim, von Papen asked local German doctors to prepare reports that Kapp was mentally unbalanced at the time of her defection. The ploy worked. Her father was forcibly retired but was not further harassed.

Contrary to later accounts, Kapp's defection gave the Americans few clues about Cicero's importance or identity. What most concerned them was Kapp's report of a German agent in the U.S. embassy. But Moyzisch assumed that Kapp had discovered Cicero's identity and revealed it to the Americans. He warned Bazna, who immediately quit his job. Knatchbull-Hugessen invited him back, prompted by the British security men, who were increasingly certain that Bazna was the spy. They hoped to use him as a disinformation channel. But Bazna did not take the bait.

Many myths have grown up about Cicero. At first, writers overstated his achievements, thought the Germans had foolishly ignored his valuable information, and credited Kapp with unmasking him. As romanticized by James Mason in the Hollywood film *Five Fingers*, Cicero became a suave gentleman's gentleman who outwitted both Germans and British.

After the revelation in the 1970s that London had broken German codes, several British and American authors claimed the whole affair was a British deception plot. The idea that any servant might gain access to such top secrets was simply too much like something out of a bad spy novel. Cicero, they argued, must have been given the material to mislead Berlin or must have been caught through code breaking and forced to work for British intelligence. Former British intelligence officers, stung by postwar failures and the well-publicized penetration of their service by Soviet spies, coyly encouraged this assumption. They implied that the Cicero case had not been a debacle but rather one of their most brilliant successes. Other former officials, intent on protecting Knatchbull-Hugessen, dropped similar hints.

These stories were all misleading. Despite the high quality of the information, Cicero only functioned at full efficiency for eight weeks, photographing documents and delivering film to Moyzisch about ten times. Moreover, during the same months, the OSS had low-ranking but proficient spies in the Japanese embassies in Ankara and Sofia and in von Papen's office as well who supplied high-grade intelligence without ever being suspected by their employers. It is thus easier to under-stand how Cicero was a genuine spy, rather than a front for British disinformation.

Nevertheless, the truth about Cicero is as compelling as the fiction-alized versions later spread by Moyzisch, Bazna himself, and other writers. The unsolved mystery lies not with Cicero's British but with his Turkish connection. There is interesting, if inconclusive, evidence that he may have been also working for the Emniyet. This Turkish intelligence agency had informants and surveillance men everywhere. It had placed at least one agent as a translator in the German embassy and other spies in Allied missions. Bazna could not easily have visited the German embassy or ridden in Moyzisch's car without attracting the Emniyet's notice. And the Turks could not fail to be intrigued by an association between the British ambassador's valet and the chief of Nazi intelligence.

An incident in December 1943 suggests that the Turks were well informed on this matter. As Moyzisch and Bazna were driving together one night, a car followed them. Moyzisch finally shook the pursuers by flooring the accelerator and screeching around several corners. The adventure left Moyzisch and Bazna pale, perspiring, and badly shaken. Moyzisch thought the Emniyet was shadowing them. A few days later, a Turkish official told him laughingly at a reception, "My dear Moy-zisch, you seem to be an extraordinarily reckless driver. You ought to be more careful, you know, particularly at night."

The Emniyet may have initiated Cicero's activity or discovered it and forced his cooperation. Moyzisch's boss, Schellenberg, later wrote, "The more I thought about [Cicero], the more likely it seemed to me that through this material Turkey had tried to warn Germany about the foolishness of continuing the war and its own unwillingness to join it." Allen Dulles, too, thought this a possibility. In a February 24, 1944, cable to the OSS, he stated that "relations between Turkish and Nazi Intelligence . . . present a possible clue to Cicero." Cicero's documents provided what Ankara most wanted to know: British plans, demands, and possible concessions toward Turkey.

The Turks also protected Bazna after the British accused him of espionage. The Turkish government claimed that spying on Britain was no crime against neutral Turkey, but these same authorities arrested, deported, or jailed hundreds of other German agents. And Bazna was a Turkish citizen. The Emniyet never dealt lightly with Turks who spied for other countries unless they cooperated with the agency itself. Bazna felt so safe from punishment that he freely appeared around Istanbul and Ankara for several months after his alleged "disappearance," at a time when there were massive roundups of others who worked for the Germans.

Whatever the true Cicero-Emniyet link, the story's end is one of delicious poetic justice. After the war, Bazna became a wealthy builder using his German payments as capital. He began constructing a resort hotel. When one of his contractors spent some of the money on a trip to Switzerland, the man was arrested for passing counterfeit currency. The money was traced to Bazna, and it was discovered that the 300,000 British pounds Moyzisch had paid him were almost all made in Berlin, not London. Bazna died in poverty.

Moyzisch had some bad moments, but he fared somewhat better than Bazna. He pleaded illness in refusing orders to return to Berlin after Kapp's defection. Von Papen protected him. Moyzisch rejected his friend Fiala's suggestions to defect. (Fiala, one of the double agents in the Dogwood ring, had already gone over to the Americans.) Returning to Germany after the war, Moyzisch was imprisoned by the British, who tried to pry intelligence secrets out of him. At first, he denied all knowledge of Cicero. After the matter became public, he wrote his own account.

Disinformation is not only a way to get enemies to accept false data but also a means of conditioning them to doubt what is true. The ultimate irony of the Cicero case is that his accurate information drew the Germans' attention eastward, toward Turkey and the Balkans. Hitler always worried about an attack in the Balkans, which inevitably diverted his attention—and a disproportionate number of his soldiers and planes—from the imminent Allied landing on the Normandy beaches.

As for the OSS, Kapp's defection made it focus on a frantic search for a spy in the U.S. embassy. Steinhardt, who had long criticized the Office of War Information (OWI), thought the enemy agent came from that group. "Many of these individuals," he complained, "have given ample evidence that besides being young and inexperienced they are most indiscreet and thus make the problem of security peculiarly difficult." The ambassador thought it no accident that an OWI security man wrote "Boo, Boo, Baby, I'm a Spy," a song that became popular in Istanbul nightclubs.

Ultimately, the agent turned out to be a naturalized U.S. citizen from Hungary who had tried to join the Foreign Service some years earlier and was now seeking a job, under German direction, at American government agencies and news services in Istanbul. The man had previously worked with British intelligence on Hungarian affairs. Although this individual provided little of value to the Germans, they had been very excited over recruiting him. Exposed by the OSS and threatened with a treason charge, he renounced his U.S. citizenship. When Hamburger defected, he also revealed that two secretaries at the U.S. consulate in Istanbul, one of them a Russian émigré, were Abwehr agents. A trusted Turkish employee of the OWI was also shown to be a German spy. But none of these people passed information of any value.

Kapp, whose defection had started all this commotion, was safe in Cairo. The ever-witty Seager wrote her there: "You have been elected a charter and original member of the 'Blue Gentian' society which consists solely of persons like yourself who have undergone similar experiences. . . . As to the gossip, your friend [Moyzisch] has had some very trying weeks." Seager joked, "It was a disappointment that I wasn't able to collect the reward [the Germans offered] for you—the idea was fascinating, but not very wise and perforce I had to drop it altogether."

The news about Rengers was not so good. "Somebody—I know who it was—spilled the beans to [Moyzisch] just as things were being worked out by our friends" to rescue Rengers. Moyzisch "immediately pulled strings and had . . . Rengers removed to another place . . . very far from Ankara. . . . Help is out of the question and escape almost impossible. . . . If it's any satisfaction to you, I have retaliated with some force upon the man responsible for giving the show away. He is suffering very much for his sins. . . . I think, on the whole, you have good reason to be encouraged—and the war isn't going to last forever. Meanwhile I trust you will be given something specific to do."

Unfortunately, Seager's latter hope did not come true, and the Americans broke their promises to Kapp. Ambassador Steinhardt and the OSS judged her information to be "of moderate value." Rather than being rewarded, Kapp was interned in New York for two months on the grounds that she had no papers and had worked at a German embassy. She protested that she had voluntarily defected, her passport was still in Moyzisch's pocket, and she wanted to work for the Allied war effort. "I trusted the Americans implicitly and have faithfully kept my part of the agreement," she wrote. After Steinhardt intervened, Kapp was released. The Justice Department, in a final bureaucratic absurdity, insisted that she temporarily leave America in order to reenter with an immigration visa. She lived the rest of her life in America and apparently never saw Rengers again.

Among the intelligence Kapp had furnished was material on the close cooperation between Moyzisch and his Japanese counterpart, a 34-year-old aristocrat named Morio Aoki. Aoki, however, found it hard to cope with the ungentlemanly atmosphere of wartime espionage. An Italian intelligence officer conned him out of a fortune by pretending to have a ring of valuable agents in American circles; he wrote their "reports" himself, using *Life, Time, Newsweek,* and *The Saturday Evening Post.*

In July 1943, Aoki returned from a trip to Berlin believing a German defeat was inevitable. The only way out, he thought, was for Germany to make a deal with Moscow. The Japanese began meeting Soviet representatives in Istanbul to promote the idea. Berlin was interested in the plan. Moyzisch's superiors ordered him to take time off from the Cicero case to meet a Russian diplomat who was supposed to come to Turkey for negotiations. Moyzisch was cautioned to determine first that the Soviet envoy was not Jewish in order to ensure that Stalin did not intend a double cross. At any rate, no Soviet emissary ever arrived.

If a Japanese diplomat could see the handwriting on the wall, so could many Axis leaders. The Russian forces were approaching from the east; each wave of the English Channel washing up on occupied Europe's beaches brought Operation Overlord's D Day closer. Would-be defectors swam for the Allied ark. The Cicero documents demonstrated to those not blinded by fanaticism that the Allies' unity and determination would continue until total victory. Some Germans, Bulgarians, and Romanians tried desperately to make a deal through Istanbul before they were drowned in the disaster of their own making.

16 | World War to Cold War

Last night, ah, yesternight when Papen came to dine
The shadow of the Big Three seemed to spread
Athwart the feast between the Sauerkraut and the wine;
But though he wooed me with Teutonic passion,
And though through Cairo Nights I kept my head,
I have been faithful to the Allies in my fashion.
—"Chanson İnönü," *The New Statesman*,
March 11, 1944

William Donovan, the OSS director, described Germany's endgame to President Roosevelt as "a picture of imminent doom and final downfall. . . . Into a tormented General Headquarters and a half-dead Foreign Office stream the lamentations of a score of diplomatic posts." Hungarians were seeking to leave the Axis, and "cagy Bulgarians are playing all kinds of tricks on [the Germans] and going off to Turkey on pleasure trips" masking secret negotiations. These events all signified "the final death-bed contortions of a putrified Nazi diplomacy."

But the Turks were slow to conclude that Hitler's Germany was, indeed, on its deathbed. They feared, wrote a British official, that "one squadron of German bombers would set [Istanbul] on fire and destroy it from end to end." He continued: "This I imagine to be the purest nonsense. If true, it seems that we have been asking the Turks to commit Hara Kiri when we are pressing them to enter the war." Turkish fears reflected both the city's real vulnerability—narrow streets, wooden homes, no antiaircraft defense—and a deception promoted by the Abwehr.

The Germans played on these concerns in order to ensure that Turkey did not come into the war against them. They warned that

German bombers would destroy Istanbul if Turkey joined the Allies. A popular Istanbul joke quoted a German diplomat as saying: "There is no need for this inconvenient black-out. When we attack, it will be in daytime." British aerial reconnaissance of Bulgarian airfields showed that the Germans had few planes left and that the Abwehr exaggerated the figures on its air power which it gave to Turkish military attachés in Sofia. When British intelligence tried to explain to Turkish generals that the Germans were incapable of such attacks, however, the Turks assumed that the British were trying to fool them.

While von Papen fought a temporarily successful holding action, the Turks were becoming convinced that Germany had lost the war. Consequently, they cooperated more with the Allies. The British worked hard—with Churchill meeting İnönü for some personal persuasion—to convince Ankara to join the winning side. But the Turks were reluctant to do anything until they received huge amounts of military equipment, far beyond what the Allies could supply. Railroad trains full of Turkish chrome continued to clatter across the Turkish border toward the Reich's factories.

"The Turks want to wait and see what happens this spring and summer," U.S. military intelligence explained. "They are not sure that the Allied second front will be a complete success and they still suspect that Russia has designs on them." In February 1944, the British gave up urging Turkey to enter the war and suspended aid shipments. One day, İnönü saw Knatchbull-Hugessen reading a book entitled *The Years of Endurance*, and asked, "Does that refer to your period as ambassador here?" A Soviet military attaché sarcastically described the Turkish stance as *"Tout prendre, jamais rendre, toujours pretendre"* (Taking all, giving nothing, always pretending).

If the Foreign Office and State Department could not get Turkey into the war, the OSS could, at least, stop the sale of chrome ore—used to strengthen tank armor and gun barrels—to Germany. Knowing that time was running out, the Germans had been speeding up the shipments. Macfarland and his British counterparts agreed that dynamiting railroad bridges in Turkey would imperil political and intelligence cooperation.

Refused permission to practice sabotage inside Turkey, the OSS decided to send Special Operations teams into the adjoining districts of

Bulgaria and Greece to blow up the railroads used to transport the ore. When the Turks refused to allow saboteurs to cross the frontier, some OSS men were so disgusted they wanted to quit. But Ankara changed its mind after the OSS bluffed—to the horror of Steinhardt and the Turks—that it was considering wrecking bridges inside Turkey.

The key man in launching the OSS's operations against the chrome shipments was Lieutenant Alexander "Alekko" Georgiades, who ran the OSS's forward post in the Turkish city of Edirne near the Greek and Bulgarian borders. This Greek-American's unique cover arrangement was serving as a diplomat in the Greek consulate. The Emniyet gave him a great deal of assistance. It gave him a special password for crossing the border, transported his supplies, and even let him wear a Turkish officer's uniform. He made about three dozen trips into occupied Greece and Bulgaria.

In December 1943 he crossed into Greece for the first time to visit the Greek anti-Nazi guerrillas after their liaison man absconded with money and supplies provided by the OSS. The partisans were now hunting for him. "I would hate to be that man today," wrote Georgiades.

Georgiades told their leaders: "I am only an intelligence man and as such I would give money or goods in exchange for cooperation in gathering intelligence to be used in fighting the enemy." Describing their response, he said, "They liked the blunt way I put it but insisted on receiving guns to carry on the struggle with more vim and said that they would be able to offer more even in the field of intelligence if they had better arms." They agreed to cooperate.

Georgiades stayed for three days with the guerrilla leader "Odysseus." "He has deeply impressed me because, though little schooled, he has a keen intellect and a very alert mind. . . . He possesses the powers of leadership. . . . Men love him." Georgiades observed no quarrels. The troops shared guns, caps, sweaters, and a great variety of political views. He described them as "mostly agrarian people whose families are either held by the Germans or were killed by the Bulgarians. . . . Their clothing is pitiful. Their arms are a collection that would do credit to a museum. . . . Living conditions and hygiene are primitive because of lack of medicines and soap." Their doctor recounted with tears in his eyes that "nine men died in the last six months who could be easily saved if they had the proper drugs." But Georgiades was somewhat disillusioned when the Communist leadership later purged "Odysseus" and several of his men as "Trotskyists" and tried to kill them.

Georgiades's travels between Edirne, occupied Greece, and Istanbul made for some strange contrasts between the guerrillas fighting in the mountains and the diplomats in the luxury-loving neutral city. And despite the common goal of the Allied forces, there was no end to bickering. The resistance bands were suspicious of each other, his Greek diplomatic colleagues worried about the Communist guerrillas' ultimate objectives, the British "plotted" to send their own men into the area, and the OSS men competed for influence. "The distrust everyone has against everyone else, most of it unjustified and magnified," added to his worries about "what is going on beyond the river" in Greece. Istanbul was a "madhouse of intrigue and counter-intrigue." Georgiades sighed, "Ambition is a terrific power which, combined with a little selfishness, can sweep everything in its way."

The lieutenant's main mission was to prepare the supply lines for an OSS sabotage team and to convince the Greek guerrillas to host it. Finally, in April 1944, he helped Captain James Kellis and two navy radiomen, Spyridon Kapponis and Michael Angelos, to cross the Evros River from Turkey onto Greek soil. Their task was to destroy bridges near Svilengrad, Bulgaria, and Alexandroúpolis, Greece, severing Turkey's sole rail links with Europe.

A five-hour march took them to the mountain camp of the Communist guerrillas. The Greeks would help the Americans only if persuaded that they had purely military objectives and would not interfere in local politics. For its part, the OSS would only supply weapons when convinced they would be used solely against the Germans, not for the incipient civil war already causing hundreds of Greek casualties.

Beginning with 200 poorly armed, untrained soldiers, the Americans recruited 1000 volunteers and 10 former Greek army officers to lead them. Noting this activity, the Germans arrested civilians and summoned special counterinsurgency units which, at one point, surrounded Kellis, Angelos, and twelve guerrillas near a village where they had stopped for food. They escaped, with three men wounded, after a seven-hour battle.

To supply the partisans, U.S. planes based in Bari, Italy, made two airdrops of plastic explosives, weapons, and ammunition. Navy Lieutenant Everette Athens piloted the OSS caïque *St. John* through dangerous waters to deliver three men and more equipment. Now possessing an arsenal of 250 rifles, 250 submachine guns, and 11 machine guns, the Americans spent a week training the little army and giving twenty men an intensive five-day demolitions course.

Captain Kellis, with Lieutenant Athens, 170 Greeks, and 1400 pounds of explosives, would assault the larger Svelingrad bridge, just across the frontier in Bulgaria. Marine Sergeant Thomas Curtis, with Angelos, 50 Greeks, and 550 pounds of explosives, would simultaneously go after the Greek span. Kellis and his men marched through relatively safe mountains for the first two days. They then crossed the exposed valleys of the Maritsa and Evros rivers, walking always at night on a zigzag course to conceal their destination. Local guides took them past German and Bulgarian posts. On May 27, they reached the objective. Kellis, Athens, and two Greeks made a reconnaissance the next day while everyone else stayed under cover. They counted ten German and twenty-one Bulgarian guards. The importance of the 210-foot-long bridge was clearly visible as the Americans watched nine freight trains —with 283 cars of matériel for the German war effort—and two passenger trains cross it that day. On May 29, Kellis assembled his enthusiastic troops, explained the mission, and prepared the charges.

Kellis sent some men as a screening force to hold off the guards and ambush any reinforcements. Once these teams were in place, the attack squad cut the guards' telephone lines. Just before 11 p.m., Kellis placed ten charges in the bridge's superstructure while Athens put four on the pier's legs so quietly that the guards noticed nothing. Eighty minutes later, just as the fuses were lit, the Germans spotted the saboteurs, fired a flare to light up the scene, and began shooting. It was too late. The bridge disintegrated in a tremendous explosion. Kellis and Athens confirmed that it had been completely destroyed.

Kellis then led his men on a forced march, crossing the Arda River at 4 a.m. A German outpost spotted them and radioed a battalion, which was soon hot on their trail. Kellis, Athens, and the sabotage crew went on ahead while the Greeks led the pursuers on a three-day wild-goose chase. They finally succeeded in ambushing and killing the German battalion commander and his staff.

The night after Kellis blew his bridge, Angelos, carrying a submachine gun, walked up to the Greek span. A Greek gendarme guarding it asked what he was doing there at such a late hour. Angelos replied that he was an American who had come to destroy the bridge. The Greek offered to help but warned that the rest of the guards might be less cooperative. Scrambling back down the hill, Angelos told Sergeant Curtis, who had his men surround the guards' barracks. Faced with this situation, twenty-five guards chose to join the guerrillas; the remaining five, fearing their families would be punished if they deserted, allowed themselves to be tied up. Just before midnight, Curtis completely destroyed the bridge.

The flow of strategic material was interrupted. Although the Germans quickly built temporary bridges, these were too fragile to carry much freight. Given continued Allied diplomatic pressure and the lesson posed by the sabotage, the Turks decided to stop selling chrome to Germany and 690 carloads of already purchased ore were permanently marooned east of the bridges.

The OSS men were impressed with the dedication of the Greek guerrillas in fighting against the Germans, though they were wary of their Communist leadership and dismayed by their bitter internal quarrels. But the Americans understood the guerrillas' urge for swift vengeance on those who collaborated with the Nazis. The OSS advisers witnessed what happened to one such man, named Kokinos, who was uncovered by a Greek civilian forced to work as an interpreter for the Germans. The guerrillas captured Kokinos with the help of a prostitute he was visiting and put him on trial.

"There is no doubt that this man has been a traitor to our country and has been responsible for the death of many patriots," proclaimed the man who uncovered him. "His hands are soaked with the blood of his own countrymen."

Kokinos assumed a hurt look and replied, "Me! Me? I beg your pardon sir, but that is not true. Why would I do such a thing?" His eloquence, an OSS observer noted, "might have convinced a less hardened jury and his acting was nothing short of superb."

"I was a poor boy with no father and a family to support," Kokinos said. "I was forced to work for the Germans and could not get away as I feared the Germans would kill my family. In my heart I was always one of you and always regretted not being in the mountains with you.

Not even the least little thing did I ever do against you or any of my countrymen. As a matter of fact, while I was working for the Germans I helped you . . . and saved many in your underground by warning them." The audience jeered.

After speaking forty-five minutes, he made a final plea: "Take me into your organization. . . . I will serve you in anything you say. I will cook, scrub, wash pots and pans; I will blow bridges by myself. I will sacrifice my life for my country. Give me a chance to prove what I say. Please, give me this one chance."

The judge and jury were unmoved. Five minutes later, Kokinos was shot on the spot.

Cheered by their successes, the local Greeks soon doubled their guerrilla force and armed themselves with captured German weapons. Lieutenant Athens printed leaflets demanding that the Germans surrender, "promoting" himself to major for the occasion to make a stronger impression. In late August, the guerrillas began a drive to seize all of northeast Greece. During the battles, church bells rang and the Greek civilians' chants of "Long live freedom!" and "Down with the Germans!" could be heard above the gunfire. The people of Férrai marched unarmed to the German positions. Women and children grabbed at the guns, and the seventy-man garrison surrendered without firing a shot. Another town fell after a thirty-six-hour battle—with Turkish border guards as spectators. By September, the whole district outside the capital had been captured. The Greeks took decent care of their 1000 German prisoners. A guerrilla leader told Lieutenant Athens: "We Greeks are not barbarians. If we treat the Germans as they have treated us, we cannot then say that we are a better race than they."

Throughout these months, the OSS men sent intelligence by radio to Cairo and by courier to Georgiades's advance post in Turkey. The haul included documents on German sabotage operations taken from a group of Bulgarian spies traveling from Istanbul. In September, Athens and a guerrilla band rowed across to Turkey to guide back a caïque, commanded by Kellis, which was carrying 3 tons of supplies to finish the liberation of northern Greece. But by then the Germans were evacuating the area.

The German troops in Greece had been thoroughly demoralized, and the Axis's dismal prospects were equally clear to the Bulgarian and

Romanian governments, von Papen, and some Nazi leaders. During the first half of 1944, it seemed as if everyone wanted to discuss surrender terms in Istanbul. The OSS was ready to talk with all parties about military cooperation or unconditional surrender, passing on political questions to higher authorities.

An OSS mission sent from Washington to negotiate with the Bulgarians included Angel Koumoudjinsky, a former Sofia banker living in New York whose friends included the king, high-ranking army officers, and leading politicians of all camps. The mission's interlocutor was the Bulgarian ambassador to Turkey, Ivan Balabanoff, a veteran collaborator now trying to portray himself as pro-American. Balabanoff shuttled between Sofia and meetings with the American envoys at the Bulgarian consul general's house in Istanbul, where both sides exchanged Old World courtesies, professions of friendship, and Chesterfield cigarettes. Balabanoff said the Bulgarian government wanted to make a deal with the Allies and asked that the bombing of Bulgaria be halted while the talks were in progress. The United States and Britain decided to do so but urged Sofia not to delay its decision to surrender.

What followed was a tragic farce, involving much useless, complicated maneuvering. The Germans were suspicious and von Papen asked Balabanoff point-blank whether he had seen Koumoudjinsky. The ambassador denied having any contacts with the Allies. But the Germans were not fooled as several Bulgarian envoys in Istanbul jealously competed, plotted, and tried to split the Americans. Koumoudjinsky told a colleague, "When two people are separately charged with the same mission it can never succeed!" Bulgaria made the same mistakes at the war's end as it had at the beginning: indecisiveness, greed for territory, and paralyzing fear of the Germans. Despite a Soviet-approved Anglo-American invitation to hold secret peace negotiations in Cairo, the Bulgarians were too frightened of Hitler to act decisively.

The Romanians were further from Berlin and closer to the advancing Russians, but they followed a pattern similar to that of Bulgaria. The OSS reported in November 1943, "Ankara and Istanbul in recent weeks have undergone an invasion of Romanians, all claiming to have been commissioned by their government to contact the Allies with a view to arranging some sort of deal by which Romania can get out of the war." The Allies dealt with delegates from both the Antonescu regime and the opposition. Despite dangerous press leaks, sporadic exchanges continued up to the moment the Soviets entered Romania.

There was almost no active resistance movement in Romania. A British officer sent to organize a struggle against the Germans in August 1943 was quickly captured and killed. Another party led by de Chastelain, director of the British SOE's Romania desk in Istanbul, had persistent bad luck. On the first attempt, in November 1943, its plane could not find the drop zone and ran out of gas over Italy: everyone had to bail out. The next month, de Chastelain made another try, landed several miles from his target, and was quickly arrested.

The fate of SOE's Bulgaria mission was worse. Led by the British Communist Frank Thompson, the group sent useful intelligence from Bulgaria until May 1944, when its radio went off the air for a week just after reporting that the Bulgarian police had discovered the group's hideout and were about to attack. When broadcasts began again, they offered only a vague account of the battle and insisted that the SOE send more men. The message was full of errors and omitted the security check an operator was supposed to use to indicate that he was not under enemy control. The British thus knew that their radio was being "played back" by the Germans, but they also understood how important it was to go along with the deception. Each operator had a distinctive style, so as long as the Germans thought they were fooling the British, the radioman would be kept safe to continue tapping out messages. After three months of SOE bluffing, Thompson's radio operator was rescued by the invading Soviet troops and evacuated to Turkey. Only then did the British learn what had actually happened: the Bulgarians had captured the entire group. After a week, when the wounded radio operator had recovered enough, the Germans made him transmit messages. His comrades were all shot.

As the war in the Balkans entered the period of most intensive fighting, the spring of 1944 was particularly beautiful in Istanbul. "There is a haze in the air and a laziness in the bones that makes one wish to sit in the sun and doze," mused the U.S. consul, Burton Berry. "The wisteria buds just outside of my office window are swelling and in a few days' time will be in full bloom." In May, the jacaranda and Judas trees sprouted their bright flowers.

Meanwhile, a few hundred miles away, the Germans were killing tens of thousands of Hungarian Jews each day in assembly-line death camps. Nazi and Soviet armies were locked in bloody combat. Hitler's realm shrank each day as the frontline moved west. Allied bombers, often guided by OSS-Istanbul's intelligence reports, were flattening the Reich's cities. The Americans and British were preparing to invade France.

Cicero's espionage had informed the Germans that the Allied plan to invade France was code-named Overlord. But it did not disrupt the major Allied effort to divert German attention toward Turkey and the Aegean. The weapons intended for the new offensive were camouflaged in England while the British pretended to create a new army in Egypt, only half of whose alleged troops actually existed. A sophisticated deception campaign was launched to persuade Berlin that this force would invade Greece and Yugoslavia in March. Pamphlets supposedly intended for soldiers landing in those countries were sent to Middle East printing firms deliberately selected for their poor security. Maps and plans of phony campaigns were circulated a bit too widely; troops were given special training that spying eyes might notice. Bombing, reconnaissance, signals traffic, propaganda leaflets dropped from planes, planted newspaper articles, and rumor-spreading were all increased in misleading directions. When the offensives did not take place as "scheduled," new cover stories were leaked to explain the delay. The result was that the Germans kept tens of thousands of troops sitting in Balkan garrisons instead of sending them to France or the eastern front.

But the Germans did know that they were on the defensive and that their situation was increasingly desperate. The Russians were advancing from the east, and the Americans and British were preparing major attacks which would come soon. Fritz Fiala, who spied for the OSS from inside von Papen's embassy, reported on April 22 that Berlin expected landings on France's Atlantic coast and in Greece between May 7 and June 30.

Faced with this tightening vice, German leaders were desperately seeking a way out. In 1943, the opposition had made overtures; now, in 1944, feelers came from leaders of the Nazi establishment. Anti-Hitler conspirators led by Colonel General Ludwig Beck, the former chief of staff, and Gottfried von Bismark, a veteran Nazi party member, contacted Germany's foreign intelligence chief Walter Schellenberg to propose eliminating Hitler and making peace with the Allies. They urged Schellenberg to convince his boss, Gestapo leader Heinrich Himmler, to help or, at least, to ignore their plan. Given the fact that dozens of people were holding meetings and talking almost openly about these ideas, one would have expected the Gestapo to round them up. Himmler's passivity signaled his willingness to take advantage of a successful coup.

The anti-Hitler conspirators understood that speed was everything. Von Bismark asked von Papen to sound out the British and the Americans; von Papen had an aide ask George Earle, who was going to Washington in May, to pass the opposition's message to Roosevelt. The proposal was couched along familiar lines, reflecting the Germans' fear and hatred of the Russians: if the British and Americans allowed an armistice on the western front so that German troops could stop the Soviet advance, the dissidents would try to remove Hitler from power. The White House did not respond, viewing the idea as a provocation designed to enrage Moscow and split the Allies. Admiral William Leahy, Roosevelt's military adviser and no softliner himself, told the president that "there is of course an element of truth in this German propaganda" about Stalin's intention to seize as much of Europe as possible. "Even if it were 100% true and 100% objectionable to Americans there appears to be nothing we can do about it until Hitler is defeated."

The German underground liberal opposition and conservative officers had each launched peace bids. Now Himmler prepared for his own coup if the dissidents seemed likely to succeed. He used a fantastic, roundabout scheme that could easily be disowned if Hitler heard about it. On May 19, the German courier plane from Vienna to Istanbul carried two rather unlikely passengers. One of them was Joel Brand, a 38-year-old businessman and a leader of the Budapest Jewish underground. The other man was Gyorgy. Brand briefed the Jewish delegation on his story while British intelligence quizzed Gyorgy.

They were a strange pair. The well-dressed, articulate Brand was a meek man who had been performing heroic deeds daily for a decade. At great risk, he had dispersed money from the Jewish delegation in Istanbul among Hungarian Jews and worked on the underground railroad to smuggle Jews out of central Europe. The squeaky-voiced Gyorgy had been a criminal and smuggler who had worked simultaneously for the Hungarians, the Germans, and the OSS.

On April 25, Adolf Eichmann, the Gestapo man in charge of de-stroying Hungarian Jewry, had ordered that Brand visit his office. It was a bizarre meeting. Eichmann, sometimes screaming hysterically, told Brand to make the Allies an offer. The Germans would release 1 million Jews if the Americans and British provided 10,000 trucks, 800 tons of tea, 800 tons of coffee, 200 tons of cocoa, and 2 million bars of soap. "Blood for merchandise" was Eichmann's formula. The trucks, Eich-mann added, would be used only on the Russian front. If Brand did not get results, all the Jews in German hands—including his own wife, two children, mother, and three sisters—would be killed. Brand was driven to Vienna in an SS officer's private car, given a German passport under a false name, and put on the Istanbul plane. All these preparations showed, a State Department report later concluded, that "Brand's mis-sion is not the brain-storm of a minor Gestapo leader in Budapest."

What was the motive behind this bizarre offer? The request for trucks seemed to echo the old idea of a deal between the Germans and the Anglo-Americans at the Russians' expense. The demand for other goods seemed a money-making scheme for the Gestapo, along with an attempt to claim a humanitarian gesture by men who knew they might soon be tried as war criminals when Germany was defeated. The move was also a suggestion of a peace feeler and, more subtly, a hint of the plans for a coup against Hitler that were already well under way.

Brand repeatedly explained that while he doubted the Gestapo's sincerity, the offer could be used to "play for time," saving hundreds of thousands of people until they could be rescued. The end of the war was already in sight, and he believed the Allies should use the threat of retribution to frighten the Nazis into stopping their crimes. Some American officials agreed. Ambassador Steinhardt wrote, "It is important that the door be kept open for further exploration of the matter and that every effort be made to convince the Germans that our government is seriously concerned with the problem of the rescue and relief of the Jews and other victims and is willing to consider any genuine proposals."

The British decided that the lifesaving plan conveyed by Brand must be rejected as a German propaganda ploy to embarrass the Allies and provoke a split with the Soviets. On June 1, the British took Gyorgy to Cairo for detention and interrogation. Brand was questioned by the Emniyet each day and returned to his room at the Pera Palace Hotel each night until the British took him off to Cairo four days later.

The British were especially determined to prevent the Americans from talking with Gyorgy. A State Department official in Istanbul correctly surmised that the British were particularly alarmed because Gyorgy was now acting as courier for a network stretching back to the chief of the Gestapo, Heinrich Himmler. Briefed by Schellenberg on the conspiracy already mounted against Hitler, Himmler was hedging his bets by refusing to interfere with that plan. If the coup succeeded, Himmler was ready to step in as Germany's new leader and would make peace with the Allies, or at least with the British and Americans. If some last-minute reprieve to the Jews was necessary to cleanse his credentials, Himmler was willing to make the gesture. The demand for trucks and coffee, made through Brand, was camouflage for Himmler's goal of seizing power in Berlin and extricating Germany from total defeat. By the same token, it was a genuine offer which could have led to the saving of many lives if the Allies stalled for time.

Ignorant about this part of the story, the Zionist delegation still frantically tried to get someone to act on Brand's message. They begged the Allies to pretend to play along with the Germans for a while in order to win the release of captives or, at least, some interruption of the mass murders. London blocked these efforts at every turn. The British refused to let Zionist leaders obtain visas to come to Istanbul; they held Brand incommunicado in Cairo. Anti-Semitism emerged once again in this refusal to help save the Jews held by the Nazis. A British interrogator asked Brand: "Where . . . shall we put these Jews if Eichmann keeps his word?" A Zionist intelligence man in Istanbul, Ehud Avriel, later noted, "We were at the mercy of our friends, and we had no power to compel them to do what we wanted."

The German opposition proceeded anyway, though the lack of help from higher Nazi officials doomed its plot. On July 20, an officer placed a briefcase containing a bomb next to Hitler during a meeting at the dictator's military headquarters. Another officer, finding the attaché case in his way, pushed it under the heavy conference table. A few minutes later, the bomb exploded; it wrecked the room, but the table absorbed most of the shock and Hitler survived. He immediately ordered Himmler to wage a bloody purge. Himmler, who was prepared to seize power if Hitler had been killed, obeyed. The Gestapo arrested, tortured, and executed scores of people whose plots or suspect loyalties it had earlier ignored. Among the victims was the former Abwehr chief, Canaris. Germany's fate was now set: it would fight for ten months more until Berlin lay in ruins and the final bunker's last resident took his own life.

Beyond the Gestapo's reach in Istanbul, von Papen stayed home and kept a low profile for the week after the failed assassination attempt. Privately, he admitted that Germany was finished, his mission in Turkey was doomed, and his own personal future was uncertain. Publicly, he called on Germans to remain united and loyal to the fatherland. "We are in a very difficult situation indeed," he told the local German community. "Everybody must be prepared to leave at a moment's notice."

As Germany's situation moved clearly toward collapse, the British and Americans now demanded that Turkey break diplomatic relations with Berlin. The Soviets took a different position. Stalin realized he could gain more by portraying Turkey as pro-fascist after the war—and demanding compensation from it—than he would if Ankara joined the alliance.

Within Turkey, the government's neutrality policy was popular. Most citizens believed that if Turkey entered the war, the Soviets would demand bases and try to take over the country. "Why," an Istanbul lawyer asked an OSS man, "should we get into this war? Just so Russia can pick up the pieces?" A student inquired: "Will the United States and Great Britain guarantee our frontiers? Will you promise to fight Russia if she tried to grab the Straits?" But the Turks were also pro-British and pro-American. Once they concluded that Germany was not going to invade their country, they favored secret help for the Allies.

This stance was seriously undermined during May and June 1944 when British intelligence counted eight German escort ships and four patrol boats moving south through the Bosporus strait into the Aegean. The antisubmarine boom blocking the Bosporus had been opened to permit their passage under cover of darkness. The British protested to President İnönü. "Somebody has been lying to me over this business," he told his cabinet. "It is either the British ambassador or Foreign Minister Menemencioglu." Menemencioglu had let the ships pass. Von Papen had claimed they were merchant ships and probably also presented a sizable bribe.

Prompted by the British complaints, the Turkish navy now searched one of the boats and found German uniforms, guns, and ammunition. İnönü flew into a rage. "Is this the time to have the Allies accuse us of secretly helping Germany? What . . . if the British had seized these ships outside the Dardanelles and proved that they were armed?" He demanded Menemencioglu's resignation but allowed him to keep the Mercedes and the sports car given him by the Germans. İnönü also forced the Turkish ambassadors in Romania and Bulgaria to resign. The former had been selling Turkish visas to Jews at high prices; the latter had sold refuge to Bulgarian fascist politicians. İnönü angrily told the diplomat returning from Bucharest: "You have been a good businessman and made enough money. I think it is time for you to retire."

Another long-awaited development further reinforced Turkish support for the Allies. British and American armies landed on the Normandy coast at dawn on June 6 and quickly established a beachhead. A special courier from Berlin brought the first German newsreel of the event to Istanbul, where von Papen screened it for a selected audience of pro-Axis diplomats. The movie falsely depicted the battle as a German victory. "No one can get through the Atlantic Wall," the hard-line Nazis boasted. "A thousand gliders have been destroyed, thousands of parachutists have been slain. We'll tear them to pieces." But few people believed Goebbels's propaganda any more.

The success of the Normandy invasion convinced Turkey that its future lay with the victors. İnönü finally acted decisively. After a ten-hour meeting of the ruling party's parliamentary delegation—many of whom only reluctantly yielded—the government announced on August 2 that it was breaking relations with Germany. The British, Steinhardt reported, thought "the Turks are naughty boys who have been misbehaving themselves and who have not yet earned the right to be treated as grown ups." They need to "rehabilitate" their status as allies. Commented the London *Daily Mail*: Turkey "has interpreted the alliance by a passivity which we have always 'understood' but which we could have wished was not quite so obvious. Still, if a stiffening of the Turkish attitude toward Germany helped to shorten the war even at this late stage, it would be worthwhile."

In response to threats by the Germans that they would now attack, Turkish antiaircraft guns rolled through Ankara past the parliament. Four British minesweepers arrived in Istanbul to keep the straits clear.

The ships were nominally transferred to the neutral Turks by the simple expedient of having the British crews don Turkish navy caps. Three days later, von Papen, in his own words, turned out "like a thief," left Turkey for the last time.

He expected a tough reception in Berlin given his enemies in Nazi circles and his record of subversive contacts with the Allies. Even British Prime Minister Winston Churchill jokingly referred to von Papen's coming punishment. But Hitler was too contrary to fulfill his arch-rival's prediction.

Von Papen's departure set off a little parade of celebration in Ankara. When Germany seized and annexed Czechoslovakia in 1939, von Papen grabbed the residence of Milos Hanak, the Czech ambassador to Turkey. For five years, Hanak had been a diplomatic nonperson. Now Ankara once again accepted him as an ambassador. Followed by a small caravan of wildly cheering Czechs, the Hanaks were driven through downtown Ankara. They marched up to the vacated embassy to reclaim it on behalf of free Czechoslovakia.

There were also, at last, some other signs that justice might still exist in the world. Peter Gabrovski, the Bulgarian minister of interior responsible for blocking the escape of Jews to Turkey and murdering those in Bulgarian-occupied territory, fled to Istanbul under an assumed name. The Emniyet identified him; the British and Americans successfully demanded his expulsion. Gabrovski would not enjoy the haven he denied thousands of others. As he was taken from the police station to the train for Sofia, reporters asked: "What about the 20,000 Jews and the 40,000 Greeks who perished in territories under Bulgarian occupation?" It was all the Gestapo's doing, he said. After the Soviets captured Bulgaria a few months later, Gabrovski was tried and executed.

Meanwhile, the German position in the Balkans was collapsing. During August and early September, the Soviets crossed into Romania and swept south and then west through that country and Bulgaria. As the Red Army arrived on their doorsteps, these two countries made their belated attempt to desert the Axis. The Romanians sent an envoy to Istanbul carrying a promise to fight the Germans if given Allied help. They would release the SOE's captured Romania expert, de Chastelain, to serve as liaison officer.

On August 23, with the Soviets deep into northern Romania, King

Michael staged a "coup" with the support of some military officers and arrested Prime Minister Antonescu. Crowds celebrated in front of the palace while inside the king tried to contact Istanbul on his personal transmitter. At that moment, de Chastelain arrived wearing his British uniform. The demonstrators insisted on carrying him around on their shoulders before letting him enter the palace.

The king asked de Chastelain to fly to Istanbul and obtain military aid. Navigating by a road map, de Chastelain made the trip. That same night the German army and air force commanders came to the palace and promised to pull out of Romania without further resistance. As soon as they left, however, they ordered a devastating three-day bombing attack on Bucharest. From the safety of the National Bank's vaults, two other released British prisoners established radio contact with Istanbul and reported German positions. Romanian forces helped the Soviets in surrounding and disarming the remaining German troops.

Next, a Bulgarian envoy approached a British diplomat on the Istanbul-Ankara train to announce his mission to remove Bulgaria from the war. He was sent to Cairo to negotiate. The secret talks between enemies was highlighted by the Bulgarian's fear that Yugoslav guerrilla officers housed in the same hotel would shoot at him in the corridors.

At the end of August, after Bulgaria had abrogated all anti-Jewish laws and asked the Germans to withdraw, Bulgarian forces went into action against their former allies. As Russian troops reached the country's border, on September 5, the Bulgarian government declared war on Germany only to find Stalin declaring war on Bulgaria. The startled Bulgarians—now at war with all four major powers—begged for peace. But Moscow did not relent until the Red Army held most of the country and the Communist-dominated Fatherland Front seized power in Sofia.

If Hungary, Bulgaria, and Romania had made a separate peace much earlier, it might not only have helped the Allies and ended the war sooner but it might also have saved those three countries from Soviet occupation. Now both Sofia and Bucharest were wrecked from the fighting and under Communist rule. "There is a shortage of everything in Bulgaria except intelligence reports," wrote an OSS agent. Although the Peasant and Social Democratic parties were participating in the nationalist governments set up in Romania and Bulgaria, Stalin began to destroy these partners and impose his own Communist protégés as dictators.

With those two capitals no longer in enemy hands, however, OSS-Istanbul was able to send in missions to gather intelligence on the Germans, observe developments, and evacuate over 1600 captured Allied fliers. The OSS intelligence team in Romania was led by Frank Wisner, who had succeeded Macfarland as OSS chief in Turkey. His men seized the files of the German air force headquarters in Bucharest; the documents included plans for advanced German warplanes and rare reconnaissance photos of the U.S.S.R.

During this interregnum when the Soviets were still being cooperative, the Haganah's Istanbul men also moved into Bulgaria and Romania to help reorganize the Jewish communities and assist emigration. In December 1944, David Ben-Gurion came to Istanbul, where he had studied thirty years earlier, and addressed the local Jewish community in fluent Turkish at Haydarpasha Station. He then boarded the *Orient Express* to Bulgaria, where he became the first Jewish leader to set foot in the formerly occupied lands.

Soviet tolerance did not last very long. In a few weeks, Moscow threw the OSS out of Romania and Bulgaria and did not allow it to return until months later and, even then, only under tight supervision. The Russians harassed official Anglo-American observers, kept out Western journalists, and arrested local people who spoke to Westerners. After trying real fascist collaborators, the Soviets began to imprison and kill non-Communist resistance leaders. Stalin had begun the process of turning central Europe into Soviet-dominated eastern Europe. The Turks watched with dread as their worst geopolitical nightmare took shape.

Meanwhile, the 3000 people holding German passports in Turkey faced their own nightmare. With Turkish-German relations now broken, pro-Nazi and anti-Nazi Germans alike were sent to three provincial camps in rural areas. The refugees from Hitler's regime, many of them Jews, feared they would be deported to Germany.

The OSS and British intelligence helped a few people who had worked with them to leave for Allied territory. Among this privileged group were two of the OSS's most prolific sources. One of them, Franz Josef Ridiger (agent "Stock"), was a genuine patriot who had been the liaison between the OSS and the ill-fated Austrian resistance movement. The other man was Fritz Fiala (agent "Dahlia"), the German embassy press counselor who had defected with his secretary/mistress. Fiala was a loyal Nazi and the last person his colleagues had expected to change sides. When Fiala was interrogated in Cairo, his long-suspected role as double agent became clear. He had produced verifiably true reports on German domestic politics and gossip which did little harm to the Axis. Once he had been accepted as legitimate, Fiala gave the OSS deceptive information on bombing targets. A careful comparison of Fiala's claims with aerial reconnaissance revealed his treachery. After the war, Fiala was deported to Czechoslovakia where he was tried and executed as a traitor.

As the Reich disintegrated, hundreds of German soldiers also deserted, crossing into Turkey from Bulgaria and Greece and arriving from across the Black Sea. The Emniyet chief in one Aegean port offered to supply his British counterpart with all the Germans he wanted at a modest price. There were so many available that the British had to hire Turkish policemen to guard them.

The German garrisons in the Greek islands also capitulated. A tiny 2½-ton British caïque, captained by an army sergeant-major, sailed into the harbor of the beautiful Greek island of Santorini and demanded the surrender of its 300-man garrison. The German commander agreed, but he insisted a larger warship be sent to keep up the appearance that he had given up to superior military force. The next day an 8000-ton British cruiser arrived for the formal ceremony of surrender.

With the Germans in full retreat, Turkey opened the straits as a supply route to the U.S.S.R. in January 1945 and finally declared war on Germany in late February. But the Emniyet now faced a new threat: instead of German spies, dozens of Soviet agents were descending on Istanbul. Stalin was determined to spread his empire and influence as far as possible.

At night, motorboats could be heard along the coast, traveling without lights or flags. In the morning, Soviet dinghies were found abandoned on beaches. Agents crossed from the U.S.S.R. or Soviet-occupied northern Iran to gather information on Turkish defenses. White Russian émigrés in Istanbul, some of whom had previously worked for the Germans, were now hired by Moscow. In February 1945, the Istanbul police arrested an armed Bulgarian Communist, landed from a Russian boat, who was carrying a large sum of money to finance these spy rings. A new international conflict was beginning.

But the old one was ending. Hundreds of miles to the west, SS

Hauptscharführer Erich Mansfeld did not know, on April 30, 1945, that this particular day was his last day of work. The 32-year-old German policeman was a guard at Hitler's Berlin bunker. The bunker's main entrance was through a tunnel from Hitler's offices on Wilhelmstrasse. But there were also an emergency exit and an escape hatch behind the building, a few yards from Hermann Göring Strasse. That day, Mansfeld was assigned to a small concrete tower next to the escape hatch when another guard dropped by at 4 p.m. to borrow a gun. As Mansfeld leaned out the tower's window to hand it down, he saw four members of Hitler's bodyguard run out the emergency door 10 yards away.

He went over to see what was happening. Out came Hitler's personal aide followed by two SS men carrying the Führer's body wrapped in a blanket. Immediately behind came another guard holding the body of Hitler's mistress, Eva Braun. Accompanied by Goebbels and Hitler's secretary, Martin Bormann, they walked a few steps from the exit. An officer ordered Mansfeld back to his post. Mansfeld complied but continued watching through the observation slit. He saw men pour gasoline onto the two bodies and set them aflame. The Third Reich was over.

The end of the war in Europe in May 1945 and Japan's surrender three months later were occasions for joyous outpourings by the millions of people who had suffered or feared the war's consequences. These events raised little emotion, however, among Istanbul's citizens. The police ordered people to put out flags, but neighbors complained about the noise from the Allied diplomats' raucous victory parties. The Turks were already preoccupied with a new Cold War in which they could not remain neutral.

On a hiking trip near Ankara, Huntington Dunn, an official of the U.S. OWI office there, came upon a small village. He was warmly received and taken to the headman's tiny, one-room hut. About thirty people crowded in. The village teacher acted as their spokesman. "Ah, America," he said. "I know your country. Your President just died and you have a great new bomb. You should drop that bomb on Moscow. And if you are afraid we will do it for you."

In August 1945, Istanbul was the scene of a tragedy hinting at the new age of Cold War. Soviet Consul General Konstantin Volkov approached a British diplomat. He and his wife wished to defect, Volkov explained, and for 27,000 English pounds he would provide the key to a suitcase of valuable documents and reveal its Moscow location. He also gave a tantalizing warning when he said there were several Soviet agents in the British Foreign Office and intelligence services that he would help unmask. Since these spies had helped Moscow break British codes, Volkov insisted that word of his own offer be sent by slower, though safer, diplomatic pouch.

Unfortunately, the message landed on the desk of MI-6 officer Kim Philby, one of the Soviet agents who faced exposure if Volkov succeeded in defecting. Philby immediately warned Moscow to eliminate Volkov. At the same time, he calmly volunteered to go to Istanbul and handle the case for MI-6, but he stalled his departure as long as possible. Well before Philby arrived, Volkov had already been drugged, tied to a stretcher, and returned to Moscow for execution. In future years, pictures of Volkov being loaded onto the plane were shown to classes of Soviet agents, warning them of a similar fate if they sought to defect. Philby and other Soviet agents including Donald MacLean and Guy Burgess would go undetected for six more years, during which they did untold damage. The most junior member of Volkov's consulate, Gaydar Aliyev, must have learned something from his boss's downfall. He later became the KGB director in Azerbaijan and, in the 1980s, the first "Moslem" Politburo member.

While in Istanbul, Philby met with an earlier Soviet defector, Ismail Akhmedov, who had exposed Moscow's involvement in the von Papen assassination attempt. Philby did not seem interested in his information about Soviet intelligence, Akhmedov later recounted, but was eager to hear about how Moscow treated those who defected to it.

At the time, of course, these affairs remained secrets known to very few. U.S. and British attention was preoccupied with Soviet political pressure on Turkey and Iran. Even before the war ended, Moscow began to criticize Turkey as treacherous and pro-fascist. "Being a neighbor of Russia," commented a Turkish journalist, "is like living in the same room with an elephant." When there were rumors that Ankara's ambassador in Moscow was going to be declared persona non grata, the Soviet military attaché in Istanbul commented: "Can you think of any Turk who would be persona grata in Moscow?" His assistant added that if Turkey developed a first-class military, the Soviets would have to take over the country.

The Turks were now subjected to a ferocious Soviet campaign of threats and intimidation. American leaders noted that the Soviet techniques seemed analogous to those Stalin employed in eastern Europe. One demand followed another throughout 1945, accompanied by a Soviet military buildup along Turkey's borders with the U.S.S.R., Bulgaria, and Soviet-occupied northern Iran.

Moscow demanded that Turkey agree to changes in the treaty covering the Bosporus which would give the U.S.S.R. a dominant role in the area and military bases near Istanbul. In addition, Stalin insisted that Turkey surrender the eastern fortress cities of Ardahan and Kars to him and other territory to Bulgaria. Since Turkey's defense line ran right through these lands, this ultimatum was comparable to that of Germany in 1939 when it demanded Czechoslovakia's strategic Sudetenland, which it then used as a springboard for occupying the rest of the country and as a base for further aggression.

The Turks kept their army mobilized and their determination to resist strong. In December 1945, around 5000 demonstrators led by Istanbul University students gathered by the Golden Horn. They carried banners stating, "We are neither Fascist nor Communist, the Nation is Democratic!" They destroyed a leftist newspaper office and marched up the Pera hill chanting, "Down with the Communists! Down with the Soviets!" Swinging onto the upper section of Istiklal Boulevard, they advanced into Taksim Square. The police stopped them short of the Soviet consulate.

The United States sought no confrontation with Moscow. On the contrary, most American leaders had been optimistic about continued cooperation following Hitler's defeat. Recognizing that Moscow had legitimate security interests along its western and southern borders, the U.S. government was willing to accept a neutralized, Soviet-influenced eastern Europe and changes in Moscow's favor on rules governing the Bosporus. What appalled the Americans, however, was the Soviet Union's total, violent subjugation of eastern Europe and apparent plans to do the same to Turkey and Iran. Observing these events moved U.S. policymakers one by one, between the autumn of 1944 and the spring of 1946, to a deep suspicion that the U.S.S.R. was an aggressive and unreliable state.

"What frightens me," wrote Averell Harriman, the U.S. ambassador to Moscow, "is that when a country begins to extend its influence by strong-arm methods beyond its borders under the guise of security it is difficult to see how a line can be drawn. If the policy is accepted that the Soviet Union has a right to penetrate her immediate neighbors for security, penetration of the next immediate neighbors becomes at a certain time equally logical."

Assistant Secretary of State Adolph Berle, a veteran New Dealer, said of Moscow's insistence that bordering states must be friendly: "If it is meant that these governments must not engage in intrigue against the Soviet Union there could be no possible objection; if it is meant that, by subsidizing guerrilla or other movements, virtual puppet governments are to be established, a different situation would prevail."

The Soviets used occupation troops, secret police, local Communist parties, labor unions, fellow-traveling or front organizations, and economic pressure, wrote Harriman, "to assure the establishment of regimes which, while maintaining an outward appearance of independence and of broad popular support, actually depend for their existence on groups responsive to all suggestions emanating from the Kremlin."

Turkey was of tremendous strategic value in this new situation. It was, as a State Department official explained, "the stopper in the neck of the bottle through which Soviet political and military influence could most effectively flow into the eastern Mediterranean and the Middle East." No other nation in the region "has a government or social order so stable and united as Turkey and none could be expected to stand against Soviet pressure after Turkey had gone down."

To discourage Soviet expansionism and to encourage Turkish resistance, President Harry Truman issued both a warning and an offer of compromise to Moscow. "It is easy to see," he stated in April 1946, "how the Near and Middle East might become an area of intense rivalry between outside powers, and how such rivalry might suddenly erupt into conflict. No country . . . has legitimate interests in the [region] which cannot be reconciled with the interests of other nations through the United Nations."

Stalin could be stopped only by counterpressure. The strain of maintaining a fully mobilized 600,000-man army was pushing Turkey toward economic collapse. On March 12, 1947, the president's "Truman Doctrine" speech asked for $400 million to aid Greece and Turkey and help defend other countries against Soviet aggression. It was the beginning of a new, permanent world role for the United States. Once again, Istanbul stood on the frontline of a global conflict and at a juncture of world history.

Epilogue

The conditions of the war, the uncertainty as to what was coming next
and the urgency of the immediate tasks, created the illusion that the
passage of time was suspended, and everyone was filled for the moment
with an extraordinarily potent sense of perpetual youth. Friendships
were rapidly born, and people revealed themselves in a day as they
would not usually do in a year.

—Colin MacInnes, *To the Victors the Spoils*

The day of victory over fascism was glorious, but it did not usher forth
a new world of unalloyed justice, peace, and plenty. Many of those
responsible for the evil prospered or escaped relatively unscathed; many
genuine heroes died in obscurity or failed to find a place for themselves
after the fighting ended.

Von Papen was arrested by the Allies in October 1945. "It is certainly
hard, as a net result of a long, devoted term of service to the Fatherland,"
he wrote with self-pity, "to be imprisoned like a criminal behind a
double barbed-wire fence covered by machine guns."

Von Papen disclaimed responsibility for Hitler's rise and reign, blaming the Nazi ascendancy on a weak intelligentsia, a decline in piety,
and broad historic trends. At his trial, he made a phony claim of having
helped Roncalli save 20,000 Jews, while actually he had only forwarded
the Vatican envoy's letters, which were usually rejected by Berlin. Ambassador Steinhardt visited von Papen during the trial, and they spent
five hours reliving their old battles. Earle, who von Papen had tried to
use as a conduit to Roosevelt, wrote a letter documenting and praising
von Papen's peace proposals. Von Papen was acquitted of war crimes
by the Nuremberg tribunal in 1946.

Franz Josef Messner, a leader of the Austrian resistance movement and a member of the Dogwood chain, was murdered by the Germans a few hours before Vienna's liberation. Wilhelm Hamburger, the Abwehr agent and Austrian resistance member, worked with the British in Cairo after his defection and then returned home to Vienna to become a successful international trade negotiator.

Some of the OSS men decided to stay in the same line of work and joined the Central Intelligence Agency (CIA). Most notable among them was Frank Wisner, OSS-Turkey's liaison man in Cairo and later Macfarland's replacement as OSS chief in Turkey. He was one of the leading critics of the Dogwood operation. In later years, he became the CIA's head of covert operations. Under tremendous stress, he committed suicide in the 1960s.

George Earle married a young Belgian woman he met in Istanbul. His behavior and thinking became increasingly erratic after the war. He returned to Philadelphia to found an extreme right-wing anti-Communist group.

Paul Leverkuehn, the displaced Istanbul Abwehr chief, became first a prosecutor and then a defense lawyer for some German officers at Nuremberg. Later, he went into politics and was elected a Christian Democratic member of parliament and president of the European Union. The Leverkuehns settled in Switzerland and became involved with conservative Catholic causes.

Ernst Reuter, one of the leaders of the German anti-Hitler refugee community in Turkey, became West Berlin's first postwar mayor. Alexander Rustow, leader of the anti-Nazi German émigrés in Istanbul and liaison between the OSS and the German underground, returned to Germany to take the chair of sociology at the University of Heidelberg. Most of the other exiled professors emigrated to the United States and enjoyed distinguished scholarly careers.

A different kind of distinguished career was followed by the Soviet assassinations expert Leonid Eitingon, who, under his alias of Naumov, had been the NKVD chief in Turkey. He was promoted to major general in 1945, and he helped establish the postwar Soviet espionage network in western Europe. In the 1950s, he organized a campaign to murder exiled Ukrainian leaders. In 1954, he was caught up in a post-Stalin purge and sentenced to twelve years in a labor camp. He eventually returned to Moscow and held a job in a Soviet publishing company that was an intelligence front.

The wartime U.S. ambassador to Turkey, Laurence Steinhardt, went on to be ambassador to Czechoslovakia and served there during the 1948 Communist coup. He later became ambassador to Canada, where he died in an air accident in 1950. Although Sir Hughe Knatchbull-Hugessen was named British ambassador to Belgium after the war, he was soon retired, his career blighted by the Cicero affair.

Multiple agent Andre Gyorgy opened a bar in Vienna after the war. Luther Kovess made his way back to Istanbul, patched up relations with the Americans, and became active in Hungarian refugee affairs. Lieutenant Colonel Otto Hatz, the Hungarian quadruple agent, survived yet another intelligence association. At first the Russians used his services, but in 1952 they sentenced him to seven years' imprisonment and fifteen years' hard labor in the U.S.S.R. Three years later he was declared innocent and allowed to return to Hungary. Hatz became a fencing coach in Budapest and lived quietly until his death in 1984.

The gallant Czech, Polish, and Hungarian intelligence men and diplomats had barely returned home from fighting the German invaders when they lost their countries to the Russian occupiers. Most of them went into an exile which, this time, would have no happy ending. Two of the main pro-Western Hungarians—Colonel Ujszaszy and Count Bethlen—were kidnapped by the Soviets at the end of the war and died in captivity in the U.S.S.R.

In contrast, the members of the Zionist delegation in Istanbul were able to establish their independent state. Out of great tragedy came constructive action. Some of Israel's builders were Jews whose lives the members had saved through their rescue efforts in Istanbul. Teddy Kollek became the mayor of Jerusalem and was responsible for that city's flowering; Akiva Levinsky rose to be treasurer of the Jewish Agency. Between 1945 and 1948, Yehuda Pomerantz became one of the leaders in Aliya Bet, bringing Jewish refugees through the British blockade into Palestine. He then became a physics professor.

The Vatican prelate Roncalli, whose career seemed to have reached a dead end in Istanbul, was named the Holy See's envoy to France in 1944. Two decades later, he became the highly popular, reforming Pope John XXIII.

The Turks themselves were much affected by the democratic ideas propagated by the Allies. After the war, İnönü allowed a multiparty state and free elections. Despite some lapses under tremendous pressure, this democratic commitment survived. The massive migration of Turks from the countryside overwhelmed Istanbul and made it one of the world's largest cities. There is now a bridge across the Bosporus. The unique flavor provided to the city's cultural life by the Greeks, Jews, and Armenians was largely diluted by their gradual emigration from the country. Still, the natural setting and old landmarks make Istanbul as uniquely beautiful as ever. In contrast, citizens of Ankara skeptically laugh at the idea that their swollen, smoggy city was once a place of beautiful vistas and open spaces.

The war had changed everyone and everything beyond recognition. "These are days of glory and of mourning," wrote the German defector Wilhelm Hamburger from Cairo in April 1945. "I am indeed dead tired after having struggled for years in vain. Once I served an idea and the idea became a crime. . . . I know that the people I knew and loved are dead or changed or robbed of all their means. . . . The homes we lived in, the forests we hunted in and the places to which I simply belong are reduced to ashes. I am to close one chapter of my life and of [the] world's history. . . . How vastly different will be the postwar world!"

Those emerging from such desperate struggles had to believe there was hope for that world. Ex-Abwehr officer Leverkuehn wrote former OSS chief Donovan in February 1946, "After six years . . . it is a tremendous relief to know that there is peace somewhere and that the friendship of good old days is helping to pave the way into that land of peace."

SELECTIVE LIST OF CODE NAMES FOR OSS-TURKEY

I. OSS AGENTS

Arbutus: Lynn Beeler, Bulgaria desk officer in Edirne.

Basil: Jerome Sperling, director of Greek chain.

Bittersweet: Dean Woodruff, Bulgaria desk officer.

Cactus: Frank Stevens, OSS-Istanbul's Romania desk officer.

Gander: Lieutenant Alexander "Alekko" Georgiades, director of OSS-Edirne outpost.

Happy: Philip Guepin, director of OSS Special Operations.

Herman/Camelia: Helmuth von Moltke, Abwehr officer and anti-Hitler conspirator.

Javelin: OSS-Turkey.

Juniper: Colonel Vala Mocarski, OSS-Cairo, who came to Istanbul in January-February 1944 to negotiate with Hatz.

Pansy: A Bulgarian officer; reported from Sofia.

Paprika: Director of Turkish secret police (also known as "Aunt Jane"); supplied intelligence particularly on Bulgaria.

Poinsetta: Polish intelligence.

Poppy: Gander's Greek courier.

Rose: Archibald Walker, director of Socony Vacuum Oil company office. Specialized in Bulgarian affairs.

Vervain: Emanuel Voska, OWI officer; gathered intelligence.

Note: OSS-Istanbul also had a "Fish" ring of agents, including Turkish and Bulgarian diplomats in Tokyo and employees of the Japanese embassies in Sofia and Ankara.

II. OSS DOGWOOD-CEREUS "FLOWER" RING (Partial List)

DIRECTORS: ALFRED SCHWARZ AND ARCHIBALD COLEMAN.

Begonia: An Austrian Nazi party member; employed by Wehrwirtschaftsant (army economic office).*

Cassia: Franz Josef Messner, managing director of Semperit Company, Vienna, and head of Austrian nationalist group (Cassia ring).

Cereus: Archibald Coleman, American OSS officer who ran the ring.

Dahlia: Fritz Fiala, German embassy press counselor and an SS officer.*

Dogwood: Alfred Schwarz. Czech businessman who actually controlled the ring's operations.

Hyacinth: Hans Willbrandt, German refugee professor in Istanbul.

Iris: Frantisek Laufer, SD agent in Budapest and Slovakia.*

Jasmine: Lt. Col. Otto Hatz, Hungarian military attaché.*

Jacaranda: Luther Kovess; handled relations with Hungarian general staff.*

Lotus: A Chinese engineer; reported from Berlin.

Magnolia: Alexander Rustow, German refugee professor in Istanbul; maintained contacts with German opposition.

Oleander: Holzmeister, German architect in Ankara.

Stock: Franz Josef Ridiger, Semperit Company official and leader of the Cassia ring; defected to Allies, September 1944.

Trillium: Andre Gyorgy,* OSS courier.

---

*German double agents.

INTELLIGENCE
ORGANIZATIONS

Abwehr: German intelligence bureau headed by Admiral Canaris; under military command but involved in all areas of intelligence collection; paralleled MI-6 and OSS.

Emniyet: Turkish secret police and intelligence organization.

MI-6: British intelligence counterpart of OSS-SI, but also handled counterintelligence outside England; in contemporary documents usually referred to as the Secret Intelligence Service (SIS).

MI-9: British intelligence unit responsible for aiding escapers and evaders.

MU (Maritime Unit): OSS unit that carried out caïque operations.

NKVD: Soviet secret police and intelligence organization.

OSS (Office of Strategic Services): U.S. wartime civilian intelligence agency; predecessor of the CIA.

OWI (Office of War Information): U.S. wartime agency responsible for disseminating information and propaganda.

SD (Sicherheitsdienst): German intelligence organization run by the Reich Security Ministry (RSHA).

SI (Secret Intelligence): OSS section responsible for gathering and evaluating information.

SO (Special Operations): OSS section charged with guerrilla and sabotage activity in occupied countries; counterpart of SOE.

SOE (Special Operations Executive): British counterpart of OSS-SO.

X-2: OSS counterintelligence section.

INTERVIEWS

Martin Agronsky
Ismail Akhmedov
Walter Arndt
Clement Auerbach
William Baxter
Victor Binns
Walter Birge
Cyril Black
Daniel Brewster
Sir Douglas Busk
Michael Cardozo
Herbert Cummings
Joe T. Curtiss
Huntington Damon
William Diamond
Nicholas Elliott
Peter Engelmann
Farnesworth Fowle
David Hacohen
Tibor Halasi-Kun
Talat Halman
Wilhelm Hamburger
Dora Hanak
Ira Hirschmann
Leo Hochstetter
Lawrence Houston
J. C. Hurewitz
Hans Juterback
Jaroslav Karpat-Pathy
Eliyahu Katan
Frank Kaufman

Kerim Key
Rolfe Kingsley
Helen Kitchen
Teddy Kollek
Frederick Latimer
Hal Lehrman
Akiva Levinsky
Yitzhak Levy
Lanning Macfarland, Jr.
Dr. Frank MacMurray
Fazilet Manyas
Lee Metcalf
Robert Minor
Charles Moore
Robert Newbegin
Earl Packer
Jaroslav Polach
Dankwart Rustow
Robert St. John
Ivan Schick
Alfred Schwarz
Dulcie Steinhardt Sherlock
Turner T. Smith
Phillip Stoddard
Aladar Szegedy
Turkish Workers Club, Bat-Yam,
    Israel (various members)
Rose Ferenc Vali
Donald Webster
C. W. Woodhouse

BIBLIOGRAPHY

I. ARCHIVAL SOURCES

George Allen papers, Duke University Library.

Burton Berry papers, Indiana University.

Central Zionist Archives, Jerusalem.

William Donovan papers, Army Historical Section, Carlisle Barracks.

Allen Dulles papers, Princeton University.

Great Britain Public Records Office, including files FO371;

WO 106 Director of Military Operations and Intelligence;

WO 201 Military HQ papers, Middle East forces;

WO 202 Military HQ papers, military missions (partial records SOE-Cairo); and

WO 208 Directorate of Military Intelligence.

Harry Howard papers, Harry S. Truman Library.

Israel State Archives, Jerusalem.

Robert F. Kelly papers, Georgetown University.

John Van Antwerp MacMurray papers, Princeton University.

Military Attaché and Office of Naval Intelligence Records, Navy and Old Army Division, National Archives.

OSS Archives, Record Group 226 including entries 88, 95, 99, 101, 106, 108, 109, 110, 116, 120, 121, 125, 134, 136, 138, 139, 144, 146, 148, 165, 168, 171, and 190, National Archives Military Reference Branch.

Franklin Roosevelt Presidential Library, Hyde Park, New York.

Laurence Steinhardt papers, Library of Congress.

U.S. Military Intelligence records, RG 319, National Archives Military Reference Branch; Washington National Records Center, Suitland.

U.S. State Department Archives, RG 59, National Archives Diplomatic Branch; RG 84, Washington National Records Center.

II. BOOKS

Akhmedov, Ismail, *In and Out of Stalin's GRU* (Frederick, Md., 1984).

Allardt, Helmut, *Politik vor und hinter den Kulissen* (Düsseldorf, 1979).

Amery, Julian, *Approach March* (London, 1973).

Andrew, Christopher, *Her Majesty's Secret Service* (New York, 1986).

Armaoglu, Fahir, *Siyasi Tarih 1789-1960* (Ankara, 1964).

Atay, Falih Rifki, *Yolcu Defteri* (Ankara, 1946).

Auty, Phyllis, and Richard Clogg, *British Policy towards Wartime Resistance in Yugoslavia and Greece* (London, 1975).

Avriel, Ehud, *Open the Gates* (New York, 1975).

Aydemir, Sevket Sureyya, *Ikinci adam: Ismet İnönü*, Vols. 1 and 2 (Istanbul, 1966–1967).

Barker, Elisabeth, *British Policy in South-East Europe* (London, 1976).

Barsley, Michael, *Orient Express* (New York, 1967).

Bartz, Karl, *The Downfall of the German Secret Service* (London, 1956).

Bauer, Yehuda, *American Jewry and the Holocaust* (Detroit, 1981).

———, *A History of the Holocaust* (New York, 1982).

———, *The Holocaust as Historical Experience* (New York, 1981).

Bayar, Celal, *Celal Bayar diyorki 1920–50* (Ankara, 1964).

Beevor, J. G., *SOE: Recollections and Reflections 1940–1945* (London, 1981).

Black, Cyril, *Floyd Black 1888–1983: A Remembrance by his Son* (Princeton, N.J., 1984).

Blood-Ryan, H. W., *Franz von Papen* (London, 1939).

Brook-Shepherd, Gordon, *The Storm Petrels* (New York, 1977).

Bruce-Lockhart, Robert, *Comes the Reckoning* (New York, 1972).

Butler, Ewan, *Amateur Agent* (New York, 1964).

Cardozo, Michael, *Diplomats in International Cooperation* (Ithaca, N.Y., 1962).

Cave Brown, Anthony, *The Last Hero: Wild Bill Donovan* (New York, 1982).

Chary, Frederick, *The Bulgarian Jews and the Final Solution* (Pittsburgh, Pa., 1972).

Cookridge, E. H., *The Orient Express* (New York, 1969).

Coser, Lewis, *Refugee Scholars in America* (New Haven, Conn., 1984).

Crankshaw, Edward, *Gestapo* (Washington, 1979).

Cruikshank, Charles, *The Fourth Arm* (London, 1977).

———, *Greece, 1940–41* (London, 1976).

Dallin, David, *Soviet Espionage* (New Haven, Conn., 1955).

Davidson, Basil, *Golden Horn* (London, 1952).

———, *Special Operations Europe: Scenes from the Anti-Nazi War* (New York, 1981).

de Novo, John, *American Interests in the Middle East* (Minneapolis, 1978).

Dos Passos, John, *L'Orient Express* (New York, 1984).

Duke, Florimund, *Name, Rank, and Serial Number* (New York, 1969).

Dulles, Allen, *The Secret Surrender* (New York, 1966).

Dunn, Robert, *World Alive* (New York, 1956).

Elon, Amos, *Timetable* (Garden City, N.Y., 1980).

Erkilet, H. Emir, *Sark cephesinde gorduklerim* (Istanbul, 1943).

Feingold, Henry, *The Politics of Rescue* (New Brunswick, N.J., 1970).

Felmy, Helmuth, and Walter Warlimont, *German Exploitation of Arab Nationalist Movements in World War Two*, unpublished manuscript.

Gafencu, Grigore, *The Last Days of Europe* (Hamden, Conn., 1970).

Gilbert, Martin, *Auschwitz and the Allies* (New York, 1981).

————, *Exile and Return* (New York, 1978).

Giritlioglu, Fahir, *Turk siyasi tarihinde Cumhuriyet Halk Partisinin mevkii*, 2 vols. (Ankara, 1965).

Glasneck, Johannes, *Methoden der Deutsch-Faschistestchen Propagandatatigheit in der Turkei vor und Wahrerd des Zweites Weltkrieges* (Halle, Germany, 1966).

Gonel, Tanju, *Mill Kahraman Maresal Fevzi Cakmak* (Istanbul, 1977).

Great Britain Naval Intelligence Division, *Turkey*, 2 vols. (London, 1942).

Greene, Graham, *Orient Express* (New York, 1933).

Gunther, John, *The Troubled Midnight* (New York, 1945).

Gyorgy, Ranki, et al., *A Wilhelmstrasse* (Budapest, 1968).

Hagen, Lewis, *The Schellenberg Memoirs* (London, 1956).

————, *The Secret War for Europe* (New York, 1968).

Hall, Melvin, *Bird of Time* (New York, 1949).

————, *Journey to the End* (New York, 1947).

Hamilton-Hill, Donald, *SOE Assignment* (London, 1973).

Hampshire, A. Cecil, *The Secret Navies* (London, 1978).

————, *Undercover Sailors* (London, 1981).

Hassell, Ulrich von, *Diaries* (New York, 1947).

Haswell, Jack, *The Intelligence and Deception of the D-Day Landings* (London, 1979).

Hebblethwaite, Peter, *Pope John XXIII* (New York, 1985).

Hinsley, F. H., *British Intelligence in the Second World War*, vols. 1 and 2, and part 1, vol. 3 (London, 1979–1984).

Hirschmann, Ira, *Caution to the Winds* (New York, 1982).

————, *Lifeline to a Promised Land* (New York, 1946).

His Majesty's Stationery Office, *Selection from Papers Found in the Possession of Captain von Papen* (London, 1916).

Hitler, Adolf, *Hitler's Table Talk* (London, 1973).

Hoettl, Wilhelm, *Hitler's Paper Weapon* (London, 1955).

——, *The Secret Front* (New York, 1954).

Hoffmann, Peter, *The History of the German Resistance, 1933–1945* (Cambridge, Mass., 1977).

Hogg, Gary, *Orient Express* (New York, 1969).

Hohne, Heinz, *Canaris* (New York, 1979).

Hollingworth, Clare, et al., *Hitler's Route to Baghdad* (London, 1939).

——, *There's a German Just Behind Me* (London, 1942).

Horthy, Nicholas, *Memoirs* (New York, 1957).

Howarth, Patrick, *Undercover: The Men and Women of the Special Operations Executive* (Boston, 1980).

Irving, David, *Breach of Security* (London, 1968).

Jackh, Ernest, *The Rising Crescent* (New York, 1944).

Jaschke, Gotthard, *Die Turken in Den Jahren 1942–1951* (Weisbaden, Germany, 1955).

John XXIII, *Journal of a Soul* (New York, 1980).

——, *Letters to His Family* (New York, 1982).

Johnson, Stevens, *Agents Extraordinary* (London, 1975).

Kadar, Gyula, *A Ludovikatol Sopronkohidaig* (Budapest, 1978).

Kahn, David, *The Codebreakers* (New York, 1967).

——, *Hitler's Spies* (New York, 1978).

Karaosmanoglu, Yakub Kadri, *Politikada 45 yil* (Ankara, 1968).

Kemp, Peter, *No Colour or Crest* (London, 1958).

Knatchbull-Hugessen, Hughe Montgomery, *Diplomat in Peace and War* (London, 1968).

Koeves, Tiber, *Satan in a Top Hat* (New York, 1941).

Krecker, Lothar, *Deutschland und die Turkey im Zweiten Weltkrieg* (Frankfurt, 1964).

Kuniholm, Bruce, *The Origins of the Cold War in the Near East* (Princeton, 1978).

Kurat, Yulug Tekin, *Ikinci Dunya Savasinda Turk-Alman ticaretindek iktisadi siyaset* (Ankara, 1961).

Larsen, Stein, et al., *Who Were the Fascists* (Oslo, 1980).

Lavra, Stephen, *The Greek Miracle* (New York, 1943).

Leverkuehn, Paul, *German Military Intelligence* (New York, 1954).

Lorand, Dombradi, *Hadsereg es politika Magyarorszagon, 1938–1944* (Budapest, 1986).

Lovell, Stanley, *Of Spies and Stratagems* (Englewood Cliffs, N.J., 1963).

Macartney, Carlile, *October 15th*, 2 vols. (Edinburgh, 1961).

MacLaren, Roy, *Canadians behind Enemy Lines* (Vancouver, 1981).

Mamboury, Ernest, *Istanbul Touristique* (Istanbul, 1951).

Manning, Olivia, *The Balkan Trilogy* (New York, 1984).

———, *The Levant Trilogy* (New York, 1984).

Mardor, Meir, *Strictly Illegal* (London, 1964).

Massigli, Rene, *La Turquie devant la Guerre* (Paris, 1964).

Masterman, John, *The Double-Cross System in the War of 1939 to 1945* (New Haven, Conn., 1972).

Meram, Ali Kemal, *Ismet Inönü ve ikinci cijhan harb* (Istanbul).

Miller, Marshall Lee, *Bulgaria during World War Two* (Stanford, Conn., 1975).

Molony, C. J. C., *The Mediterranean and the Middle East*, vols. 5 and 6.

Moravec, Frantisek, *Master of Spies* (Garden City, N.Y., 1975).

Morley, John, *Vatican Diplomacy and the Jews during the Holocaust* (New York, 1980).

Morse, S. B., *While Six Million Died* (New York, 1968).

Moyzisch, L. C., *Operation Cicero* (London, 1969).

Myers, Edmund, *Greek Entanglement* (London, 1955).

Nadi, Nadir, *Perde Araligindan* (Istanbul, 1964).

Neumark, Fritz, *Zuflucht am Bosporus* (Frankfurt, 1980).

Newman, Bernard, *Turkish Crossroads* (London, 1951).

Nicosia, Francis, *The Third Reich and the Palestine Question* (Austin, Tex., 1985).

Office of Strategic Services, *Official History* (New York, 1976).

Orlow, Dietrich, *The Nazis in the Balkans* (Pittsburgh, Pa., 1968).

Paloczi-Horvath, George, *The Undefeated* (London, 1959).

Paneth, Philip, *Turkey: Decadence and Rebirth* (London, 1943).

Parker, Robert, *Headquarters Budapest* (New York, 1945).

Patmore, Derek, *Balkan Correspondent* (New York, 1941).

Peis, Gunter, *Hitler's Spies and Saboteurs* (New York, 1958).

Playfair, I. S. O., *The Mediterranean and the Middle East*, vols. 1 to 6 (London, 1954–1987).

Popov, Dusko, *Spy Counterspy* (New York, 1974).

Rendel, George, *The Sword and the Olive* (London, 1957).

Righi, Vittoro Ugo, *Papa Giovanni sulle rive del Bosforo* (Padua, Italy, 1971).

Rittlinger, Herbert, *Geheindienst mit KO beschrankter Haft* (Stuttgart, 1973).

Roshill, S. W., *The War at Sea*, vol. 1–3 (London, 1976).

Rubin, Barry, *The Arab States and the Palestine Conflict* (Syracuse, N.Y., 1980).

——, *The Great Powers in the Middle East* (New York, 1981).

Rustow, Alexander, *Freedom and Domination* (Princeton, N.J.: 1980).

St. John, Robert, *From the Land of the Silent People* (New York, 1942).

——, *It's Always Tomorrow* (New York, 1944).

——, *The Man Who Played God* (Garden City, N.Y., 1962).

——, *The Silent People Speak* (Garden City, N.Y., 1948).

——, *This Was My World* (New York, 1953).

Schellenberg, Walter, *The Labyrinth* (New York, 1956).

Schmidt, Paul, *Hitler's Interpreter* (New York, 1951).

Sertel, Zekeriya, *Hatidladklarm* (Istanbul, 1977).

Sherwood, Shirley, *Venice Simplon Orient Express* (New York, 1983).

Slessor, John, *The Central Blue* (New York, 1957).

Smith, Bradley, *The Shadow Warriors* (New York, 1983).

Smith, R. Harris, *OSS* (Berkeley, Calif.: 1972).

Sokolnicki, Michael, *Memoirs* (New York, 1965).

Spiro, Edward, *Inside SOE* (London, 1966).

———, *Set Europe Ablaze* (New York, 1967).

Stafford, David, *Britain and European Resistance* (London, 1980).

Stern, Fritz, *Ernst Reuter* (Berlin, 1976).

Stirling, Wilfred, *Safety Last* (London, 1953).

Stowe, Leland, *No Other Road to Freedom* (New York, 1941).

Sulzberger, C. L., *A Long Row of Candles* (New York, 1969).

Sweet-Escott, Bikham, *Baker Street Irregular* (London, 1965).

Sykes, Christopher, *High-Minded Murder* (London, 1944).

———, *A Song of a Shirt* (London, 1953).

Tebelen, A. Mennan, *Carnet d'un Diplomate* (Paris, 1951).

Thompson, E. P., and T. J. Thompson, *There Is a Spirit in Europe* (London, 1947).

Tobin, Chester, *Turkey, Key to the East* (New York, 1944).

Tomlin, E. W. F., *Life in Modern Turkey* (New York, 1946).

Us, Asim, *Hatra Notlari* (Istanbul, 1966).

Vali, Ferenc, *A Scholar's Odyssey*, unpublished manuscript.

von Papen, Franz, *Memoirs* (New York, 1968).

Voska, Emanuel, *Spy and Counterspy* (New York, 1981).

Walker, David, *Death at My Heels* (London, 1942).

———, *I Go Where I'm Sent* (London, 1952).

———, *Lunch with a Stranger* (New York, 1957).

Ward, Barbara, *Turkey* (London, 1942).

Weisband, Edward, *Turkish Foreign Policy, 1943–1945* (Princeton, 1973).

Weller, George, *The Crack in the Column* (New York, 1949).

West, Nigel, *The Circus* (New York, 1983).

————, *MI-5* (London, 1981).

————, *MI-6* (New York, 1983).

————, *A Thread of Deceit* (New York, 1985).

White, Leigh, *The Long Balkan Night* (New York, 1944).

Widmann, Horst, *Exil und Bildungshilfe* (Frankfurt, 1973).

Wilson, Lord Henry, *Eight Years Overseas* (London, 1948).

Winks, Robin, *Cloak & Gown* (New York, 1987).

Winstone, H. V. F., *The Illicit Adventure* (London, 1982).

Wistrich, Robert, *Hitler's Apocalypse* (New York, 1985).

Woodhouse, Christopher, *Apple of Discord* (New York, 1948).

————, *The Struggle for Greece* (London, 1976).

Wyman, David, *The Abandonment of the Jews* (New York, 1984).

Yalman, Ahmet Amin, *Turkey in My Time* (Norman, Okla., 1956).

Ziyaoglu, Rakim, et al., *Tourists Guide to Istanbul* (Istanbul, 1951).

Zoltan, Makra, *Honvedelmi Miniszterek Szolgalataban, 1940–1944* (Munich, 1986).

ARTICLES AND PAPERS

"Al-domi: Palestinian Intellectuals and the Holocaust, 1943–1945," *Studies in Zionism*, Spring 1984.

Epstein, Mark, "A Winter in Turkey," paper presented at the Woodrow Wilson Center Conference on German refugee intellectuals.

Gelber, Yoav, "The Mission of the Jewish Parachutists from Palestine in Europe in World War II," *Studies in Zionism*, Spring 1986.

Gyula, Juhasz, "Visszatekintes madartavlatbol," *Ujiras*, June 1978.

Polach, Jaroslav, "The 1939 Attack on Hitler and 'ON,' " *Journal of Czechoslovak and Central European Studies*, Summer 1986.

Porat, Dina, "The Transnistria Affair and the Rescue Policy of the Zionist Leadership in Palestine," *Studies in Zionism*, Spring 1985.

Senate Internal Security Subcommittee Report, "Interlocking Subversion in Government Departments," Oct. 28, 1953.

Trever-Roper, Hugh, review of *Donovan: The Last American Hero*, *New York Review of Books*, Feb. 19 and Apr. 1, 1976.

"Zionist Policy and the Fate of European Jewry, 1943–1944," *Studies in Zionism*, Spring 1983.

INDEX